PRAISE FOR *A SPECTRE, HAUNTING*:

"In *A Spectre, Haunting*, China Miéville, mind, soul, and pen ablaze, guides his readers through Marx and Engels's unignorable, inextinguishable, eternally uncomfortable, and always essential *Manifesto*. This is both a history of critical thought and a magnificent exemplar of reading and thinking critically. Miéville has written a thrillingly lively and lucid exegesis on the *Manifesto*, its contents and its discontents. He's gathered together an astonishingly heterogenous array of voices and responses, making a case for the *Manifesto* as a locus of politically engaged analysis and argument for nearly two centuries. Miéville adjudicates and synthesizes with unfailing clarity, wit, courage, decency, and passion, writing brilliantly about nationalism, race, gender, literary style, and—my particular favorite section—about the perils and necessity of hate. He gives us a *Manifesto* that is simultaneously a central artifact of our species and a means for understanding our present, hazardous moment, a historical work that remains absolutely, ferociously alive." —TONY KUSHNER, author of *Angels in America*

"It's thrilling to accompany Miéville, one of the greatest living world-builders, as he wrestles—in critical good faith and incandescent commitment—with a manifesto that still calls on us to build a new world." —NAOMI KLEIN, author of *On Fire* and *No Is Not Enough*

"China Miéville's elegant book patiently explains composition—style, structure, class—to reveal *The Communist Manifesto*'s spectral energies. Reading with him today sharpens our senses to contemporary internationalist movements from below." —RUTH WILSON GILMORE, author *Abolition Geography* and *Change Everything*

"The *Manifesto* is one of history's most profound prophecies. In Miéville's brilliant interpretation it is like a great comet whose periodic return blinds the sky with its light and urgency. Read this and be dazzled by its contemporaneity." —MIKE DAVIS, author of *City of Quartz and Set the Night On Fire*

"With diligence and a ruthlessly critical eye worthy of Marx himself, China Miéville expands upon the *Communist Manifesto*, calling us into renewed struggle for the best of what humanity could be. Against the million little cruelties and death-making of capitalism, this book builds a case for the value of the *Manifesto* to today's struggles without demanding fealty. It turns long-standing complaints about Marx on their heads to challenge the reader even while seducing with luminous prose. I didn't know I needed this book, but I did." —SARAH JAFFE, author of *Work Won't Love You Back* and *Necessary Trouble*

"An excellent book, very lively and engaging, written in clear and readable prose . . . much more than a contextual and analytical reading of the *Manifesto* . . . For today's readers Miéville does excellent work presenting and reviewing a huge amount of twentieth-century history" —PROFESSOR TERRELL CARVER

"It would have been enough to have a thorough, learned, clear introduction to *The Communist Manifesto* from one of the greatest leftist authors of our time, but China Miéville's *A Spectre, Haunting* is also a serious and singular exploration of the vital principle of the *Manifesto* as a work of writing, a rhythmology of its bottomless fury and impassioned faith in a communist horizon."
—JORDY ROSENBERG, author *Confessions of the Fox*

"A book about another book might sound boring, but *The Communist Manifesto* is more than a book: it represents a bulging galaxy of historical struggle, ever moving and shining, even if only on the periphery of our vision. Here, China Miéville opens up the pages of the *Manifesto* and transmits the energy of communism across the pallid present. Close reading, historical essay, political commentary, and a manifesto of sorts: *A Spectre, Haunting* is a rich, luminous reflection of and on a light that never quite goes out."
—ANDREAS MALM, author *How to Blow Up A Pipeline*

"Very enjoyable and well done . . . properly scholarly and thorough in its apparatus of discussion and issue identification . . . lively, politically driven appreciation." —PROFESSOR GREGOR MCLENNAN

**PRAISE FOR CHINA MIÉVILLE:**
"You can't talk about Miéville without using the word 'brilliant.'"—*Guardian*

"One of our most important writers." —*Independent*

"Miéville is gifted with an incomparable visionary imagination."
—*Financial Times*

"Miéville is regarded as one of the most interesting and freakishly gifted writers of his generation." —*Daily Telegraph*

# A SPECTRE, HAUNTING

# CHINA MIÉVILLE

ON *THE COMMUNIST MANIFESTO*

Haymarket Books
Chicago, Illinois

© 2022 China Miéville  First published in the UK in 2022 by Head of Zeus Ltd

This edition published in 2022 by Haymarket Books, P.O. Box 180165, Chicago, IL 60618,
www.haymarketbooks.org

ISBN: 978-1-64259-891-9

The works from which the epigraphs in this book are gratefully taken are:
Agnes Denes, *A Manifesto* (1970) © Agnes Denes,
courtesy Leslie Tonkonow Artworks + Projects, New York. The full text, of which the epigraph
in these pages is only a short extract, can be seen on the artist's website, at
www.agnesdenesstudio.com/works15.html.
Helen Keller, *The World I Live In* (Hodder and Stoughton, 1908)
Helen Macfarlane, "The Democratic and Social Republic"
(*Red Republican*, 12 October 1850)
Mira Mattar, *Yes, I Am A Destroyer* (MA BIBLIOTHÈQUE, 2020)
Carolyn Rodgers, *How I got ovah: new and selected poems* (Anchor Press, 1975)
Eve Kosofsky Sedgwick, "Paranoid Reading and Reparative Reading, or, You're So Paranoid,
You Probably Think This Essay Is About You," in *Touching Feeling* (Duke University Press,
2003), 123–51
Assata Shakur, *Assata: An Autobiography* (Lawrence Hill Books, 2001)
Rebecca Solnit, *Hope In the Dark* (Nation Books, 2004)

Distributed to the trade in the US through Consortium Book Sales and Distribution
(www.cbsd.com) and internationally through Ingram Publisher Services International
(www.ingramcontent.com).

This book was published with the generous support
of Lannan Foundation and Wallace Action Fund.

Special discounts are available for bulk purchases by organizations and institutions.
Please email info@haymarketbooks.org for more information.

Cover design by Jamie Kerry.

Library of Congress Cataloging-in-Publication data is available.

1 3 5 7 9 10 8 6 4 2

*To Rosie Warren, salvor.*

"When someone asked me what communism was, i opened my mouth to answer, then realised i didn't have the faintest idea. My image of a communist came from a cartoon. . . . We're taught at such an early age to be against the communists, yet most of us don't have the faintest idea what communism is. Only a fool lets somebody else tell him who his enemy is."

—ASSATA SHAKUR, *Assata: An Autobiography*

# Contents

# Introduction

I'm a communist, you idiot.

Ash Sarkar, *Good Morning Britain*, July 12, 2018

Midway through the nineteenth century, a tiny group of embattled leftist reprobates grandiosely declared that their enemies, the great powers of Europe, were haunted. So opens *The Communist Manifesto*.

The *Manifesto* predicts and demands the overthrow of industrial capitalism, a system then still burgeoning. It looks urgently forward to its replacement with a new form of society, based not on ruthless competition for profit, and the social atomisation and mass human misery that inevitably accompanies it, but on a new collective reality, the fulfilment of human need and the flowering of human potential, on the basis of communal, democratically controlled social property. The parameters, pitfalls, and possibilities of this goal were, and remain, controversial, including for the Left. But what it would be is *communism*. This is the spectre that's invoked in the opening sentence of the *Manifesto*.

The *Manifesto* itself is short and rude and vivid and eccentrically organized—and its impact has been utterly epochal. "It is difficult to imagine," wrote Umberto Eco with palpable awe, "that a few fine pages can single-handedly change the world." Admirers celebrate that fact; detractors decry it. But they're united in acknowledging the book's astounding sway over the minds of its readers, and its historical power.[1]

Now that ghost is back. No surprise, perhaps: repress something, and it's as a spectre that it's likely to return. Still, there's something truly bizarre about what Richard Seymour has called today's "anticommunism without communism." Three decades on from the collapse of the Soviet Union and its allies, states ostensibly committed to the *Manifesto's* vision (for all that that commitment was in large part a cruel joke), and absent any serious mass far-left presence in world politics, "today's reactionaries are hallucinating a communist threat."[2] This threat is, indeed, a hallucination: what genuine advances for the Left occur today, however welcome, tend to be embattled outliers. They certainly don't imply any systemic shift. And yet, for a small but growing and increasingly vocal minority of mostly young activists, the concept of "communism" is beginning to lose a taint that has, for so long, been taken for granted. And that has been invaluable to those in power.[3]

Every political generation must encounter the *Manifesto* anew, learn what to focus on within it, find problems, questions, analyses, answers, gaps, and aporia and solutions for and of their own time. This is not, in some partisan cliché, to bullishly assert that the text is relevant "now more than ever." But just as it was without question a distinct experience to read the *Manifesto* in the context, say, of decolonization and neo-colonialism, so too was it to read the text during the rise of the welfare state, or of that system's deliberate diminution, the ascendancy of unregulated financial speculation, the drawn-out exhaustion and collapse of Stalinism, the era of the hard centre, and so on.[4]

These words are written in 2021. Close to half of humanity subsists on less than $5.50 per day. The world's few billionaires own more than the poorest 60 percent of the planet. Wealth taxes are at historic lows for the rich and for corporations. Twenty percent of the world's children—more than a quarter of a billion—cannot attend school. Ten thousand people die unnecessarily every day, from causes directly related to poverty.[5] The new jostling over the idea of communism occurs in the dragged-out aftermath of the 2007–08 economic crash, at a time of accelerating climate catastrophe and the sixth mass extinction, of soaring social anxiety, a slide into growing political toxicity and sadism; it arises in the rubble of the extraordinary rise and quick fall of unprecedented left challenges to the doctrines of neoliberal capitalism, and of the "austerity" policies that were until very recently touted as necessities, in the Corbyn leadership of the Labour Party in the UK and the Sanders insurgency in the US: it proceeds in milieux shaped by the hard-right regimes of Trump and Johnson, buffeted by a virulent and appallingly mismanaged global pandemic that has, at the time of writing, killed more than four and a half million people, disproportionately affecting minority and impoverished groups, with the resulting lockdowns exacerbating underlying weaknesses in the world economy and very possibly resulting in the worst depression in the history of capitalism. And this is also the context of the most dramatic social upheaval in the US in more than half a century. Sparked by the slow public murder of George Floyd by the Minneapolis police, thousands of citizens have recently faced down brutal and heavily militarized police in protest at a system of racist carceral oppression. They've inspired huge solidarity protests and political discussion internationally. The world has been shaken by chaos and instability, and by popular protest against repression. In Bolivia, a short-lived right-wing regime installed by military coup in 2019 was overturned the following year, after mass demonstrations violently and lethally put down by the authorities, with an election victory for the Left so resounding that even those committed to imagining fraud could not question it.[6] Upheaval has shaken Hong Kong, against the increasingly interventionist and heavy hand of the Chinese state. In May 2021, Palestinians across the whole of historic Palestine rose in furious reaction to the ethnic cleansing of the Sheikh Jarrah neighborhood of Jerusalem by Israeli authorities, an uprising to which Israel responded with its usual indiscriminate and provocative violence, including the shelling of the crowded prison that is the Gaza Strip. Thirteen Israelis, including two children, were killed—and twenty times as many Palestinians, and thirty-three times as many Palestinian children.

And on and on. To such lists of violence and resistance, countless more examples could be added. What is *The Communist Manifesto* in *this* moment?

---

The book you hold doesn't pretend to be an exhaustive evaluation of the *Manifesto* or its arguments. It's intended as a short introduction to an indispensable text with the curious and open-minded reader in mind. I presume no prior knowledge. I include synopses of, and quote liberally from, all the *Manifesto*'s sections. I've tried to make this book as freestanding as possible, while honoring the work of scholars and activists on which it draws. That's why the text is full of echoes, not shy to quote, to name names, even in passing, to speak words spoken best and first by others. And for those readers interested in investigating the sprawling literature further, in the endnotes I've alluded to and expanded at reasonable length on various debates, discussions and references to which I can only gesture in the main text.

Of course, no quotes or arguments can substitute for the original document. The *Manifesto*, barely 12,000 words long, is reproduced here as an appendix. If this introduction achieves nothing else, I hope it'll encourage new readers to explore that remarkable work.

The booklet was written in German in 1848 by Karl Marx and Friedrich Engels—though, as will become clear, that assignation isn't uncontroversial. Many, including Engels himself, grant Marx sole authorship: as I'll explain, I don't take that tack here. Over the years the text has seen an enormous number of editions and translations into countless languages.[7] By far the most prominent English translation is the 1888 version by Samuel Moore (also the translator of Marx's masterwork *Capital*), made in collaboration with Engels himself. It isn't, of course, beyond reproach. In his discussion of his own 1996 translation, Terrell Carver demolishes "the strongly held view that this English text, being blessed by the translator of *Capital*, vol. 1, and friend of Marx, and by Marx's political partner of some 40 years, is simply sacrosanct."[8] Apart from anything else, on such grounds one should have seen the substantial rehabilitation of the first English translation, of 1850, by the extraordinary Helen Macfarlane. Her version though, when not ignored, is mostly now traduced and mocked for some of its idiosyncratic renderings—Macfarlane, for example, introduces communism not as a spectre but, notoriously, as a "frightful hobgoblin." But far from being significant "only because the translator seems to have consulted Marx or . . . Engels," as Eric Hobsbawm puts it with hauteur,[9] Marx himself thought highly of Macfarlane as a radical intellectual, and attempted to have her translation printed as a brochure, and both he and Engels made repeated use of it and sent it to international comrades.[10]

In any case, however, particularly for the new reader, the Moore translation is certainly the best starting point. Whatever quibbles one may have, it's not only canonical but a fine and rousing translation, and thus an indispensable cultural port of call. It is this version, fractionally tweaked and updated, that is reproduced as an appendix here. Here it's numbered by section then paragraph, in the format "1.1," etcetera, and quotations and synopses from it are referred to in this introduction according to that system, for easy cross-reference. Of course, a purely "accurate" translation can never exist—"translation is interpretation"[11]— and I don't refrain from citing various other versions as they prove useful or interesting.

---

In what follows, Chapter 1 is a brief proem on the manifesto form itself. Chapter 2 outlines the historical context of *The Communist Manifesto*, and explores the place of the text in the broader thought of Karl Marx and Friedrich Engels. Chapter 3 comprises an expository precis of the *Manifesto*, and of various important afterwords it accumulated over the years. In Chapter 4, I unpack some of the *Manifesto*'s key claims, in order to consider it as a work of history, politics, economics and ethics.[12] In Chapter 5, I engage with certain important criticisms of the text, from several perspectives. The boundary between chapters 4 and 5 is porous: broadly, the former attempts to explicate and evaluate core claims and concepts of the *Manifesto*, and engage relatively briefly with criticism as part of that process, whereas the focus of the latter is more directly on some of what I consider the most important critiques of the document. Chapter 6 considers the *Manifesto* at our febrile moment, to bring its invective and exhortations to bear on the accelerating crises that face us, to ask what we must discard and what we might take from the *Manifesto* now. Whether it's in any way a guide. Whether it ever was.

The horizon for such questions isn't only intellectual. Like the authors of the *Manifesto*, I don't believe that the generalized mass misery of the world, all the unbearable checklists of deprivation and depravity, is irrelevant, nor unrelated to the economic system that runs the current order of things. Nor that the poverty of the poor is unrelated to the riches of the rich, nor the powerlessness of the disempowered to the power of the powerful. We're all familiar with inventories of inequality like the one quoted above, eliciting anguish from some and eyerolling from those for whom such anguish is politically gauche. I don't believe, for reasons outlined below, that such invidious realities are sad facts of human nature, nor that they are inevitable—though certainly changing them would not, will not, be easy. The question is whether it's worth the attempt. Whether those countless discarded and disempowered lives are worth fighting for and alongside.

Where I articulate my own views here, I try to do so in ways that will allow readers of various opinions to find value in the discussions. Only in the brief afterword are such issues engaged with without restraint. But nowhere do I pretend to be dispassionate or neutral. I hope I've been neither uncritical nor dogmatic, that I've avoided surrendering to the habits of cosplay leftism. Still, it will be obvious that this book is written from a perspective according to which the *Manifesto* is no mere historical curio, but a restless, urgent, vital document.

Which is why, for all the due-diligent exorcism above, a spectre haunts this text: that of a hunch, that the *Manifesto* does loom *now more than ever*.

This can never be a given. It might, however, be earned.

# 1

# On the *Manifesto* and the Manifesto Form

working with a paradox
defining the elusive
visualizing the invisible
communicating the incommunicable

Agnes Denes, *A Manifesto*

A manifesto embraces contradiction. It's unafraid of paradox. It delights in outrage. It provokes and insists and jokes and it's quite serious. It oscillates between registers. It is, as Marjorie Perloff puts it, "not quite 'theory' or 'poetry'" but "a space between the traditional modes and genres."[1] Manifestos are "flippant and sincere, prickly and smooth, logical and absurd, material and immaterial, shallow and profound . . . [f]leeting and permanent, serious and ridiculous," "unstable texts in the extreme." And they are "theatrical": "[p]erformance is part of the manifesto's materiality."[2]

Manifestos are everywhere. They've proliferated, particularly in the field of art, ever since the early modernist outbreak of "manifesto fever," stridently demanding this or that approach to this or that phenomenon, at the start of the twentieth century.[3] Most discussions of the form focus on such artistic manifestos, taking Marinetti's supremely seminal—and profoundly reactionary—1909 *The Founding and Manifesto of Futurism* as foundational. But it wasn't the first: Jean Moréas's *Symbolist Manifesto* dates from 1886, for example. Meanwhile, beyond the field of art, there's a much older tradition of politically revolutionary, often "revelatory" and millenarian, religious pamphlets. And for all the real distinctions between the aesthetic interventions of the avant-gardes and that earlier kind of manifesto as political statement, there's also continuity. Such simultaneous continuity and break is crucial in the case of *The Communist Manifesto* itself.

It was not the only politically radical self-styled manifesto of its moment—it emerged on the heels of the 1840 manifesto of the utopian socialist Robert Owen, Victor Considerant's 1841 *Manifesto of the Societarian* [sic] *School*, and its 1847 revision as the *Manifesto of Democracy*, the radical Krakow Manifesto for Polish freedom in 1846.[4] But *The Communist Manifesto* was a uniquely astonishing development and transformation of that earlier religio-political pamphleteering tradition—the unintentional creation of "a new genre" birthing the artistic manifesto.[5] "Anyone who manifestoed after Marx," as one curator of the form has it, "had the spectre of that sainted longhair hovering somewhere nearby."[6] In its radical "No," its extraordinary exigent rhetoric, its rushing hypnotic prose, even in the stridency of its typography,[7] *The Communist Manifesto* was and is an archetype, "the ur-manifesto of the modern period."[8]

Its declamatory tenor, "perhaps the most unabashedly rhetorical and flamboyant of Marx and Engels' writing,"[9] is immediately clear to any reader. Which is why it should be no less clear that the book is anything but a judiciously, cautiously laid-out set of scholarly propositions. That's what makes it all the more tone-deaf that very often it's treated as such—usually by critics, but often enough by friends. It's approached as if its tenets could be falsified or verified like mathematical proofs. The form and style of this performative text, so full of the "violence and precision" that Marinetti would later insist a manifesto needed, are in fact inextricable not only from assertions but from its transformative project.[10] In its "apocalyptic and poetic style," the *Manifesto* certainly makes various claims—but that very style also "serves a precise political purpose."[11] So, is lambasting the *Manifesto* for inaccuracy a category error, akin, say, to fact-checking a slogan? (And would it be self-evidently wrong to do that?)

Take one example. Responding to the *Manifesto*'s assertion that the bourgeoisie "produces its own gravediggers," Garry Runciman airily avers that "[t]his, as everyone knows, turned out to be mistaken," "falsified by unpredictable contingent events," and based on factual errors. Now, that counter-argument deserves to be investigated—and is, below. But so, too, does the context in which the *Manifesto*'s claims are made, and just how it makes them. That is to say, its *manifesto-ness* is relevant. And it calls into question Runciman's triumphalist conclusion that "[n]o rereading can alter or circumvent" the failure he discerns.[12]

An officer prepares troops for battle. She indicates on a map where intelligence suggests the enemy are gathered. She describes the landscape, lays out the plan of attack. Then, seeking to inspire her soldiers, she declaims: "We will win!" In fact, though the terrain itself is well-mapped, her intelligence about the enemy's whereabouts is somewhat less certain. And she has reason to believe, in any case, that the balance of forces may be against her. It would be nonsensical to read her claims that "This is a stretch of hard terrain," "The enemy perimeter is here" and "We will win!" as correct or incorrect *in the same way*. The assertions perform different, if overlapping, functions. But it's just such an approach that characterises a good deal of the discussion of *The Communist Manifesto*. In its pages, analysis, provocation, warning, aspiration, and inspiration are inextricable.

As we'll see, the text slides between registers, laying out policy, explaining the analysis that leads to it, condemning enemies, expressing ultimate hopes, glorying in language, all sometimes in one freighted phrase.

None of this inoculates the *Manifesto* against criticism. Nor does it mean that none of its assertions of fact can reasonably be evaluated. We'll have no truck with a certain zealously defensive reading according to which no offending or problematic statement in the *Manifesto* is meant as it's critically interpreted, but must be considered rhetoric rather than, say, historical claim. This is a kind of Marxist apologetic theology—hardly unknown on the Left.

The truth is, as one would expect of a rush-written pamphlet, that "[f] lawed and hastily conceived passages sit alongside brilliant insights."[13] The only reasonable way to read the *Manifesto*—or anything—is to be as flexible as the text itself. To proceed with rigor that's both sympathetic and suspicious, allowing for grey areas, uncertainties and good-faith disagreements. What errors and fallacies there are must be counted as such, without inferring that in and of themselves they necessarily fatally wound the text. We should strive to read as generously as possible—and to read ruthlessly beyond that generosity's limits. Both bouquet and brickbat should be predicated on an understanding of how the text works. That it performs distinct tasks, and deploys distinct, if overlapping, voices.[14]

One such is the voice intending to recruit and bolster comrades. It's perfectly understandable that our imaginary officer insists to her soldiers that they will win, whatever private doubts she may have. And what's more, delivered well, such an inspirational claim *increases the chances that it will be the truth*. This is the rational kernel behind Julian Hanna describing a manifesto "as a magic spell . . . a performative speech/act that attempts to bring a new reality into existence."[15] Inextricably from its analyses and polemic, and above all, *The Communist Manifesto* is hortatory, "a call to arms in the service of the revolution."[16]

The text is prophetic, poetic, melodramatic, and tragic: the proletariat "has nothing to lose but their chains" (4.11); in the rush of capitalism, "[a] ll that is solid melts into air, all that is holy is profaned" (1.18); competing socialist currents wear "a robe of speculative cobwebs . . . steeped in the dew of sickly sentiment" (3.33); and now, "[s]ociety suddenly finds itself put back into a state of momentary barbarism" (1.27).[17] All this, and more, to show that "society can no longer live under this bourgeoisie, in other words, its existence is no longer compatible with society" (1.52)—that is, to diagnose capitalism as a bleak and laughterless comedy. Vivid with fury and sarcasm, as well as with admiration for its enemies, the *Manifesto* demands to be read aloud, to savor the poetry of its imprecations, its repetitions. Its piling-up of litotes and enjambment presume an ethics of engagement, insisting that its readers join the movement and project that it proclaims. This is a rhetorical act of recruitment underlining that a campaign is necessary.[18] It's an interventionist speech act. "It is a manifesto: accordingly it not only works upon the material it analyses—it also intends for its analyses to work upon the readers."[19] This it obviously does in its declamatory final demand, capitals and all, that "WORKERS OF ALL COUNTRIES, UNITE!" (4.12); but it does so too in, say, the swagger with which it dispenses with capitalism's partisans—"let us have done with the bourgeois objections to Communism" (2.67)—to communicate their utter inadequacy. Evaluating the text's success has to mean gauging its impact, as well as the understanding of the world by which it arrives at its conclusion.[20]

What, then, is the relationship between such exhortation, stylistic flair and substantive claims?

For thousands of years, an influential strand of thinking has regarded rhetoric with deep suspicion. At best surplus and irrelevant to the substance of arguments, at worst it has been understood as mesmeric and dangerous—"the artificer," said Plato, "of a persuasion which creates belief about the just and unjust, but gives no instruction about them."[21] A vulgar version of this approach shores up an anticommunism for which "[i]n the beginning there was *The Communist Manifesto* . . . the first piece of communist propaganda."[22] The central role of "Marx's rhetorical gifts," as one implacable enemy of the *Manifesto* has recently put it, is to catch the reader up in a "stirring" work despite the danger of "such nonsense."[23] Rather more subtly than seeing logic and rhetoric as so starkly counterposed, other critics understand the two as "blended" in the *Manifesto*, making the text "more forceful and more moving."[24] Which doesn't at all mean they don't remain suspicious of its rhetorical flair.

And it's not only anticommunists who are concerned about the slippages facilitated by rhetoric. Consider a debate between Perry Anderson and Marshall Berman, both distinguished Marxists. In their wrestling over the relationship between revolution and "modernity" (which Anderson glosses as "neither economic process nor cultural vision but the *historical experience* mediating the one to the other")[25] a fascinating dispute arises over the *Manifesto*'s lush register. Berman's *All That Is Solid Melts Into Air* is a masterwork on the nature of capitalist modernity, and is itself one of the most lyrical investigations into the lyricism of the *Manifesto*, its "theme of insatiable desires and drives, permanent revolution, infinite development, perpetual creation and renewal in every sphere of life; and its radical antithesis, the theme of nihilism, insatiable destruction, the shattering and swallowing up of life, the heart of darkness, the horror."[26] For Berman, inhering in the *Manifesto*'s rush of "luminous, incandescent" prose is a protean modernism embodying change, and therefore undercutting a certain teleological outlook evident in the same text[27]—that is to say, a vision implying a final purpose or goal of history, begging questions and inverting causality, presuming a particular end. For Anderson, by contrast, such a focus on linguistic techniques risks obscuring the text's concrete arguments. Considering Berman's discussion of the "permanent revolution" of modern life evoked by the text, Anderson chides that "'[r]evolution' is a term with a precise meaning: the political overthrow from below of one state order and its replacement by another. Nothing is to be gained by diluting it across time or extending it over every department of social space. In the first case, it becomes indistinguishable from mere reform . . . in the second case, it dwindles to a mere metaphor."[28]

Now, Berman is attuned to the dangers here, and keen to distinguish his approach from a depoliticized "postmodernism" more enthralled by than critical of fragmentation, let alone cynical, as is much known by that name, about the potential for any liberatory project. Conversely, for Anderson it's important to see *through* rhetoric, and, wanting "to find some sort of closure in Marx' and Engels' text,"[29] here at least he understates the complex traction and politics of language itself. This complexity is particularly relevant for writers like Marx, for whom style is a matter of fascination and exacting attention.[30] One may certainly argue that "revolution" has a particularly important sense, a center of gravity in this text. But what it doesn't have is a single "precise meaning."[31] No language does, whether writers are conscious of that fact or not. All texts are, always, to various degrees, contradictory, multifarious, polysemic.[32]

This is not licence for epistemological anarchy, according to which anything, any reading, always goes. But it is to acknowledge that no text, whatever its author's (or reader's) intent, can have a simple, singular meaning. Every text will generate something like a tangle of meanings and connotations, more or less concentrated around a core, and more or less protean or stable, according to political, social, and linguistic context. As one playful formulation has it, rather than being straightforwardly "about" something in particular, every text is inevitably surrounded by a "vibrating aboutness cluster."[33] The context, content, and range of that cluster must be accounted for as part of an analysis. Some writers in some situations may strain against rhetorical shenanigans, for example striving for the specificity of logical notation: the cluster of reasonable meanings of such texts may well thus be less diffuse than for those which, say, revel in pun and performance. But a text with one "true" meaning is a chimera. Analysis is not closure, but an attempt to discern reasonable meaning(s) close to the core of that cluster, and to contest those that range too far from it.

In this case, in the *Manifesto* "revolution" is certainly, as Anderson insists, a crucial category with a particular meaning. But the echoes that surround it are neither irrelevant, nor supererogatory to that key sense.

The brilliant Venezuelan poet and philosopher Ludovico Silva has laid out how constitutive metaphors are to the text of the *Manifesto*, indeed to the whole of Marx's project. As he insists, metaphors can't be conflated with explanations, but they're not irrelevant to them, and we do need a *stylistic* reading of Marx, to acknowledge the centrality of such formulations and rhetoric, without collapsing them into analysis.[34] *The Communist Manifesto* is lavish with language and its play. It's full of ghosts and sorcerers and clothes made of cobwebs and rent cloth and gravediggers, and whatever else can be said about such metaphors, and *pace* Anderson, there's nothing "mere" about them. Chosen to express reality and politics more vividly than would be possible in their absence, they are constitutive and perspicacious—and persuasive.

There are those critics for whom wordplay—regrettably—trumps rigor. Echoing Plato's suspicion, for them it's "not by the veracity of its arguments" that the *Manifesto* recruits readers, but "by means of its rhetorical techniques."[35] Certainly these *can*, of course, be deployed in the service of conscious falsehoods, and/or barbarity. But whatever one might think of their rhetoric, the authors of the *Manifesto* are thunderously uncynical. Marx and Engels, rightly or wrongly, are convinced by their own claims. And precisely in expounding them so masterfully, they aim to make their claims about the future more likely.

# 2

# *The Communist Manifesto* in its Time

The bulk of the world's knowledge is an imaginary construction.

Helen Keller, *The World I Live In*

## In the Shadow of Revolution(s)

The *Manifesto* was published in February 1848, on the very eve of a revolutionary upheaval that shook Europe. For sixty years up to that point, Europe and the Americas had been defined by what's sometimes called a "dual revolution": the intermingling events and effects of the political revolution in France, and the industrial revolutions in Britain and elsewhere. Both of these in turn were in part culminations of the shake-up in political and scientific ideas under way since the seventeenth century that we know as the Enlightenment.[1]

Spreading out from Britain, the industrial revolution transformed economic organization with new techniques and sources of power, productive and transport technology, and the spread of the factory, which concentrated human labor and machinery together. Large sections of the European population still worked the land, though under changing conditions, while the growing industrial working class—the proletariat— were rapidly becoming centrally important to the economy. They lived and worked in generally appalling conditions, inevitably coming into bitter conflict with the bosses and owners for whom they extracted profit. Predictably, this led to the growth of political militancy.

The great French Revolution of 1789–94, meanwhile, was still a living memory. This convulsive overthrow of power had replaced a system of absolutist monarchy and peasant serfdom with a new republic that proclaimed liberty, equality, and fraternity as ascendant, over outdated feudal "virtues" such as hierarchy, stability, and obedience.[2] Internecine political squabbles and pressures, along with attempts by the other European monarchies to destroy the revolution, meant the new regime would follow a strange trajectory. Soon it fell under the contradictory rule of self-proclaimed emperor Napoleon Bonaparte, who defended certain legal and economic advances of the revolution, while limiting political rights, and sending his armies across the world to build an empire for the benefit of bourgeois France. After his defeat in 1815 by the United Kingdom and the reactionary and autocratic regimes of what then became known as the "Holy Alliance"—Russia, Prussia (in what's now Germany), and Austria—France was briefly run by the retrograde monarchical regime of Charles X. That rule would be replaced in short order, after three days of barricades and street fighting, in the July Revolution of 1830, by the reign of Louis Philippe d'Orléans, the last French monarch. Known as the "bourgeois king," Louis Philippe's was a cliquish, venal, and corrupt constitutional monarchy that consolidated the political rule of the property-owning middle class.

No sooner were they triumphantly expressed than those radical ideas of the revolution, *liberté, égalité,* and *fraternité,* came up against the hard limits of bourgeois society itself. Whatever some of its radical advocates might have believed or wanted, that society was—and is—fundamentally driven by the maximization of profit, and the power over it. That's not to say that those ideals that its partisans professed, or professed to profess, were completely arbitrary, without any structural relation to that mode of social organization. Nor, however, were they—or are they—the driving force of society, but part of an organizing ideology functional to it, on the basis of accumulation that is predicated on, and policed by, ferocious and barbaric violence. Most glaringly, as the great C. L. R. James points out, "[t]he slave-trade and slavery were the economic basis of the French Revolution."[3] That bourgeois society was, and still is, resistant to any change that might put profit maximization in jeopardy or threaten the stability on which such profit and power relies. This stability was not just able to accommodate oppression and repression, but was shored up in part through it, proclamations of liberty and equality notwithstanding. Women, for example, were not granted suffrage. With the Law of May 20, 1802, Napoleon Bonaparte overturned the earlier law of February 4, 1794 that had abolished slavery in French colonies.[4] Such appalling racist and reactionary acts as these, and the norms they expressed, were never just regrettable political atavism, "mere" backwardness: they made clear certain real priorities of actually existing republicanism and liberalism.[5]

But nor were those liberal ideals simply *lies*. Rather, their meanings were always *contested*. On the one hand they were, as James puts it, deployed "with a fencer's finesse and skill," proclaimed—and extended, radicalized and made a material force—by great revolutionary rebels against oppression, such as Toussaint Louverture during the Haitian slave uprising and revolution of 1791–1804. In a letter of 1792, Louverture proclaimed: "Let the sacred flame of liberty that we have won lead all our acts. Let's go forth to plant the tree of liberty, breaking the chains of those of our brothers still held captive under the shameful yoke of slavery. Let us bring them under the compass of our rights, the imperceptible and inalienable right of free men." At the same time, such ideals were also proclaimed by those who betrayed the insurgent slaves for the sake of power and property. In an extraordinary poem of 1804, "In Praise of

Suriname," the Dutch-Surinamese writer and merchant Paul François Roos made vividly clear how inextricable "liberty" could be from its opposite. "Instruct your children . . . to raise up temples in praise of liberty!" he enjoined the reader, before enthusiastically predicting that "Africa's coast . . . / Will serve us as a warehouse packed with sturdy slaves!"[6]

Even fought over, contradictory and complex, as they travelled, often with the victorious French armies, such ideas were opposed by partisans of the Holy Alliance. Whatever meaning they took on in different contexts, the spread of republican ideas in this turbulent epoch threw up questions such as free speech and freedom of the press, the liberation of nations under colonialism, the consolidation of fractured post-feudal polities, the rights and conditions of workers, and, crucially, democracy itself. These were all immensely controversial, and immensely important, issues. They inspired popular unrest and were central to tumultuous popular struggles.

In Europe, the 1840s were a time of political and economic crisis, of harvest failure and terrible deprivation. During these "Hungry 40s," the famines and the cruel refusal of governments to alleviate starvation caused over a million deaths, many of them in the British colony of Ireland.[7] From the 1830s on, the largest organized expression of radical opposition arose in England, where the Chartists, an independent working-class group, demanded, among other things, universal male suffrage. But across the continent and beyond, oppositional groups of radical republicans proliferated further to the left, too, in a mass of associations and clubs, often illegal—and very often involving émigré German workers, in Paris, Brussels, Geneva, and London. These were considerably more liberal environments than those the refugees had fled, and there they could capitalize on certain social freedoms.[8] In their hopes of overthrowing an unjust society, many of these groups held to romantic models of secret conspiratorial organizations. This skulduggerous, dashing lineage was reflected in the elusive, allusive poetry of some of their names: the Society of the Families; the Society of Seasons; the League of the Proscribed.

In 1834, German workers in Paris formed the Bund der Geächteten—the League of Outlaws. At its peak, this organization had fewer than 200 members. Within three years these outlaws succumbed to the fissiparous tendencies of the politically dissident, with the splintering off of many of the more working-class members under the leadership of Wilhelm Weitling into the religiously inflected communist Bund der Gerechten: the League of the Just.

It was this Justice League which would be central to the creation of *The Communist Manifesto*.

## Marx and Engels

By the time they came to collaborate on the *Manifesto*, Marx and Engels had already established themselves as leading figures in the radical movements. That was, in large part, why the League of the Just offered them the commission to write the text of the document that has long outlived the Bund der Gerechten.

Marx was born in 1818 in Trier, Engels in 1820 in Baumen, both in the Rhineland. These are now German towns, or parts thereof, but at the time there was no such political entity as "Germany." Rather, the German Confederation, born out of the 1815 Congress of Vienna, was a coagulum of forty-one states and statelets of various degrees of power, political form, economic advancement, and cultural ambience. Among these, the Rhineland was somewhat unusual. It was a province of Prussia, one of the authoritarian, neo-absolutist great powers of the Holy Alliance, very different from the bourgeois republic of France, and fallow ground for liberal or democratic hankerings.[9] But the Rhineland itself had been controlled by Napoleon until 1813, and its culture had been touched by French revolutionary ideas, and was considerably more liberal and intellectually open than was the Prussian norm.

Marx's was an affluent liberal family of Jewish origin, though his father had strategically converted to Protestantism when the Rhineland passed back to those reactionary, officially anti-Semitic Prussian hands. As a student, Marx junior had an enthusiasm for radical ideas and milieux, and for poetry over the law that he was supposed to be studying. In 1836 he transferred from Bonn to Berlin University, where he became fascinated by the notoriously complex and abstruse works of the great philosopher G. W. F. Hegel.

The crucial element in Hegel's thought was the "dialectic." This, to hugely simplify, is a dynamic model of totality, including society, according to which the world is not at base static, but in which fundamental grand-scale change and development occurs through epochs, and in which such motion derives from tensions and dynamics intrinsic to phenomena, rather than as the result of contingent stimuli from outside. Such social phenomena contain the seeds of their own developments—and their own overturnings. For Hegel, *Weltgeist*—"world spirit," a sort of soul of the age—developed through history, moving towards ever-greater freedom. This was exemplified for him by Napoleon's liberal reforms in Prussia after the French Revolution, of which he was an initial enthusiast. Which raised a question: what is the trajectory of that *Weltgeist* when those reforms were then replaced by the repressive policies of Prussia, in what looked, surely, like a backward step?

Hegel died in 1832, and in his later years he turned somewhat towards reaction, moving towards squaring this circle by seeing in a version of that Prussian state Reason itself. It's important not to overstate this: Hegel's own position was considerably less enthusiastic about the existing state than later representations might imply.[10] For all that, a certain articulation of that later Hegelianism could be made appealing to the powers that were. For which reason, irrespective of the nuances of his thought, after his death he was "to all intents and purposes, the official Prussian philosopher."[11]

Against such quiescent theorizing, the atheist and, by certain markers, liberal thinkers known as the "Young Hegelians" adopted radical interpretations of his earlier positions—including against Hegel himself. For them, "the Absolute," which for Hegel had been God and reason, was humanity, and any implication from any epigone that the Prussian state might be its embodiment was a contemptible betrayal of the model. Philosophically, these ill-tempered contrarian disciples tended towards "idealism": that is to say, for them the fundamental motor of the world was the realm of ideas. For many, then, it was thus in that realm that social change occurred.[12] Marx was initially attracted by Young Hegelianism. His political radicalism manifested at first in spirited, often courageous attacks on Prussian absolutism, and in demands for reform, such as for freedom of the press. But what distinguished it wasn't only the trenchancy of its attacks on reaction, but Marx's withering impatience with the pusillanimity and inadequacy of the liberal opposition. "God save me," he wrote in 1842, "from my friends!"[13]

This radicalism was underlined by his soon being won over from idealism to an opposing position of philosophical "materialism." To this day, critics of materialism regularly recite the tenacious canard that the model crudely counterposes "economic" factors to "culture, ideology, and mentality," and that "[t]he realm of pure human thought and idea is relegated by the Marxist to a state of jejune non-effectuality."[14] That for materialism, thought is epiphenomenal froth. This is bogus.

The point is emphatically and explicitly not that culture and ideas are irrelevant. Nor that, so toothless, they can in a reductive, mechanical way be "decoded" as mere echoes of economic, material interests. What the model suggests instead is that in all their specificity and rich texture, such cultural and psychic factors are ultimately, in highly complex ways, thrown up by and functions of underlying material social reality. This is not to say that they have no impact, nor that they are smoothly functional *to*, even if functions *of*, a given system.[15] The affective, the symbolic, the of-the-mind, need not and should not be outcast elements in Marxism—as what follows will attempt to make clear.

Such a textured perspective on materiality and subjectivity would become increasingly clear over the maturation of Marx and Engels's work (not that that would get in the way of the calumnies). Still, though their terminology changed and their analysis developed, the model is limned fairly clearly as early as 1845–46, in the co-written *The German Ideology*. And it informs the *Manifesto*.

Marx gained his PhD in philosophy in 1841, but any path into academia was blocked by official opposition to certain ideas, such as those of the Young Hegelians. Instead, he went into journalism. When his work was suppressed by those censorious Prussian authorities he left for Paris. There he encountered the radical German émigrés of the League of the Just, alongside various other squabbling leftist currents, and the beginnings of an organized working-class movement. Marx was vastly impressed, eulogising "the pure freshness, the nobility which burst forth from these toil-worn men," and asserting that it was "among these 'barbarians' of our civilised society that history is preparing the practical element for the emancipation of mankind."[16] Such a milieu, along with an intensive study of political economists such as Adam Smith, as well as an important and inspiring 1844 rebellion by German (Silesian) weavers, pulled him firmly to the left. In that year—the same year that his first child, his daughter Jenny, was born—he became a communist.

Exactly what this meant was, of course, no less vexed then than it is today. An outline of the historical context of the tradition, and the specifics of Marxist communism, will be developed below. Broadly speaking, to be a communist in the 1840s was to assert a principle of radical equality and of a community of goods, in opposition to private property.

Marx developed his theories in various important essays of this time, including "On the Jewish Question" (1843), "Towards a Critique of Hegel's Philosophy of Right" (1843) and the "Economic and Philosophic

Manuscripts" (1844). In the first he argued that another French-style "political" revolution—that is, one that ushered in a new governmental form, even in a reactionary polity such as Prussia, without fundamentally altering the underlying political economy of a newly entrenching capitalism—would leave the social atomization of individuals in place, and could not usher in "human emancipation." In the second, he suggested that the German bourgeoisie was too weak to bring about such a revolution, and that the workers were the only group in a position to play a leading role. And in the last and perhaps most important, he focused on that proletariat as the key productive group within capitalism, and the one, therefore, that in liberating itself would liberate humanity as a whole. These writings contained a vital early formulation of the core relation, for Marx, between revolution, the working class as the central agent that might bring it about and universal liberation. "From the relationship of estranged labor to private property it follows that the emancipation of society from private property, etc., from servitude, is expressed in the *political* form of the *emancipation of the workers*."[17]

Engels came from even more privileged stock than Marx, being the son of a wealthy businessman. In his early years he was a rakish partygoer. He, too, gravitated to the Young Hegelians, and to what was then the cutting edge of that movement, the work of Ludwig Feuerbach. Already an "ardent communist" by 1842—fully two years before Marx—Engels traveled to Manchester to work for his father's company. He was appalled and enraged by the poverty and degradation suffered by the English proletariat, and in 1845 he published, in German, the furious and pioneering study *The Condition of the Working Class in England*. Of which more below.

Marx and Engels met briefly in 1842. They did not think much of each other. It was in 1844 when they met again, in Paris, that they established the close personal friendship, intimate political comradeship, and impressive intellectual collaboration that would last until Marx's death in 1883. Soon after this second meeting, the two young men co-wrote *The Holy Family* and *The German Ideology*. These bear on the *Manifesto* in important ways. The former was in part an attack on that "idealist" radical thought according to which the moving principle of history was "spirit." Here, Marx and Engels argued instead for a materialist basis to their radical politics. They developed this point of view in *The German Ideology*, among other things an attack on Young Hegelianism. In this text, Marx and Engels defined "alienation" as a material, social, and psychically deleterious process whereby workers must sell their productive activity, becoming a means to an end not their own, and are thus estranged from their own creativity, from other humans and from nature. They concluded that to overcome this baleful condition, private property, the absolute right of an owner to determine the use of what they "own," most particularly with regard to the ownership of the means of production themselves, must be abolished.

*The German Ideology* is now perhaps best known for its tersely expounded claim that "[t]he ideas of the ruling class are in every epoch the ruling ideas, i.e. the class which is the ruling material force of society, is at the same time its ruling intellectual force." The section "Ruling Class and Ruling Ideas" in which this model is developed offers a considerably more nuanced development than is sometimes implied of the relationship between the ruling class's interests, and its vastly disproportionate opportunities both to expound ideas that further such interests, and to abstract such ideas so that they may—while not uncontested—tend to take on the semblance of common sense and/or eternal truths. An analysis of the contested approaches to ideology—Marxist and other ways into the question of how we apprehend and misapprehend our relationships to capitalism—ranges far beyond us here.[18] Still, the discussion that follows is informed by a sense of the power of such ideology, the social tenacity of sets of ideas thrown up by and functional to systems of inequality and oppression, including among those who suffer from those systems, such as one might, with caveats and care, derive from this *German Ideology* model. What will also become clear in what follows is a distinct if related model of the central ideological importance of the *circumscription* of possible thought.

Beyond this question, in *The German Ideology* Marx and Engels drew four conclusions from their conception of the alienated nature of labor in a system of private property, that would inform the *Manifesto* that followed. First, that the economic development of society would reach a point when its organizational norms were in tension with those of social organization and thus "only cause mischief," when its forces "are no longer productive but destructive," and that "connected with this a class is called forth"—the working class—"which has to bear all the burdens of society without enjoying its advantages . . . and from which emanates the consciousness of the necessity of a fundamental revolution, the communist consciousness." Conscious, perhaps, of their own non-proletarian circumstances, the authors allowed that such consciousness might also "arise among the other classes too through the contemplation of the situation of this class."[19]

Second, that over and against this productive class is another, a ruling class, with opposed interests, and whose social power, "deriving from its property, has its practical-idealistic expression in each case in the form of the State." In this model, the state itself, with all its bureaucracy and power, is not the neutral arbitrator of conflict, including between the classes, as it's often described, but ultimately expresses ruling-class power. For Marx and Engels, it is, as it has been through history, against the ruling class that the revolutionary struggle must be waged.

Third, that revolutionary upheavals had hitherto been political, that is, concerned with reorganizing power *in*, rather than with the overturning *of*, existing economic "relations of production." But they argued that a communist revolution must be different. Such a revolution must fundamentally alter the social and economic composition of the existing order, and be "directed against the preceding mode of activity" to abolish "the rule of all classes with the classes themselves," as "the expression of the dissolution of all classes, nationalities, etc." The struggle to do away with the iniquities of the system is necessarily on a total social scale, a fundamental overturning of capitalism, its dynamics, norms, and structures. Which is to say, the abolition of structural social inequality—class itself.

Finally, that such a revolution is necessary, "not only because the ruling class cannot be overthrown in any other way, but also because the class overthrowing it can only in a revolution succeed in ridding itself of all the muck of ages and become fitted to found society anew." In this model, capitalism may be tinkered with, but it cannot be made a system worth living in. It must be replaced. And, no less crucially, only by effecting such change can people change themselves, as they deserve to and must, to live in the better world they—we?—usher in. Everyone knows that Marx and Engels wanted to change society: less emphasized, but no less important, is their belief in people's self-empowerment, through that radical activity, their self-alteration "on a mass scale," into, as Engels puts it in an early draft of the *Manifesto*, "an entirely different kind of human material."[20] The self-liberators of the future will remake themselves, too. Ours is a humanity defined by unfreedom: central to theirs will be freedom.

## The Context of Communism

"Communism" as a political concept rose to rapid prominence in Europe through the 1840s.[21] "[W]hen it was written," Engels said of the *Manifesto* in 1888, "we could not have called it a *socialist* manifesto . . . [I]n 1847, socialism was a middle-class movement, communism a working-class movement. Socialism was . . . "respectable"; communism was the very opposite."[22] This opposition to "respectability" was a residual commitment to *Geächtet* status, to being outlaw, a renunciation of polite norms that one might read as childish provocation or liberatory recalcitrance, depending on your generosity. This distinction between socialism and communism would soon lessen in cultural importance, and Marx and Engels would come fairly quickly to be content to use either term to describe their own positions. But when the *Manifesto* was written, "socialist" broadly described anyone concerned with the social problems of capitalism, whatever piecemeal and/or eccentric solutions they might propose. By contrast, the communism of *The Communist Manifesto* is committed to some model of communal democratic ownership, in place of the existing system of individual private property, profit, and competitive accumulation.

And it's not just the end result that's centrally important, dreamed of as some ultimate horizon, but the notion of how it might be reached. At the time of writing, communists were those, Engels said, who "proclaimed the necessity of total social change."[23] For them, what was vital was a fundamental radical break with the status quo—to use a key word from the *Manifesto*, a *rupture*.[24]

Proto-communism extends back at least to the radical religious sects of the sixteenth century, which attempted to hold property in common, often in opposition to the power and wealth of established churches, and to the modernisation of such ideas in the insurgent ideologies calling for private property's abolition in the eighteenth century. It's late in that century that the words "communist" and "communism" in such radical political iterations first appear, influenced by the hard-left egalitarian minority in the French Revolution, exemplified, for example, by Gracchus Babeuf.[25] Such an ultra-radical wing of republicanism re-emerged in France's July Revolution of 1830, committed to a deep egalitarianism, and a community of property against the private property they saw as central to social power and inequality. This tendency spread, informing pre-existing political dissent and taking on various colors around Europe and the world—to local ruling-class horror.[26] While acknowledging the prehistory and history of communism, for Marx and Engels socialism and communism "proper" arrive with the struggle between bourgeoisie and proletariat.[27] In the first half of the nineteenth century, a plethora of socialist, communist, and anarchist individuals and groups stood in opposition to capitalism (as well as, very often, to each other). Some drew on radical religious doctrine, some on utopian thinkers such as Saint-Simon, Fourier, Robert Owen, Victor Considerant, and Proudhon, setters-up of "humane" factories, dreamers up of unlikely new communities, writers of impassioned visionary prose, preachers of a social gospel.[28] Some were idealists committed to peaceful change in, of and by the human spirit; others were conspiracists plotting the violent overthrow of governments by a tiny, ruthless, enlightened minority. In 1846, Marx and Engels, now working together, inaugurated what they called a Communist Correspondence Committee, to forge ties with various such radicals. These included the left-wing leaders of that mass working-class British movement, the Chartists, and, at the other end of the scale, the few hundred members of the League of the Just.

By 1847 the two friends had become leading lights in the radical movement. They committed to join the League—and struggled to win control of it. Engels came to London in June for its Congress, at which it renamed itself the Communist League and reorganized itself along less conspiratorial, more democratic lines. It also notably shifted in its tone. Its previous slogans had been strong on philosophically idealist, moralist propaganda, abstract sentiments about love and equality. (As will be argued, one might just make a persuasive case for the political salience of love, but only insofar as that phenomenon is understood as part of a broader concrete political totality, perhaps inextricable from, but hardly reducible to, the love on which one focuses.) Now the organization adopted the call: "Workers of all countries unite." This was evidence of the growing impact of Marx and Engels's ideas and political approach.

Engels quickly produced a draft of a communist "confession of faith," its question-and-answer form laying out the group's positions in the form of a religious catechism.[29] "Question 1) Are you a Communist?" it demanded. Then in answer: "Yes." It continued:

**Question 2:** What is the aim of the Communists?

**Answer:** To organise society in such a way that every member of it can develop and use all his capabilities and powers in complete freedom and without thereby infringing the basic conditions of this society.

**Question 3:** How do you wish to achieve this aim?

**Answer:** By the elimination of private property and its replacement by community of property.

And so on, in similar form, twenty-two questions in total. In October, the League mandated Engels to produce a longer second version, now known as "Principles of Communism."[30] Engels had come to see limitations in this didactic structure, however, and, ruminating on what kind of document the League and wider movement needed, he wrote to Marx: "I believe that the best thing is to do away with the catechism form and give the thing the title: Communist Manifesto. We have to bring in a certain amount of history, and the present form does not lend itself to this very well."[31]

Preparations were afoot. Six years previously, before he knew Marx, Engels had anonymously published a long satirical poem, *The Triumph of Faith*, in which he had mocked the left philosopher Arnold Ruge, having him demand of listeners "hear my Manifesto, all of you," as part of his depiction as a revolutionary in word but not deed.[32] Now, Engels saw more use for the manifesto form as a political intervention.

From November 29, for ten days, the League held its second Congress in London. This time both Marx and Engels were present for the fervent and furious debates between their materialist, class-struggle-based communism, and the remnants of idealist(ic), universal-brotherhood-style quasi-religiose communism. Marx gave a speech, one old comrade would report years later, that was "brief, convincing and compelling in its logic," and "[t]he more I realized the difference between the communism of Weitling's time and that of the [soon to be written]

*Communist Manifesto*, the more clearly I saw that Marx represented the manhood of socialist thought."[33] This gendered language sticks in the throat today, and undoubtedly expresses unexamined nostrums about the movement. At an intentional level, however, the implication was intended to be of "maturity" as much as of masculinity.

Marx and Engels won the organization to their views. "The old idyllic "community of goods" was replaced by the new realistic political-economic program of the class struggle to abolish private property"—a materialist politics in an attempt to ground and give teeth to an ethical aspiration.[34] As a result, Marx was tasked to draft the official program. After the Congress he returned to Brussels and set to.[35]

He drew heavily on Engels's earlier work, his two catechisms. As we've seen, after Marx's death Engels disavowed any credit for the document. This was entirely characteristic of the man in his relationship with Marx. He was too modest. For all that Marx was the key force behind the text that we know, not only was Engels's general influence on him very important, not only was it he who proposed the manifesto form, but those catechisms were a crucial concrete foundation for the *Manifesto*, in terms of structure and of key concepts, overall approach and tone. It's not, then, out of mere sentimentality that Marx and Engels are often jointly credited as the *Manifesto*'s writers—as they are here.[36]

His comrades eagerly awaited their promised document. But Marx did not deliver. He kept toiling over the *Manifesto*, the work dragging and dragging, an early example of what would become a lifetime's practice, Marx's "abiding brinkmanship with deadlines."[37] He was writing against a backdrop of growing tumult and upheaval, across Europe and beyond, but not even an epochal convergence of world history itself, as if to prove his point and validate his thesis, and on which he could reasonably hope his manifesto might actually have an impact, could prod him into delivering on time.

The year 1847 had been one of economic crisis, the worst year of the Irish potato famine, one of the hungriest of those Hungry 40s. Only in

Britain did the industrial bourgeoisie have any real weight in political systems: elsewhere, institutional tension between intransigent reactionary regimes and the economically powerful middle class continued, as the conditions of disenfranchised workers remained dire. Prognosticators of left and right predicted revolution. In the last months of 1847 Switzerland was shaken by the Sonderbund War, a conflict between Catholic and Protestant cantons of the Swiss confederation, best understood less as a religious than a political confrontation between conservative and liberal-democratic bourgeois forces. Alarmed conservatives around Europe viewed it, indeed, as such, and as a prefiguration of political upheaval, an attempt to sweep away old monarchical structures by middle and working classes. "See what is preparing itself amongst the working classes," warned the great French political scientist Tocqueville at the start of 1848. "We are sleeping on a volcano . . . Do you not see that the earth trembles anew? A wind of revolution blows."[38]

This was the heady nature of the time, and still Marx wrote. On January 12, 1848, the revolutionary year, known as the Springtime of the Peoples, properly began. Insurrection broke out in Sicily, provoking similar uprisings across what's now Italy. This was the era of the telegraph, and word spread. Engels himself published articles—"Movements of 1847," "The Beginning of the End in Austria"—on the rumblings of revolution. Still Marx wrote. The earth was trembling anew, and the communists did not yet have their manifesto. Representatives of the League sent Marx a dark and agitated warning that if the manifesto didn't reach London by the following week, "further measures" would be taken against him.

Whatever those nebulous measures might have been, and whether for fear of them or not, Marx did at last manage to draw the document to a close—though, as we shall see, the ending feels, to put it politely, truncated. The manuscript arrived in London and was rushed into print. In mid-February, a dark green pamphlet at last appeared.

*Manifest der Kommunistiche Partei*, its cover read. *Proletarier aller Länder vereinigt Euch!*

The Manifesto of the Communist Party. Proletarians of all countries, unite!

This was not the manifesto of the Communist League, per se: that name appeared nowhere on or in the book, for all that it was a legal organization in Britain. The aspirations of the authors and their comrades were greater than that. "At this time, well before the development of modern party systems in politics, the word 'party' (in any European language) meant primarily a tendency or current of opinion, not an organized group." In declaring itself the manifesto of the Communist Party, the title thus claimed, with extraordinary audacity, "This is the communist point of view."[39]

This declaration of such an insurgent perspective arrived into a world in upheaval. Engels had been expelled from France at the end of January, by a government made skittish by the prospect of revolution. Revolution which was indeed beginning in Paris by the time the *Manifesto* appeared, after that government banned political banquets, a favored form of middle-class opposition to the regime. Crowds of Parisians, working-class and liberal middle-class, filled the streets, throwing up barricades in what Marx called the "beautiful revolution," fighting the city guards and dying in large numbers. Louis-Philippe fled for his life, and the French monarchy was—once again, and finally this time—done.

Revolution continued and spread elsewhere, into what would become "the only truly European revolution that there has ever been" and "in some respects a global upheaval."[40] In March, the Belgian government expelled Marx from Brussels, and he and Engels and other members of the League repaired to Germany, where they were active in the revolution there. Uprisings would imminently shake Berlin and Vienna. There would be tumult in Norway and Palermo, Moldavia, Hungary, Portugal, and repercussions as far away as Ceylon, the Caribbean, and Australia.[41] As well as demands for liberal civil rights, the crowds called for independence for European nation-states under the control of the imperial powers. In Britain, the Chartists, that working-class mass movement for reform, organised large demonstrations.

The hope of Marx and Engels, by March both in Cologne, was that the German middle class would perform their "historic mission." This would be to sweep away the appurtenances of feudalism, ushering in a liberal modernity that would dispense with the muck of the old autocratic system, bettering the political conditions for workers as well as the bourgeoisie, allowing the flowering of capitalist development, and clearing fertile ground for the growth and swift political triumph of workers' power thereafter. "Bourgeois Germany," they had just written in the *Manifesto*, "will be but a prelude to an immediately following proletarian revolution." (4.7)

Workers should have "the clearest possible recognition of the hostile antagonism" (4.6) between them and capitalists, but should "fight with the bourgeoisie whenever it acts in a revolutionary way." (4.5) Utterly committed to the cause of the working class as the far-left edge of the democratic revolution, they held that, as a bourgeois revolution, this democratic republic had to be ushered in by the bourgeoisie as part of a class alliance against the old rulers. Marx's "policy was to spur on the bourgeoisie from an independent base on the left, organizing the plebeian classes separately from the bourgeoisie in order to strike together at the old regime, and to prepare this democratic bloc of proletariat, petty bourgeoisie and peasantry to step temporarily into the vanguard should the bourgeoisie show signs of cold feet."[42] To push, that is, working-class politics, including to the receptive elements of the bourgeoisie which Marx believed in and considered a necessary agent, from and to the left. Hence he took up editorship of the *Neue Rheinische Zeitung*, a political newspaper opposed to German reaction, and funded by the furthest-left wing of local capitalism, with an intended readership of those funders, workers, peasants and petty traders.

But far from cementing middle-class rule over the *ancien régime* as the revolution's working-class advocates and militants had hoped, the bourgeoisie across Europe proved considerably more fearful of the revolutionary threats from below to the status quo than they were opposed to that status quo itself.[43]

Initially, it looked as if the German bourgeoisie, for all its obvious lack of mettle, might take the kind of revolutionary action the Left expected of it. Under popular pressure, some political gains were made. But by the middle of the year a palpable wave of reaction was setting in across the continent. Over several days in June, the new Republican government of France ruthlessly smashed a workers' uprising in Paris, killing more than 3,000 people. In September, a popular insurrection in Frankfurt was quelled by the authorities calling in Austrian and Prussian troops. Martial law was proclaimed in Cologne and, in November, in Berlin, and an uprising in Vienna was crushed by the Habsburg Empire. Ultimately, the German middle classes, rather than stand even reluctantly alongside the radicals and working-class movements opposing the Prussian monarchy, made peace with that shaken but ultimately triumphant power, in exchange for a few constitutional crumbs.[44] The European revolution fell to shattering defeat.

In his "The Bourgeoisie and the Counter-Revolution" of December 1848, Marx tried to make sense of what had gone so very wrong. "The German bourgeoisie had developed so sluggishly, so pusillanimously and so slowly, that it saw itself threateningly confronted by the proletariat, and all those sections of the urban population related to the proletariat in interests and ideas, at the very moment of its own threatening confrontation with feudalism and absolutism. . . . It had sunk to the level of a type of estate . . . inclined from the outset to treachery against the people."[45] The impact of this realization on Marx's thought, and, retrospectively, on the *Manifesto*, is touched on in Chapter 4.

Facing a wave of counter-revolutionary reaction throughout Europe, in 1849 Marx and Engels relocated to the relative freedom of England. There they would consider, among other things, how best to relate to a necessary bourgeois revolution when the bourgeoisie refuses to play its allotted role; there they would see the Communist League wither and die; there they would continue their lifetime of radical work.

And the *Manifesto*, that quintessential young writers' book?

The *Manifesto* had seemed a text "arising from the revolution even as it sought to trigger the revolution,"[46] had drawn thousands to discuss it in Amsterdam in June 1848, had been eagerly disseminated in Cologne throughout that revolutionary year.[47] Now it seemed as if counter-revolution might sweep it away.

Interest in the *Manifesto* did not dry up completely. Demand continued sporadically in the initial aftermath of 1848,[48] and Macfarlane's pioneering English translation appeared in the weekly *Red Republican* in 1850. The 1850s in general, however, were something of a desert for the *Manifesto*, and a low point in Marx's own life.[49] "With the disappearance from the public scene of the workers' movement that had begun with the February Revolution," Engels would write in the 1890 preface to the reissued book, "the Manifesto too passed into the background." It enjoyed a small upsurge of fortune in the late 1860s, with the publication of Marx's *Capital* Volume 1 in 1867, partly simply a matter of name recognition of its author, partly because *Capital* includes substantial quotes from the earlier book. Still, one scholar can describe the *Manifesto*, by the early 1870s, as "a nearly forgotten little work."[50]

In the preface to the 1872 publication, Marx and Engels stressed that various editions had been published in the twenty-four years since the book's first appearance, but in truth its influence wasn't particularly extensive. The rhythms with which it was republished and cited, however, are telling. After an initial small burst of references, a fallow decade followed from the early 1850s, during the reactionary crackdown after 1848. Thereafter arose little waves of new editions, and/or citations to the text, at moments of political upheaval, evidence of the *Manifesto*'s modestly growing influence, until new editions begin to proliferate again in the 1870s.

The bloody suppression of the Paris Commune, the radical government that arose in that city in 1871 at the end of the Franco-Prussian War, a remarkable and all-too-brief experiment in working-class rule, had a substantial clarifying impact on some of Marx and

Engels's own ideas, including in the *Manifesto*, as will become clear. It also abruptly increased interest in the text. This was in part due to Marx's new notoriety as a supporter of the Commune, and partly due to his leadership of the organization he attempted to wield as an organ of working-class solidarity, the International Workingmen's Association.[51] Given the lessons taught to Marx and Engels by the Commune, with regard to questions of political organization, and in the context of their insistence against the anarchists within the IWA that workers must organize within political parties, from this point the *Manifesto* could be read in a renewed way, as a renewed intervention, as an even more direct call than previously for political action by workers' revolutionary parties, and for a reconfiguring of the state as part of that revolutionary action.

After the Commune, it was in part the very antipathy to communism, often in the shape of thunderous attacks on the text, that fed curiosity in the *Manifesto*. Alongside this continued more sympathetic interest, leading to various new translations, and pressure for a new English version, culminating in the Moore translation of 1888.[52] This edition, in the context of the "new unionism," the increasing militancy and wider recruitment practices of British trade unionism in the 1880s, accelerated the growing interest. This peaked again in 1905 and 1917—these, of course, were years of revolutionary upheaval in Russia. All of which is to say that "the distribution of the *Manifesto* tracks the periods of revolutionary upheaval of 1848, 1871, 1905, and 1917."[53] The *Manifesto* "increasingly became an index of revolutionary activity."[54]

It may have failed in its initial speech act, as an incitement to political rupture. But the *Manifesto* did not go the way of all the hundreds of other angry radical documents of the nineteenth century. If the 1870s began the turnaround for the text in earnest, there commenced then forty years of the rise of social-democratic labor parties, during and due to which "the Manifesto conquered the world."[55] 1917, the Russian Revolution, was a key turning point. Not only did the leaders of the massive and powerful state that would come to be the USSR declare their fidelity to the text, but, over the years that followed, that state turned its resources to publishing it, along with other works of Marx and Engels, in vast numbers of cheap editions.[56]

On a considerably less world-historic scale, recent years suggest that even without such revolutionary activity or the productive capacity of a state printer, other moments, too, can attract attention to the *Manifesto*. These aren't always without their ironies or bleak humor: in 1998, a handsomely produced red-and-black 150th anniversary edition very nearly made it into the window displays of the high-end clothing store Barneys in New York.[57] That was a moment of bullish capitalist swagger; more often, though, it's during the opposite that the *Manifesto*'s profile rises. A "return to Marx" occasioned by the financial crisis of 2008, a substantial spike in sales for his texts, provided much wry laughter from the commentariat. But even anecdotally, this fascination, in the aftermath of the banking collapse, is intriguing.[58] In Berman's words: "Whenever there's trouble, anywhere in the world, the book becomes an item; when things quiet down, the book drops out of sight; when there's trouble again, the people who forgot remember. . . . When people dream of resistance—even if they're not Communists—it provides music for their dreams."[59]

Such dreams can be highly ambivalent, as can the moments that give rise to them. As one of the most haunting images of the *Manifesto* attests.

In 1919, the Soviet artist V. V. Spassky released an official poster celebrating the new Communist International, the organization for the coordination of communist parties across the world in the wake of the Bolshevik triumph in Russia. Drawing on Géricault's illustrious 1819 painting *The Raft of the Medusa*, Spassky depicts a lone figure on a raft in the waves, close to a wrecked ship, straining agonisingly towards a glimmer on a far-off, dark shore. "To the Lighthouse of the Communist International," the inscription reads. The raft itself is a giant, opened copy of *The Communist Manifesto*.

As part of a brilliant discussion of the iconography of revolution, Enzo Traverso, allowing that it is an evasive symbol, reads the ship as probably representing either the recently collapsed Tsarist regime, or the Second International, the pre-existing grouping of socialist parties whose members had disgraced themselves by rallying around their "own" governments, and against international working-class solidarity, during the First World War. "The message of the poster is clear nonetheless," Traverso concludes. "[T]he socialist future is not compromised, since the Communist International embodies a light of hope. And the instrument of this salvage is a text: *The Communist Manifesto*."[60]

But what is deeply striking here is the poignancy, the melancholy, and danger in this image. Far from the clichés of socialist Prometheanism or the traditional rah-rah of propaganda, the central figure is lonely, bent, thin, pained. A survivor, but only just. Yes, he makes for the light, but it is a long way off, deep in darkness, and it seems far from assured that he will make it. And consider the moment the image was born, with the new Soviet Union wracked by a civil war of almost unimaginable savagery, the workers' state constrained and forced into a fortress of repressive measures very far from the Bolshevik leaders' notions of socialism, with the international revolutionary wave on which the Russian revolutionaries had always staked their future seeming stalled, uncertain, the Soviet ship of state listing. In that context, whatever the intent of the artist, it's impossible not to discern in that polysemic ship—among other things, no doubt—the possible wreck of the socialist polity itself. Poised between triumph and catastrophe, this is an expression neither of optimism nor of defeat but of a superposition between the two. To live according to radical politics, perhaps more than with any other approach to the world, can be to experience moments in which hope and lament, utopia and apocalypse, are inextricable. In this extraordinary image, the *Manifesto* is a literal life raft to survive such instants of what we might call apocatopia.

All of which raises the questions of what *The Communist Manifesto* is and what it does, what it could be and what it might do, now, faced with a quite new and extraordinary coagulation of crises—of a sclerotic global economy, of reconfiguring political agency and toxicity, of assaults on even the thinnest democratic norms, of the existentially catastrophic climate emergency. Why we should read it again, and how.

The *Manifesto*'s post-fall rise became inextricable from insurgency. And from anxiety. And from the longing for betterness, that unique yearning that is in German called *Sehnsucht*, that the best unease can bring.

# 3

# An Outline of the *Manifesto*

---

Yes, we will change the existing state of things.

Helen Macfarlane, *The Democratic and Social Republic*

## OVERVIEW

The *Manifesto* opens by stating its intent to dispel myths about communism. It achieves considerably more.

In Section 1, the authors stress the central importance of classes and class conflict to history. They describe the rise of the bourgeoisie, its shift from a progressive force to a fetter on development, and the rise of a mass proletariat that will end capitalism. Section 2 outlines how organized communists (should) relate to the working class, and the communist tenet that the abolition of private property—in its bourgeois sense—is necessary for human development. Marx and Engels also respond to common criticisms of communism. In Section 3 they criticize left-wing tendencies other than their own. Finally, Section 4 looks at how communists view non-working-class opposition parties.

(This section is brief enough to suggest it was dashed off in response to that grumpy note from Marx's comrades.) The *Manifesto* ends with a famous clarion for revolution.

Here, each section is outlined in some detail. As mentioned, for those wishing to cross-refer to the original text, reproduced as Appendix A, the paragraphs under discussion are identified by section and paragraph number, there and in quotes that follow.

## PREAMBLE

What opens the *Manifesto* is that legendary moment of phantasmagoria: "A spectre is haunting Europe: the spectre of communism" (0.1). With the image of the ghost terrifying the old powers, the authors mock their enemies for their histrionic anticommunist propaganda ("Where is the party in opposition that has not been decried as communistic by its opponents in power?" (0.2)), for being frit of a "nursery tale" (0.3), or, perhaps more accurately, "horror story,"[1] and/or of spreading it. At the same time, the authors revel in that foreboding spectrality invoked, that flattering vesting in communism of dread powers.[2] Swaggering, they claim the *Manifesto* will lay out "in the face of the whole world . . . their views, their aims" (0.3). This from a pamphlet of which perhaps 1,000 copies were initially printed by a small group of squabbling émigrés. The hubris of speaking for communism, as a potentially vast movement, is breathtaking. And it would come to be essentially accurate.

## SECTION 1: BOURGEOIS AND PROLETARIANS

This section opens (1.1) with another famous claim, the core of the authors' materialist analysis of history: that, excepting egalitarian "primitive communistic societies,"[3] "[t]he history of all hitherto existing society is the history of class struggles." They cite various historical examples (1.2–1.3), and describe the rise of modern bourgeois society as emerging from crises within feudalism. It's worth saying that in immediately stressing the role of class *struggle*, rather than ineluctability, from the start Marx and Engels invite readers to activism.[4] They outline the rise of the bourgeoisie (1.6–1.11), stressing the role of international trade, with traditional feudal organization unable to keep up with the growing demand such trade helped spur, and which in turn spurred the industrial revolution and "an immense development to commerce, to navigation, to communication." This development fed back into the growing power of the bourgeoisie itself, which benefited from and encouraged it.

It has become a truism that what's often astonishing to the newcomer to the text is how fervently these two partisans for insurrectionary working-class power praise the bourgeoisie. Historically, we read, they played "a most revolutionary part" (1.13). Marx and Engels outline the bourgeoisie's capturing of political power and eulogise its political, economic and spiritual impact on the world (1.12–1.26)—accomplishing "wonders far surpassing Egyptian pyramids." These paragraphs contain many freighted aperçus, formulations over which debates continue to rage, such as that "[t]he executive of the modern state is but a committee for managing the common affairs of the whole bourgeoisie" (1.12); that in bourgeois society "personal worth" has been "resolved" into a quality called "exchange value" (1.14); that its "single, unconscionable freedom" is "Free Trade" (1.14); of the putative effacement of national distinctions and the rise of an international culture. In the disruption and destruction of old norms and justifications, the *Manifesto* suggests that bourgeois society—capitalism—is exploitative in a newly open, "bare" way. Here are the text's most arresting, admiring descriptions of the bourgeoisie's abilities and remorseless drive to submit the world to a maelstrom of change, to the ripping away of old veils, described in near-religious poetic terms.

The bourgeoisie . . . has put an end to all feudal, patriarchal, idyllic relations. It has pitilessly torn asunder the motley feudal ties . . .

It has drowned the most heavenly ecstasies of religious fervour, of chivalrous enthusiasm, of philistine sentimentalism, in the icy water of egotistical calculation. [1.14] . . . The bourgeoisie cannot exist without constantly revolutionising the instruments of production, and thereby the relations of production, and with them the whole relations of society. . . . Constant revolutionising of production, uninterrupted disturbance of all social conditions, everlasting uncertainty and agitation distinguish the bourgeois epoch from all earlier ones. All fixed, fast-frozen relations, with their train of ancient and venerable prejudices and opinions, are swept away, all new-formed ones become antiquated before they can ossify. All that is solid melts into air, all that is holy is profaned, and man is at last compelled to face with sober sense his real conditions of life and his relations with his kind [1.18].

Far from simply being a catalogue of antagonism, one sympathetic commentator describes the *Manifesto* as "an impassioned, enthusiastic, often lyrical celebration of bourgeois works, ideas, and achievements," and that is nowhere so clear as here.[5] Even a conservative critic calls this "a panegyric upon bourgeois achievement that has no equal in economic literature."[6]

Only having hailed its power do the authors announce the bourgeoisie's downfall (1.27–1.28). Just as they did under feudalism, existing economic arrangements ("relations of production") come into conflict with developing productive forces: economic crises repeatedly "put on . . . trial" bourgeois society. The great difference now is that due to the intense competition between capitalists, mass impoverishment, and immiseration result not from *inadequate* production, but from *over*production, a glut of products that go unsold. Bourgeois society responds in three main ways to this: with the destruction of productive forces, as, for example, in catastrophic slumps; by expanding into new markets, as in the global spread of imperialism; and/or with increased exploitation, where it's already entrenched. Which, of course, sets up more crises to come.

Hand in hand with the bourgeoisie's rise is that of the working class that produces the profits (1.29–1.35). With the consolidation of industry, the proletariat are massed in large concerns, under "a perfect hierarchy of officers and servants" who control their labor for the benefit of the bourgeoisie. Women and children enter the workforce alongside men. There's a strong tendency toward de-skilling and—to use that term from Marx's then unpublished *Economic and Philosophic Manuscripts*—"alienation." Which is to say that work, for countless millions, is soul-crushing drudgery.

De-skilling reduces capital's costs, lower-skilled workers being paid less than higher (1.33). Here is implicit an early, underdeveloped formulation of Marx's "labor theory of value," by which any commodity's "value," on which its price is based, is derived from the average amount of "abstract labour" needed to produce it.[7] The ability of workers to work is itself a commodity, after all—the only one workers have to sell—the value of which underlies the wage necessary to keep them alive. And, crucially, this is not an eternally given but a contested sum, the result of class struggle (1.38, and implicitly elsewhere). From this hard-won amount, workers must pay out to landlords and shopkeepers and the like, for the means of life (1.34). Certain less powerful sections of the middle class—the petite or petty bourgeoisie—especially those whose traditional activities grow outdated, Marx and Engels see as under pressure, potentially even pushed towards the proletariat (1.35).

Workers have always struggled against exploitation: the *Manifesto* describes resistance such as Luddite attacks on machinery, riots, early struggles *alongside* the bourgeoisie against feudal restrictions, and combination into trade unions to fight for improved wages and conditions (1.36–1.40). Workers must compete against each other under capitalism, but this tendency constantly jostles its obverse, that towards working-class collectivism (1.39), the "organisation of the proletarians into a class, and consequently into a political party" (1.40).

The struggle of the bourgeoisies of different nations against both feudalism and against the bourgeoisie of other countries can lead them to offer sops to "their own" proletariats, to get them on-side with the bourgeois project, including through education—which workers can then turn against the bourgeoisie itself (1.41). Under capitalism, even a few members of the bourgeoisie will be pitched into the working class, and may politically go "over to the proletariat" (1.42–1.43). In contradistinction to others, the proletariat is "a really revolutionary class" (1.44): the lower middle classes tend to be socially nostalgic in their fight against the corrosive power of big capital (1.45);[8] and the "lumpenproletariat"—literally "proletariat in rags," that we might now call the "underclass"—excluded from or profoundly insecure in the workforce, tends towards "reactionary intrigue" (1.46). This is a structural, rather than a moralizing, argument: what might seem like the harsh exclusion of one of the most vulnerable, precarious and exploited sections of society from a progressive destiny is, right or wrong, a sociological claim. It's predicated on the specific political and cultural milieux, and the pressures towards generalized antagonism, brutal and petty competition and suspicion, that we could call negative solidarity, experienced by those in such a position.[9]

From here to the section's end (1.47–1.53), the text unfolds in a fervent, rhetorical rush. It's important to be clear that the authors describe tendencies they see as implicit and growing in capitalism, such as the stripping of the worker of national or religious particularity, as if they were already flowering. The proletariat, having "nothing of their own to secure and to fortify," cannot consolidate power by taking control of an emerging regime of accumulation: it can only usher in democratic political control and communal ownership of productive capacity. As its members are (or will become) the majority, so they must become a self-conscious movement *of* the majority, take control and throw all givens of state power into question. Such struggle will occur initially within individual countries, against the working class's "own" bourgeoisie, as a phase of what is a necessarily international revolution (1.50–1.51).

Capitalism cannot exist without mass poverty, and—what is not quite the same claim—workers sink "deeper and deeper below the conditions of existence" (1.52), in a process of relentless pauperization. Capital cannot exist without the wage labor of workers—who are pushed towards "revolutionary combination" and whose self-realization requires the end of capitalism itself.

"What the bourgeoisie therefore produces, above all, are its own grave-diggers" (1.53).

## SECTION 2: PROLETARIANS AND COMMUNISTS

Marx and Engels propose relations between the communists and the working class and its parties (representative organizations in a wider sense than that term would mean today, including, for example, trade unions and the Chartists, as well as looser political tendencies), to stake out a position as the best grouping to achieve proletarian power (2.1–2.9). They repudiate sectarianism, insisting that communists struggle as part of the working-class movement whether or not the wider class agrees with their specific positions. The communists, "the most advanced and resolute section" of working-class activism (2.6), with a rigorous historical understanding born out of the class struggle, aim to "overthrow . . . bourgeois supremacy" to replace it with working-class power (2.7).

The authors stress that the communist aim—the "abolition of existing property relations"—is not new (2.10–2.17): throughout history, political revolutions have replaced such outdated norms with those better suited to a new ruling class. *Bourgeois* private property, against which the communists set themselves, is capitalism, "the final and most complete expression" of a system based "on the exploitation of the many by the few" (2.12). And because there's no "higher form" of private property with which to replace it, "the theory of the communists" can be summed up as "[a]bolition of private property" (2.13)—"private property," importantly, here understood as the private exploitative control of the economy, rather than, as per a common misrepresentation, as the fact of any personal possessions (2.14). Capitalism's advocates insist that "property" is the result of an individual's hard work: the *Manifesto* counters that capitalism itself has abolished any such property for countless striving peasants and others, and that all the proletariat's hard work only shores up the property of the bourgeoisie (2.15).

The writers describe how the "social power" of capital perpetuates itself (2.18–2.22), according to that early version of Marx's labor theory of value, by which workers are paid according to the value of their ability to work—"that quantum of the means of subsistence, which is absolutely requisite to keep the labourer in bare existence" (2.22). The implication, following the economist David Ricardo, is that wages would always be driven to the minimum possible level. As we'll see, the authors themselves would come to repudiate this particular position. They repeat that the abolition of private property doesn't mean the end of personal possessions, let alone the means to live, but the private property in the means of production, which is to say, the relations whereby social surplus is appropriated to enrich the bourgeoisie (2.22).

In communism, they fleetingly tease (2.23–2.24), the baleful power of capital, which operates like a living predatory presence, will end, and the productive capacity of society will work for the benefit of all. Rather than communism being the end of individuality, as its enemies claim, it's under capitalism that, controlled by inhuman forces, most people cannot develop such a quality.

Marx and Engels go on to dispense with more anticommunist canards (2.25–2.58), finding such objections wanting. Repeatedly, they diagnose this as due to an inability or unwillingness on the part of their opponents to imagine that existing, historically specific norms of bourgeois society could be anything other than eternal truths (2.58). This long sequence skilfully deploys the rhetorical tropes of *procatalepsis* and *concessio*, pre-emption and concession: that is, they concede the accuracy of certain classic attacks on communism, but in ways that redound on their opponents. For example (2.25): "And the abolition of this state of things is called by the bourgeois, abolition of individuality and freedom! And rightly so. The abolition of bourgeois individuality, bourgeois independence, and bourgeois freedom is undoubtedly aimed at."

At this point, the writers effect a remarkable shift in voice, into the second person, "you" (2.28 on). Abruptly, now, the *Manifesto* doesn't merely discuss its class enemy, the bourgeoisie, but excoriates it directly as an interlocutor. "You are horrified at our intending to do away with private property . . . You reproach us . . . with intending to do away with a form of property, the necessary condition for whose existence is the non-existence of any property for the immense majority of society. . . . You reproach us with intending to do away with your property. Precisely so; that is just what we intend." (2.29) It seems implied that, while the *Manifesto* is a rallying call for proletarians and radicals, it is also written to be *overheard*, as it were, by the bourgeoisie.[10] On the one hand, this mode of double address flatters the communists, in implying that their enemies *need* to pay them attention. Simultaneously, coming as it does after fulsome praise for the bourgeoisie, as if to lull them, the switch of registers allows an all-the-more powerful direct attack on its enemies.

The "individual," the loss of whose "individuality" under communism the bourgeoisie laments, is only "the middle-class owner of property" who "must, indeed, be swept out of the way, and made impossible" (2.31). This, however, is to say nothing about the development of alternative modes of individuality, currently precluded for the vast majority by want and alienation (2.30–2.34). Here again is that key insight we saw in *The German Ideology*: in totally changing a society, people must inevitably radically change their own ideas, and the nature of being human itself. Under communal ownership and democratic control, it would be socially impossible to be someone whose selfhood is predicated on the exploitation of others. A subjectivity that would *desire* such power would be meaningless, and have no social traction.

Marx and Engels repeatedly stress that revolution is the transformation of people and ideas as well as social structures.

Against the tenacious slur that without bourgeois property humanity will surrender to universal laziness, the *Manifesto* points out that the working class by and large already has nothing—and yet it continues to work.[11] The bourgeoisie (2.35–2.37) is also fearful that, absent its version of property, culture itself will wither and die, to which the authors retort that for most of humanity this vaunted culture manifests merely as training to produce profit for others, and that the disappearance of particular cultural norms hardly means that culture *in toto* will end. The *Manifesto* pillories its opponents for that category error, a "selfish misconception" (2.38), for presuming that historically particular standards and ideas thrown up by and for their class are universal. They are, in fact, neither inevitable, nor necessarily just (2.37–2.38).

There follow (2.39–2.51) several paragraphs about the "infamous" communist suggestion of the abolition of the family. The *Manifesto* stresses that this sentimental bourgeois concern for the family is predicated on work that splits real families apart, through, for example, drudgery and child labor. Advocating social education, rather than privatized and familial education, is not to propose indoctrination, but countering the doctrines of the ruling class. To the moralist concern about a communist "community of women"—some version or other of "free love," a breakdown of the monogamous and privatized model of marriage—the authors (unlike some communist thinkers) don't outline or defend any such model (in keeping with their career-long preference for critiquing what exists, rather than pre-empting post-capitalist norms). They do, however, insist that such fear bespeaks a bourgeois conception of women as property. With gusto, they point out the hypocrisy of the bourgeoisie, for whom sanctimonious familial piety co-exists with systematic bed-hopping, infidelity, coercion, exploitation, and abuse.[12] This hypocrisy they see as baked into the system.

In their discussion of nationhood, the authors famously declare that "[t]he workers have no country" (2.52–2.56), having more interests in common with workers in other countries than with their "own" bourgeoisie. This, unsurprisingly, is one of the most contentious and questionable passages of the *Manifesto*, and various objections to it will be a particular focus below. For the *Manifesto*, internationalism is a sine qua non of the workers' movement, and of any successful revolution. The authors again expound the tenets of their philosophy of historical materialism (2.57–2.65), not so much defending the ethical/political positions of communism as the historicizing of ideas and social structures from which, for them, communist politics stem. "What else does the history of ideas prove, than that intellectual production changes its character in proportion as material production is changed?" (2.59)

Dispensing quickly again with the claim that "[t]here are ... eternal truths, such as Freedom, Justice, etc." (the "etc." is pleasingly waspish), they then ventriloquize a far more interesting and sophisticated critique of communism: that in abolishing such "eternal truths" *rather than* "constituting them on a new basis," communism itself "acts in contradiction to all past historical experience" (2.63). In this model, imputed to their enemies, eternal truths *do* exist, and/but they are given specific form in different societies. This is a complex position. It marries aspects of the more conventional bourgeois abstraction of its own norms into eternal truths, with a certain diluted common-sense version of historical materialism that *does*, in fact, historicize such ideas, implying that they should exist, only in new forms. Here, Marx and Engels imagine a version of their own critique of bourgeois ideology deployed against communism itself: that it is communism, in actually *abolishing* certain truths, that should rather be somehow transformed and made historically appropriate, which is in fact ahistorical.

In its answer, the *Manifesto* allows that certain "common forms, or general ideas," do, in fact, generally survive epoch to epoch, in distinct forms—but precisely because the revolutionary upheavals by which particularities have changed represent the replacement of one ruling class with another. Communism, by contrast, though it's not ahistorical, *is* different from any formulation that has gone before, in a key respect. This is not down to its abstract moral worth but is a corollary i) of the specific, dynamic, and universalizing nature of the class society in which the working-class movement arises; ii) of that working-class movement itself; and iii) of the politics by which that movement must overturn the capitalism that gives rise to it. Because such an overturning must mean, for the first time in the history of class struggle itself, the end of *all* class exploitation.

It's *this* that makes "[t]he communist revolution . . . the most radical rupture with traditional property relations," and thus "no wonder that its development involves the most radical rupture with traditional ideas" (2.66).

The sheer scale of that rupture with the existing social totality cannot be overstated.

It is, then, somewhat surprising to see the modesty of the concrete proposals which follow (2.67–2.72). It's by these that the *Manifesto* suggests the working class can begin to change the world when—temporarily, in the process of eradicating classes altogether—it takes power.

"[T]he first step in the revolution by the working class is to raise the proletariat to the position of the ruling class, to win the battle of democracy" (2.68). This sentence, in the words of one scholar, is "crucial to the entire *Manifesto*."[13] The traditional counterposing of democracy and communism is the result of decades of anticommunist propaganda. But in fact the problem for communists has, rather, been that the parliamentary democracy which is the only version on offer is not nearly democratic enough. Excepting certain left anarchists and so-called "ultraleftists," for whom any involvement at all with the existing state is to be shunned, most revolutionary communists, including Marx, consider the push for reforms by whatever means are available to be crucial to the process of gaining strength towards the ultimate aim. That would be communism: a new kind of collaborative collectivity, more empowering *and more democratic*, at all levels, than any form of democracy hitherto seen. In the words of Martin Hägglund, "[f]or Marx—contrary to a persistent misconception—the overcoming of capitalism is not meant to abolish democracy but to make *actual* democracy possible."[14]

Allowing that such measures will be locally specific, the *Manifesto* lists ten as appropriate to the most economically advanced countries, with the most developed capitalist economies (2.71–2.72).

1. Abolition of private ownership of land, and land rent applied to public works. (The authors later allowed that they would exempt ownership of a small amount of land.)
2. High progressive income tax.
3. Abolition of inheritance.
4. Expropriation of "emigrants and rebels," those who would leave to avoid workers' power.
5. The abolition of private banks for a single state bank in charge of credit.
6. Centralization of transport in state hands (to which, after the invention of early telephony, the authors added communication).
7. The increase in the industrial holdings of the state, and the improvement of the natural environment, degraded by capitalism.
8. The necessity for all to work if they can, and a program of public employment.
9. "[G]radual abolition of the distinction between town and country": the synergizing of agriculture and manufacturing.
10. Free public education and abolition of child labor.

Some of these now read as remarkably mild: proposals 2 and 10, for example, hardly necessitate the overturning of capitalism. Others, by contrast, such as 3 and 4, even if in the abstract compatible with capitalism in some form, seem highly unlikely ever to be permitted by actually existing capitalists. The important fact is that, far from being descriptions of communism, none of these particular measures were shibboleths even as stepping stones, to be insisted on in all circumstances; different contexts might suggest different demands. This the authors would come to make clear in their 1872 preface, where they insisted that "no special stress is laid on the revolutionary measures" listed, and that given the "gigantic strides of modern industry," measures called for would likely be very different were the *Manifesto* written then. All these demands, however, particularly in combination, were intended to undermine the logic of capitalist society *itself*, even though, and in the context of being, still constrained and stained by it.

Finally in this section (2.73–2.74), the *Manifesto* does briefly advert to the communist horizon. The authors reiterate that, taking power, under conditions of productive plenty, the proletariat will dispense with class antagonisms in total, "and will thereby have abolished its own supremacy as a class." Class society will thus be replaced by a society fit for humans. They underline again that, far from destroying individuality, freed from the deadening constraints of class antagonism and the remorseless pursuit of profit, as opposed to human need, "we shall have an association, in which the free development of each is the condition for the free development of all."

Therein true individuality, and community, might flourish.

## Section 3: Socialist and Communist Literature

Here the authors lay out their criticisms of, and occasional praise for, other left theories.[15] They divide this literature into "reactionary socialism" (3.1–3.35), that is criticism of capitalism that looks backwards for its proposed solutions: "conservative or bourgeois socialism" (3.36–3.43), which proposes various ameliorating reforms while leaving the fundamentals of capitalism intact; and "critical-utopian socialism and communism" (3.44–3.57), radical proposals for alternative systems which, however sincerely meant and motivated by hatred of exploitation, are fanciful and dreamlike. The first category, reactionary socialism, they confusingly subdivide further into "feudal socialism" (3.1–3.11); "petty-bourgeois socialism" (3.12–3.18); and "German or 'true' socialism" (3.19–3.35), a particularly obscure category today.

*Reactionary Socialism: A—Feudal Socialism*

"Feudal socialism," the first species of "reactionary socialism," is the province of the (particularly French and English) aristocracy. In France, the aristocracy's recrudescent champion the Bourbon monarchy had been overthrown in 1830, replaced by the constitutional monarchy of Louis Philippe; in England, in 1832, the Reform Act weakened certain atavistic features of the system and slightly expanded the franchise, diminishing the power of the declining aristocracy relative to the bourgeoisie. For the *Manifesto*, the socialism of this political current is "half lamentation, half lampoon" (3.3), the protestation of a now-supplanted ruling class. It's capable of mocking its bourgeois antagonist with, at times, "bitter, witty, and incisive criticism," and of mourning the chaos, upheaval, and loss of its ascendency. These "socialists" lament that the old order is destroyed, and warn that catastrophe is coming, attempting to recruit the working class "to formulate their indictment against the bourgeoisie in the interest of the exploited working class alone" (3.2).

Such criticisms of capitalism aren't wholly wrong: indeed, for "feudal socialism" to have any traction at all, it must make some reasonably persuasive points. The *Manifesto*, too, sees catastrophe as possible, and is clear about the destabilising upheaval of capitalism. But for feudal socialism such aristocratic attacks are deployed for the doomed end of turning back the clock to a time that was also exploitative. This fact these feudal-socialist critics conveniently forget. And the aristocracy may lament the passing of a system it once controlled, but it will still certainly make peace with the new masters, for the sake of profit, trading under new conditions, particularly in agriculture, even as they mourn their golden age. Which is to say, "they join in all coercive measures against the working class" and "despite their highfalutin phrases . . . barter fidelity, love, and honour for traffic in wool, beetroot-sugar, and potato spirits" (3.9).

The authors conclude with two abrupt paragraphs on Christianity (3.10–3.11), seeing "clerical socialism" as tending to accompany feudal socialism. They focus on a strand of ascetic Christian ideology that criticises riches, property, and the state (and, they add, marriage), to advocate simplicity, charity, and poverty. But such seemingly critical ideas are in fact exculpatory, solace to guilty aristocrats: "Christian Socialism is but the holy water with which the priest consecrates the heart-burnings of the aristocrat" (3.11).[16]

### Reactionary Socialism: B—Petty-Bourgeois Socialism

It's not only the aristocracy whose existence is rendered unstable by bourgeois society. In some countries, the old medieval burgesses and small peasants still existed, and they, too, were increasingly left behind (3.12). Of particular interest to the authors of the *Manifesto* were the petty bourgeoisie, small farmers or manufacturers, shopkeepers and the like. This "new class," as a class, was intermediate between, thrown up by and "ever renewing" by that fundamental relation between worker and bourgeoisie.[17] Members of this class are under constant risk of sinking to a proletarian level or lower, an anxiety that can make them receptive to criticisms of capitalism. Particularly in countries such as France, with a large peasantry, criticism of the bourgeoisie might then take on a "petty bourgeois" idiom (3.14).

This is a politics that is sensitive to the dissolution of norms, the inequalities and iniquities of capitalism, and, too, about the disastrous results of its tendencies towards monopoly, economic crisis, and "war of extermination between nations" (3.15). But, expressing the subjectivity of a class defined by a position between capital and labor, its proposals aren't about overturning that exploitative relation. Some petty-bourgeois socialism is, like the feudal socialists, simply backward-looking. An alternative to such straightforward nostalgia is an impossible dream of compromise, of "cramping the modern means of production and of exchange" with outdated social relations (3.16), social protections inspired by a bygone era, quasi-medieval "corporate guilds," for example (3.17).

This position is "both reactionary and Utopian," hankering for something that has been swept away and cannot return. No wonder the petty-bourgeois socialists are doomed to disappointment, to a "fit of the blues" (3.18).

### Reactionary Socialism: C—German or "True" Socialism

This is a separate discussion of various German writers, such as Moses Hess, who styled themselves the "True Socialists."[18] They were a variety of the petty-bourgeois socialism already rhetorically dispatched, as the *Manifesto* clarifies: "German socialism recognised . . . its own calling as the bombastic representative of the petty-bourgeois Philistine" (3.34). This loose alliance took a philosophical approach to social problems in Germany by deploying certain ideas from radical French writing. These notions had been created for and under very different conditions: French radicalism was born "under the pressure of a bourgeoisie in power, and . . . was the struggle against that power," whereas in the backward German polity, the bourgeoisie had not overcome the reactionary *status quo ante* (3.19). Transplanted like this, the French work "lost all its immediate practical significance and assumed a purely literary aspect" (3.20). This fannish misapplication led its German enthusiasts to a uselessly abstract conception of real social problems. Strongly influenced by the philosopher Feuerbach, this tendency broke from any class perspective, away from the proletariat towards a nebulous "humanism" and recourse to an abstract spirit of Love (upper case and all), hoping to inspire people against bourgeois selfishness.

It was a peculiar and questionable decision for the authors of the *Manifesto* to include at such length a discussion of this one particular obscure strain of would-be socialist ideology. There seem to be three plausible reasons for the decision. One was personal and political investment. Neither Marx nor Engels ever shied from polemic, sometimes out of all proportion to the importance of their targets. One of the leading "True Socialists" was Karl Grün,[19] with whom Marx had had an intense rivalry, and the rhetorical demolition of whose tendency would likely satisfy him. And the spleen here had its roots in the debates which had formed Marx and Engels: the True Socialists were related to that Young Hegelian tradition from which they had broken. The True Socialist way of thinking was the opposite of Marx and Engels's own approach of, as Marx would later describe it, "rising from the abstract to the concrete,"[20] that is, the translation of previously idealist categories from Hegel into concrete formations, such as the state. For Grün and his comrades, the reverse was the method.[21] The True Socialists were a vivid illustration of the thesis of historical materialism that ideas cannot float free of underlying reality. Here the problem wasn't obviously wrong ideas per se, but of importing otherwise decent ideas into an alien context, where they became meaningless, or actively reactionary. In French socialist and communist literature, for example, radical demands from a proletarian criticism of liberalism assailed the shortcomings of actually existing liberal institutions—"hurling the traditional anathemas

... against representative government, against bourgeois competition, bourgeois freedom of the press, bourgeois legislation, bourgeois liberty and equality" (3.28). In the German context, however, to repeat such slogans, as did the True Socialists, was not to strengthen a critical left current, but the hand of the reactionary powers, such as the Prussian monarchy, striving to foreclose those institutions from coming into being.[22] Here, putative radicalism strengthens reaction against liberalism, and the True Socialists "served as a welcome scarecrow against the threatening bourgeoisie" (3.29).

No surprise that the True Socialists were vehemently opposed to the communist program, with its class-partisan nature. It must have been a small pleasure to Marx and Engels that, virtually as the *Manifesto* appeared, to quote Engels"s later footnote again, "[t]he revolutionary storm of 1848 swept away this whole shabby tendency," leaving us with what's now an extended and rebarbative epitaph.

## Conservative or Bourgeois Socialism

In this short section, the authors discuss various middle-class reformists who allowed that social problems exist due to capitalism, and wanted to address them "in order to secure the continued existence of bourgeois society" (3.36). Not to sweep a sick system away, but to save it from itself.

Obviously enjoying himself, Marx indulges in a withering litany of do-gooders, hand-wringers, and—from his perspective—cranks: "economists, philanthropists, humanitarians, improvers of the condition of the working class, organisers of charity, members of societies for the prevention of cruelty to animals, temperance fanatics, hole-and-corner reformers of every imaginable kind" (3.37). There are clear modern-day analogies to ragbags of the sanctimonious who are nebulously anguished at the iniquities of capitalism, but far more so at any thought of fundamental change. "The Socialistic bourgeois want all the advantages of modern social conditions without the struggles and dangers necessarily resulting therefrom" (3.39). Their proposed reforms aren't merely inadequate sticking plasters, but are designed to protect "the continued existence of these relations" (3.40) that throw up such problems in the first place.

It's a paradox of this "bourgeois socialism," according to the *Manifesto*, that some variants of it can frantically suggest certain reforms while pooh-poohing others, particularly those of "political reform," on the grounds that "only a change in the material conditions of existence, in economical relations" (3.40) will really help the working class. In fact, even their proposed economic reforms are for the benefit of capitalist administration, the effect being to "lessen the cost, and simplify the administrative work, of bourgeois government"—reform, that is, "based on the continued existence" of capitalist relations. And, in any case, it's misleading to counterpose such work to "political" reforms: this was written at a time when the struggle for bourgeois, liberal political freedoms was a fierce and vital contest, including, for Marx and Engels, for the working class.

A peculiarity of this section is the *en passant* citation of Pierre-Joseph Proudhon's recent *Philosophy of Poverty* (*Philosophie de la Misère*) "as an example of this form" of bourgeois socialism (3.38). This is questionable. Proudhon was and is famous as an anarchist thinker committed to fundamental social change, and profoundly opposed to the bourgeois state. But Marx was deeply opposed to anarchism in general and Proudhon in particular. For the *Manifesto*'s authors, an insistence on revolution without a sense of the agency necessary to and capable of carrying it out precluded actual political change, which is what they saw in anarchism, with its perceived antipathy to power *tout court*: it's possible that the authors characterized Proudhon as they did because his anarchist opposition to political authority meant he opposed any notion of a proletarian party, let alone one taking state power, thus placing him, for them, in the category of those who want "the existing state of society, minus its revolutionary and disintegrating elements" (3.39).

It's also possible that this categorization was designed as much as anything to troll Proudhon.

## Critical-Utopian Socialism and Communism

Here, the authors start by clarifying what they are not criticizing: that is, the sincerely working-class radical theory of, for example, Gracchus Babeuf, a radical egalitarian who led a failed conspiratorial *coup d'état* in France in 1796, intended to usher in a form of top-down communism. The authors describe such early working-class communism as a product of times of "universal excitement"—social upheaval, the accession of the bourgeoisie—expressing the needs and interests of the working class, in conditions wherein that class was still developing. In a nascent phase of capitalism, these schemes were heroic and honorable, but doomed. Proposing egalitarianism and common property in an underdeveloped economy, driven by a tiny section of the class rather than its mass, inevitably meant advocating "universal asceticism and social levelling in its crudest form" (3.44–3.5).

Marx's steadfast disinclination to outline his imagined communism—to "write the cook-books of the future"—beyond a few vague intimations, has been much debated.[23] What's clear, as this negative example with regard to Babeuf shows, is that there were certain visions of communism from which Marx vigorously distinguished his own. Despite the authors' great respect for Babeuf, there's enthusiasm here neither for "ascetic" communism, nor even for egalitarianism *as an intrinsic good* per se. The latter, going back to Section 2, is desirable, rather, for the end of "the free development of each [as] . . . the condition for the free development of all" (2.74). And it's vital to stress that the communal property and individual flowering of communism is predicated, for the *Manifesto*, on an economy more advanced than capitalism itself, and unfettered from it: that is, a post-scarcity communism.

The utopian communism considered here also arose in the early development of the struggle between working class and bourgeoisie, though its influence continued beyond that in writers such as Saint-Simon, Fourier, and Owen (3.46). They saw, often very clearly, the antagonisms and crises of capitalism. But their analyses and prescriptions did not emerge from the working class itself, and tended to regard that class as passive (3.47). And the conditions of economic development under which their thought developed not being adequate to any serious political action by the working class, their politics tend to take the shape of fanciful schemes (3.48–3.9). In such dreams as these there's always a danger of savior complexes. The *Manifesto* charges the utopians with concerning themselves with the working class insofar as it is "the most suffering class" (3.50), and, seeing themselves as "far superior to all class antagonisms" (3.51), thus dispensing with class politics.

It's not that an ethical position against suffering is wrong, of course, but that one cannot derive meaningful politics from such an ethic in the abstract, without an analysis of a particular balance of political forces. This is even more the case when that essentially moralistic standpoint makes such utopias actively hostile to radical class politics—when "they reject all political, and especially all revolutionary, action" (3.52). Instead, these utopians pursue rarefied social experiments—alternative modes of living, for example—of kinds that can never exist more than fleetingly and interstitially in capitalism.

For all this, the *Manifesto* is notably more generous to such writers than to its other targets. In their critique of social relations "they are full of the most valuable materials for the enlightenment of the working class" (3.54). Their transformative aims, such as social harmony and the abolition of the family, the *Manifesto* doesn't scorn, but describes as predicated on "the disappearance of class antagonisms" (3.54), and thus as, at best, thought experiments or provocations. But though the founders of such groups may have been "in many respects, revolutionary" (3.55), their followers have developed "mere reactionary sects," prioritizing the maintenance of their little communities, irrespective of or in opposition to movements of the working class. Some of their representatives in England and France, for example, were opposed to the Chartists and the left wing of the French republican movement (3.57).

## SECTION 4: POSITION OF THE COMMUNISTS IN RELATION TO THE VARIOUS EXISTING OPPOSITION PARTIES

This brief, clearly unfinished section claims (4.1) that the *Manifesto* has previously clarified the relationship between communists and existing working-class parties such as the Chartists. This it doesn't in fact do other than by implication. Most of the section is devoted to progressive, but not specifically working-class, parties, such as the French Social Democrats, the Swiss Radicals, and the Polish Democratic Society,[24] progressive forces in Germany, and how the communists should relate to them (4.2–4.5).

Of course, these parties have now gone the way of all flesh, and, in later editions, the authors readily allowed that their specific suggestions were outdated. Certain principles, however, remain relevant. In each case, the communist program was to support such parties insofar as they push radical programs—against, for example, feudal remnants in agriculture, for national liberation against imperial powers (as in Poland) and against the conservative bourgeoisie. And the communists proceed with clear understanding of the limitations of the programs of all such parties, and of their class natures—never "losing sight of the fact," for example, that the Swiss Radicals "consists of antagonistic elements, partly of Democratic Socialists . . . partly of radical bourgeois" (4.3). Communist support for or collaboration with these parties is not unconditional: the communists reserve the right "to take up a critical position in regard to phrases and illusions" (4.2).

The *Manifesto* advocates paying particular attention to Germany and the German workers (4.6–4.7), because, though the German political system was retrograde and reactionary, its workers' movement, in its attitudes and influence, was relatively advanced. Some critics have seen in this focus a contradiction with the historical materialist insistence that capitalism can only be surpassed when the bourgeoisie has established power, given the incompleteness of bourgeois institutions in Germany at the time.

For the authors, this circle was squared in the claim that Germany was precisely a politically reactionary but advanced "civilised" country, "on the eve of a bourgeois revolution . . . to be carried out under more advanced conditions . . . and with a much more developed proletariat" than in previous bourgeois ascensions (4.7).[25] They make clear that readying this fight means stressing to the working class the "hostile antagonism" between them and the bourgeoisie (4.6), and preparing to fight with whatever political weapons political reform granted them.

As we've seen in Chapter 2 above, the actual history of the 1848 revolutions, of course, makes this section glum reading, and would provoke a rethink of the relations between the working class and the pusillanimous bourgeoisie, even in states dominated by reactionary powers. What hedged and suspicious aspirations there were to any alliance between the proletariat and the bourgeoisie in the *Manifesto* were soon to wither.

For all that forthcoming disappointment, the stress here on workers fighting in Germany does nuance any reductive model of a rigid historical sequence in Marxism—of the bourgeoisie necessarily coming first to power before the working class can assert itself in its own right. This nuancing in turn invalidates any implication that the working class should be politically quiescent at a "premature" moment, when it's allegedly not developed enough to stake its own claim. Indeed, the model here views that very concept with suspicion. Vitally relevant to the necessary working-class militancy on which the authors insist, as later laid out in a celebrated preface to a Russian edition (see Appendix C), is the nature of capitalism as an *international* system. The judgement of whether or not the time is right for working-class struggle anywhere is never a matter of conditions in that country alone. Thus the German revolution the authors advocate "will be but the prelude to an immediately following proletarian revolution" (4.7). This, as we will see, has been one of the most vexed strategies and prognostications in the *Manifesto*.[26]

In the last five short paragraphs (4.8–4.12), the *Manifesto* makes clear that no historical evaluation of context should blunt revolutionary ardor: in a wonderful and important formulation, they insist that "the Communists everywhere support every revolutionary movement against the existing social and political order of things" (4.8). "The Communists disdain to conceal their views and aims," and their program, even when collaborating with non-revolutionary parties or agitating for reforms, requires "the forcible overthrow of all existing social conditions" (4.11). In every struggle "they bring to the front . . . the property questions"—whatever stage it may be at (4.9). All this in the service of the communist revolution, at which prospect the ruling classes should "tremble" (4.11).

"WORKERS OF ALL COUNTRIES," the last paragraph reads in its entirety, capitals and all, "UNITE!"

## Prefaces

To the *Manifesto* are often appended one or more prefaces, including those from the German editions of 1872 (reproduced as Appendix B), 1883 (Appendix D) and 1880; a Russian edition in 1882 (Appendix C); an English in 1888 (Appendix E); Polish in 1892; and Italian in 1893. These documents defend the *Manifesto*'s positions, while allowing that intervening years have impacted its arguments. A few particulars are worth noting.

In the 1872 German preface (see Appendix B), the authors discussed the disappearance of many of the organizations discussed in Section 4, and it was here that they discouraged excessive focus on those "revolutionary measures" at the end of Section 2, given the consolidation of capitalism and of business, and of various economic and political crises rising from increasing class polarization. It was also here that, very importantly, they stressed that the concrete political program of Section 2 had been superseded—"has in some details become antiquated"—by the "improved and extended party organization of the working class, in view of the practical experience gained, first in the February Revolution [of 1848], and then, still more, in the Paris Commune, where the proletariat for the first time held political power for two whole months." After which point it was brutally and bloodily crushed. This, too, was a lesson. Key to what they drew from the Commune's brief existence, crucial for later readings of the *Manifesto*, was that "the working class cannot simply lay hold of the ready-made state machinery, and wield it for its own purposes," but must transform it. The list of ten measures suggested in the *Manifesto* are economic policies—in the aftermath of the Paris Commune, the authors returned to this section with a new focus on questions of politics and political form, by which economic change might be attempted.[27]

In the 1882 Russian edition (see Appendix C), Marx and Engels considered the belated, partial opening of Russia, "the last great reserve of all European reaction" to capital, which rapidly took on monopolistic features. Intriguingly, in this economic and political context, a revolutionary break to communism—only possible by emerging out of the productive crucible of capitalism—seemed to them no longer so unlikely as it once had. Noting that in Russia, unlike most of Europe, land communally owned by peasants in a system called *obshchina* comprised more than half of all land, they mused on whether the radicalization and expansion of that system might allow a distinct path to communism, without passing through "the same process of dissolution," the shattering of feudal norms "such as constitutes the historical evolution of the West."

This concrete question, vitally important as it was, also underlines the continued deviation of Marx and Engels from what's sometimes maligned as a teleological and stage-ist vision of historical development—of feudalism inexorably giving way to fully developed capitalism and then and only then to communism. If the *obshchina* had operated as a "staging post" to fully developed communism, in this model it would not portend, as even one thoughtful commentator claims, that "the materialist conception of history would . . . be broken,"[28] but, as the authors had hinted in their discussion of Germany in the *Manifesto*, that such a conception is not a procrustean bed into which complex reality must be shoved. Specific material circumstances, including the unusual and anomalous, require careful analysis without preconception. And whatever the prospects might be for revolutionary upheaval in Russia or extending the commune model, if any such thing were to occur, it would be necessary for "the Russian Revolution [to] become the signal for a proletariat revolution in the West, so that both complement each other." Again, revolution, just like capitalism, is necessarily international.

Marx and Engels answer their own question as to whether the *obshchina* might conceivably "serve as the starting point for a communist development" positively—but only in the context of this global focus. Such focus allows them—to deploy some of the language of the Hegelian dialectic that so inspired them—to synthesize particularity and generality, that is, tendencies as well as their exceptions, trends and contingencies. To ask such a question of the *obshchina* in *isolation*, abstracted from all that messy history and geography, would, of course, be to do violence to their method. As it is, their answer is a sort of "yes and no." Such a response may very often be an infuriating evasion, but it can, in certain contexts, to certain questions, be the only rigorous and enlightening—dialectical—response.

The brief 1883 German preface (see Appendix D) was written alone by a grieving Engels. Marx had recently died. Here, with much self-effacement, is where Engels grants to Marx "solely and exclusively" the foundational insight of the manifesto. This he restates in admirably terse form.

[T]hat economic production, and the structure of society of every historical epoch necessarily arising therefrom, constitute the foundation for the political and intellectual history of that epoch; that consequently

. . . all history has been a history of class struggles . . . between exploited and exploiting, between dominated and dominating classes . . . that this struggle . . . has now reached a stage where the exploited and oppressed class (the proletariat) can no longer emancipate itself from the class which exploits and oppresses it (the bourgeoisie) without at the same time forever freeing the whole of society from exploitation, oppression, class struggles . . .

# 4

# Evaluating the *Manifesto*

Hope, often a fracturing, even a traumatic thing to experience, is among the energies by which the reparatively positioned reader tries to organize the fragments and part-objects she encounters or creates.

Eve Kosofsky Sedgwick, "Paranoid Reading and Reparative Reading, or, You're So Paranoid, You Probably Think This Essay Is About You"

## HISTORY

The tour of history in the *Manifesto* is brisk, schematic, not always free of contradiction or ambiguity, and hardly sacrosanct. The tale it tells of the birth of capitalism in the context of class struggle, the book's focus on international trade and the medieval towns, remains vigorously debated, including among those committed to Marx's politics and methodology.[1] This is hardly surprising, given the nature of the *Manifesto*'s "historical analyses" in the text as fleeting and somewhat vague abstractions about European development.

Underlying all the disputed details, and important as such disputation is, is what Marx would soon describe as his key contribution in the *Manifesto*:

What I did that was new was to prove 1) that the existence of classes is only bound up with particular, historic phases in the development of production; 2) that the class struggle necessarily leads to the dictatorship of the proletariat; 3) that this dictatorship itself only constitutes the transition to the abolition of all classes and to classless society.[2]

The "dictatorship of the proletariat" is a term now understandably embarrassing to many admirers of Marx, and one that has been used to justify and promote brutal one-party rule. Marx never fleshes out the concept (which wasn't his coinage, but that of his interlocutor, Weydemeyer). At its core, what Marx implies by it is not bloodthirsty, ruthless suppression but i) a necessary transitional stage between capitalism and communism, after ii) the forcible overthrow of the former, involving iii) the construction of a government by and for the working class.

Certain suggestive ideas for what such a government might look like were unexpectedly thrown up in 1871 with that seventy-two-day life of the Paris Commune, which inaugurated radical innovations to maintain organic links between the administrative apparatus and the working class. Measures ranged from the radical liberal through to glimmers of something beyond, from the disestablishment of the church, vast improvements in working conditions, the end of juridical and moralizing distinctions between "legitimate" and "illegitimate" children, to the establishment of an armed people's militia in place of a standing army, the paying of the Commune representatives workers' wages and making all such representatives, in military, legislative and executive branches, subject to immediate democratic recall and replacement. In Marx's words, "[i]nstead of deciding once in three or six years which member of the ruling class was to misrepresent the people in Parliament, universal suffrage"—at this point universal male suffrage, it must be allowed—"was to serve the people."

Thus it was that in the 1872 edition of the *Manifesto*, after that profoundly instructive example of the Commune, Marx and Engels insisted that, the state being an instrument of class rule, "the working class cannot simply lay hold of ready-made state machinery and wield it for its own purposes"—those purposes culminating ultimately in the end of all classes and all states.[3]

History, in the *Manifesto*'s model, then, is characterized by struggles between those at the top, who have power over the productive forces of society, and those over whom they exercise control in various ways, and who perform the productive work. Work over which, and over the fruits of which, those workers in turn have no meaningful say. And, as Marx wrote, "necessarily"—a controversial word, containing multitudes—the exploited will, and/or must, overthrow that system of exploitation.

It's often claimed that the *Manifesto* crudely depicts the disappearance of all classes but the bourgeoisie and the proletariat under capitalism. This is false, and predicated on minor infelicities in translation, and a context of hostile reading.[4] The *Manifesto* doesn't imagine the replacing of all the intricate complexity of class hierarchy with such a simple binary face-off, but rather that that opposition between the two "great hostile camps" is so powerful a motor of antagonism within capitalism that it tends to subordinate other class conflicts to its logic.

With regard to that freighted "necessarily," it is the case, without question, that various of the *Manifesto*'s formulations seem to invoke a kind of inevitability in regard to the proletarian revolution, among other events. What's not so often stressed is that such passages contrast with *explicitly anti-inevitabilist* formulations that are also in the document. We'll return more than once to this important point, particularly in Chapter 5. For now, it's worth pointing out that this is why a generous rigor with regard to the manifesto form is vital. Simply to read such contradictions as if they entirely invalidate the work and its project, in the context of so incantatory a polemic, is vacuous.

Whatever the contested details of the *Manifesto*'s historical/political story, to hole it below the waterline, a truly substantive, truly damaging critique would have to focus on what Marx saw as his key contribution.

And thus to insist: i) that class divisions do not exist; ii) and/or that they do not cause fundamental social problems; iii) and/or that any attempts to overturn this iniquity is doomed and pointless; iv) and/or that any such attempt will worsen the world, or be so likely to as to make it not worth the wager; v) and/or that this class divide is desirable.

The lies to the first two propositions, the fact that class differences exist and have deleterious consequences for countless people, are surely self-evident, including to conservatives. The fifth claim, that such distinctions are in and of themselves desirable, isn't as rare as it should be: see, for example, the socially sadistic trolling of such articles as "Why Inequality Can Be Beautiful."[5] But the overt depravity of such a position means it's still relatively uncommon. The third and fourth positions, that change is impossible, or can only be for the worse, are by far the most common. It's easy to see why. A totalizing system such as capitalism encompasses not only the economic motor of society, but its politics, culture, and ideology. Whatever particular, contradictory ideological notions arise in such a society, the very structures of such thought that it engenders have a tendency to project it as a seamless totality, without a chink in its carapace. This kind of thinking Mark Fisher famously described as "capitalist realism"[6]— not an acceptance of capitalism, but a belief that, regrettably or otherwise, it represents the boundaries of the possible. The hold of such deadening common sense, inimical to social change, is understandable.

But whether despairing or celebratory, this is a faith position, no less than is some kitsch Stalinist certainty in the glorious proletarian future. As Ursula Le Guin magnificently put it: "We live in capitalism, its power seems inescapable—but then, so did the divine right of kings. Any human power can be resisted and changed by human beings."[7] The *Manifesto* itself is clear that history is a long sequence of the upending and overturning of seemingly unshakeable systems. Capitalism *may* be inevitable. But we have no grounds for claiming this a priori.

It's a certain sign of ideological weakness when one has to explicitly demand something that was hitherto simply a given. Thus, for example, the recent official guidelines by the British Department of Education instructing schools "not under any circumstances" to use any resources by organizations which have expressed a desire for the abolition of capitalism,[8] are on the one hand a grotesque moment of thought-crime policing, on the other an intimation of capitalist unease. In the last few years, capitalist realism has been shaken. This is not least because a permeable membrane exists between the questioning of certain nostrums of the system, and questioning that system *in its entirety*. By no means do all of those who recently demonstrated around the world against savage police brutality, for example, hold that capitalism can or must be dispensed with. But in the US, thousands of people now firmly advocate the defunding, even abolition, of the police—demands that would have been unthinkable scant months before. And once certain givens are no longer given, a questioning of the system which insisted upon them can follow.

This is why it's a risk for its advocates to insist that capitalism must take certain forms and only those forms (generally, of course, those most profitable and comfortable at any moment for those in power). For example, when, under conditions of mass pandemic and economic shutdown, to save itself capitalism provides economic resources and structures of support, even if inadequate, that it very recently insisted were quite impossible, its grander claim that it is the only available option is also undermined. Given the fact of class struggle—in the broad sense of structural opposition and antagonistic interests, not necessarily entailing open hostilities—and the misery and powerlessness it entails, capitalism must constantly negotiate a narrow band of actual reform, and "reformability" itself, titrating how much to alter its structures, how much and when to allow that any such alteration is possible, to preclude opening the door to greater demands.

This is clearer now, in a global context of advanced capitalism, than when the *Manifesto* was written. Then, bourgeois civilization wasn't firmly established. Rather than the nature of today's "late capitalism"—of which more below—it was its "earliness" that was a complication for Marx and Engels, those fascinated critics.

## POLITICS AND THE BOURGEOISIE

It was precisely because it was a product of a moment of unfinished transition and political instability that the *Manifesto* paid such particular attention to how communists should relate to the bourgeoisie. Tumbling out of the pen on what seemed to be the eve of bourgeois revolution, liberalism and democracy, with the possibility of a swift move from such a situation to proletarian revolution, the *Manifesto* formulated strategies to overthrow the bourgeoisie as swiftly as possible, while at that moment supporting them. The lesson that followed, that the German bourgeoisie was more afraid of workers than of the reactionary absolutist state it despised, prompted the disquieted authors to depart from any hedged, partial, tactical alliance with, or patience for, the bourgeoisie, and "a fundamental reorientation of the proletariat away from a strategic alliance with the bourgeoisie and toward its own political independence."[9]

Marx and Engels never lost a scintilla of commitment to the urgency of the overthrow of bourgeois society, but after the failure of the uprisings they "returned to the original proposition, this time as pessimists rather than optimists. They had accepted that the overthrow of bourgeois capitalism was more necessary than ever, given the craven quality of bourgeois leadership in 1848; but the contest with the bourgeoisie was seen as darker and more bitter."[10] It was such revolutionary pessimism that saw them begin to dispense, shortly after they published the *Manifesto*, with the vestiges of any notion of a sequence of inevitable historical "stages." They moved instead towards a sense that even the struggle for liberal democratic rights must be the preserve of the working class, as part of a revolutionary process culminating in socialist revolution.[11]

That it just predates this Damascene shock goes a long way to explaining that most remarked-upon qualities of the *Manifesto*: that two such trenchant critics of capitalism, in a screed devoted to its overthrow, provide so unrestrained a paean to the revolutionary nature and Promethean power of the bourgeoisie, their admiration that it "has played a most revolutionary part" (1.13), "pitilessly torn asunder" outdated feudal ties (1.14), "stripped of its halo every occupation hitherto honored and looked up to with reverent awe" (1.15), "accomplished wonders" (1.17).

Even within such paragraphs, the admiration is ambivalent. But admiration it is. This respect for the bourgeoisie stems, in the words of Michael Löwy, from an "insufficiently critical stance in regard to modern bourgeois/industrial civilisation."[12] The encomia to the destroyer of all feudal bonds would ring hollow just a few months after its appearance, as those supposed destroyers scurried to the safety of those very bonds.

A similar faith in the historic role of the bourgeoisie internationally was also at best naive. Certainly, "[t]he need of a constantly expanding market . . . chases the bourgeoisie over the whole surface of the globe" (1.19), transforming the world. But when the *Manifesto* mentions colonialism in terms of compelling "all nations, on pain of extinction, to adopt the bourgeois mode of production" (1.21), and bourgeois society's capacity to draw "even the most barbarian" nations into "civilisation," the image is of a "modernising" transformation of the world, not only economically and politically but culturally (as in the obscure and questionable prophecy of the rise of a "world literature" (1.20)). A certain global flattening, to which we will return.

Never sanguine about it, Marx would come to be even more critical of the utterly brutal role of colonialism, and skeptical of the extent to which it might, in fact, "modernise" colonised nations. Clear signs of such suspicion are already evident in the *Manifesto*. It even ironizes that common image of the dynamism of "civilisation," for example, breaking from the default Eurocentric, racist distinction between "barbarian" and "civilised" by referring cynically to the latter as "what it calls civilisation" (1.21). The market processes by which the world is opened up are described as "the heavy artillery with which it batters down all Chinese walls." This is an unsubtle reference to the Opium War of

1839–42, during which the "heavy artillery" that the British used to force the Chinese to open their economy to British imports, including opium, was in literal fact heavy ordnance. Thus is the relationship between the "dynamism of capitalism" and murderous imperial violence made starkly clear—and the line between them blurred. And there's more than a little skepticism about the "developmental" role of capitalism in the *Manifesto*'s description of the bourgeoisie making "barbarian and semi-barbarian countries dependent on the civilised ones" (1.22). In the decades since the *Manifesto*'s publication, theorists in and beyond the Marxist tradition would extend such germs to analyze how the relationship of colonial metropole to the "periphery" was fundamentally driven by exploitation rather than any historic mission of "development," which, if it occurred at all, did so contingently, piecemeal, and in violently contradictory fashion. The conflicted and suspicious but real admiration for the bourgeoisie in the *Manifesto* would come to be corrected.

None of this is to suggest that the depiction within the *Manifesto*'s pages of the sheer upheaval of modernity isn't vivid and, if sometimes too generous, crucially important. There's deep insight in its depiction of bourgeois *society* as an aggregation of countless dynamics and as a profoundly destabilizing and disintegrative form—if not always in the ways the *Manifesto* sometimes seems to imply. Under capitalism, for example, pre-existing norms and cultures are often transformed, rather than simply swept away. Such transformation, neither at the behest nor for the benefit of those at its sharp end, is profound, and a matter of constant upheaval. It's no wonder that modern life is rubbish, generative of anxiety, deracination, a deep psychic as well as economic instability, not to say disempowerment and death, for millions.

## Politics and the Proletariat

The authors of the *Manifesto* stress tendencies against working-class unity, caused by the competition between workers under capitalism. But for all that due diligence, they are still too optimistic about the class's development when they suggest that, in countervailing tendency, "[t]his organisation of the proletarians into a class, and consequently into a political party" is progressing on an ever "stronger, firmer, mightier" footing (1.40).[13]

As so often in the *Manifesto*, the line between claim, prediction, and exhortation is hazy. The trajectory described here is as much aspiration as it is prediction or description. The lack of global proletarian victory would certainly have surprised and disappointed Marx and Engels. But to invalidate the *Manifesto* as analysis would require disproving the existence of class struggle itself. And, again, with regard to prescription, one would have to argue that democratic grassroots control of society's productive capacity would be *worse* for the mass of humanity than capitalism itself. While the struggle may be considerably harder than Marx and Engels imagined, this doesn't in and of itself invalidate their view of the working class as the "agent of history" capable of overturning oppression and exploitation.

Rightly or wrongly, they view the working class as the only group capable of rendering that change. This isn't because the working class are, as for the True Socialists, the "most" oppressed or exploited group. Nor is it out of sentimentality, "an assumption" imputed to Marx and Engels by some of their opponents "that the proletariat were more altruistic than other classes."[14] The point is, rather, that for historical materialism, class is not one axis of oppression among others, all related one to the other simply arithmetically.[15] Radicals can and do debate in good faith the extent to which various axes of oppression are inextricable from capitalism itself, and thus the extent to which one can reasonably hope that the ending of class society would see their end (more on this below). For all that, in the *Manifesto*'s model, class is a distinct social relation—though one intersecting with oppression in profoundly important ways—in that it is constituted on axes of i) productivity and ii) exploitation. That is to say, it's *as workers* that workers create capitalism's wealth. It's that position, and the power implicit in it, that underlies why the working class is uniquely placed to change the economic system—to take control of society and its productive capacity, which does not exist without it.

This is the sense in which the *Manifesto* stresses the working class as the agent of revolution. And it's because of the particular position of the working class at this point in history, unlike that of the bourgeoisie, that to overthrow its own exploitation is ultimately to end class exploitation of all kinds: "universally dispossessed," the proletariat "lacks any particular interest to defend."[16] With nothing to lose but chains, the working class's interest doesn't lie in applying chains elsewhere, but in dispensing with them all.[17]

## Economics

The *Manifesto* doesn't lay out a developed economic theory,[18] though it gestures at certain analyses and predictions, many extrapolated from Engels's earlier work on the condition of the working class in Manchester.[19] There are economic lacunae, too, such as the lack of engagement with the role of money and finance capital, which may have been partly behind the "rather episodic and contingent" treatment of financial flows and structures in the Marxist tradition.[20]

Marx's economic theory would come to be developed in the later mature works, culminating in the magisterial *Capital*, but crucial early investigations predate the *Manifesto*. In the *Economic and Philosophic Manuscripts*, for example, the model, inherited by the *Manifesto*, is of the relentless *alienation* of the workers from the fruits of their labor, from each other, and from their own essence—thus linking the economic and philosophical critiques of capitalism.

Other positions in the text are less persuasive. As we've seen, in the authors' model, wages are inevitably pushed ever lower, towards a state of absolute poverty and immiseration (1.52), a theory drawing from Ricardo, and one that Marx and Engels themselves would come in later works to see was wrong. The fact of this error would come to be central to many "revisionist" takes on the *Manifesto*, which turned away from its revolutionary conclusions, advocating instead a steady ameliorative reformism.[21] This is despite the fact that germ seeds of a more nuanced position, of downward pressure on wages that is real but *contested*, are implicit in the *Manifesto*'s pages. When, for example, the authors describe workers forming unions "in order to keep up the rate of wages" (1.38), they envisage the value of labor-power (the capacity to labor) and, concomitantly, of the wage varying in changing contexts, and such variation, crucially, being in part due to class struggle.

This is the embryo of what Marx would come, in *Capital*, to call the "moral-historical component" of labor-power, and it directly contradicts the immiseration thesis. The fruits of such struggles can impact the value of labor-power itself. When the working-class movement succeeds in insisting that, say, a reduction in hours isn't a temporary concession but that it sets a new socially acceptable baseline, or when social and political pressure and changing living standards redefine what were once "luxuries" into necessities and/or basic rights (fridges, holidays, televisions, computers, etc.) the value of labor-power will alter to reflect the changing norms of that labour-power's replication—which is to say, working-class life itself. That doesn't mean that all workers will have access to such amenities, but that where once it might be a surprise if they did, it can become something like a social shame if now they don't.

In certain circumstances, such shifts in, to use the modern phrase, the "Overton window" with regard to what's minimally acceptable to working-class life, can, of course, also occur in the other direction. This is always a question of class contestation.

Far more persuasive than the "immiseration thesis," in the *Manifesto*, are the references to the consolidation and monopolizing power of large capital, and its imbrication with nation-states. Today's anxiety over megacorporations, and their hold over and relationships with the machineries of state, is hardly surprising, nor is it restricted to the Left.

Or consider the *Manifesto*'s brief discussion of economic crises. One particularly unedifying commonplace of capitalism is the regular claim of its apologists that it has superseded the "boom and bust" cycle.[22] Marx and Engels—along with a few unsentimental advocates of hard free-market libertarianism—scoff at this. The *Manifesto*'s position is that such crises are absolutely inevitable features of capitalism, that it will as long as it exists be wracked by such catastrophes of waste and human misery.[23] Claims that crises can be tamed are thrown up in anxious disavowal, and they, too, will continue, and they will continue to be false.[24] Frankly, more useful to the capitalist class than such lullabies, particularly at this point in history, is that unsentimental and growing current that sees acquisitive opportunity in the inevitable crises—the "disaster capitalism" so bitterly and brilliantly outlined by Naomi Klein.[25]

Another claim in the *Manifesto* that stands the test of time is of "the need of a constantly expanding market for its products [that] chases the bourgeoisie over the entire surface of the globe." This is a trenchant depiction of the kind of globalization that was, at the time of writing, only in an embryonic stage. Even various of Marx's opponents praise the perspicacity of the *Manifesto* on this point.

That they do so is, of course, not politically uncomplicated. "[C]apitalist apologists have always been more than happy to concede"[26] such "prophecies," because by this point in history, what were once insights such as these have now become hard to contest. They are *merely*, and reasonably obviously, true. And what's more, impressive as such prognostication of the internationalizing tendencies of capitalism was, in and of themselves those tendencies are not threatening for the bourgeoisie, and nothing for them to disavow. As economic analysis, in fact, they shine a light on something to be approved, even proud, of. Hence the extensive cottage industry of leadenly "provocative" edgelord pro-capitalist "returns to Marx," that often take as their point of departure the *Manifesto*'s analysis of globalized capitalism's dynamism.[27]

In fact, the young authors' genuine perspicacity on this economic point is somewhat constrained by other limitations of their theory, with regard, for example, to the tenacity of the nation-state itself. The sense that globalization is not the dissolution of states, but has been a dynamic of a system *of* regulatory states, has been understated by many commentators—and is in the *Manifesto*.[28] And at least as important, that admiration for their enemies, what we might call the "bourgeoisphilia," in the text, leads the authors to underestimate both the sheer destructiveness of the depicted international process, and, in describing "universal inter-dependence of nations," to overstate its effacement of particularities and differences. In the context of the power dynamics and drivers of bourgeois society, what this leaves inadequately interrogated is the way "[h]ierarchical organisation and fragmentation are inherent in the very form of globalisation that capitalism carries out."[29]

Obviously, too, for all such "prophetic" insight, the specifics of capitalism are not static. The changes in the system since the *Manifesto* was written are vast: the growth in importance of telecommunications, logistics and data technology, the incredible acceleration of flows of commodities and data. But seeing this simply as evidence of the outdatedness of the *Manifesto* would be to focus on the changes—epochal as they certainly are—in the surface level of specifics, rather than the continuities on the basis of the fundamental dynamics with which the *Manifesto* is concerned. Those are of profit-extraction by a minority, through the exploitation of the labor of a majority, in the context of competitive accumulation. On *that* basis, in fact, as Jodi Dean puts it in her introduction to the *Manifesto*, its "description of capitalist society is more accurate today than when it was written. The world in the twenty-first century is entirely subsumed by capitalism. The capitalist system is global. Competition, crises, and precarity condition the lives of and futures of everyone on earth."[30]

As we would expect, on questions of post-revolutionary economic organization, the *Manifesto* has little to say. The mechanisms of collective control of the economy are left for future communist subjects to discover and create, as they discover and create themselves. One aspect of communist economics, though, is important: to repeat, this is a communism of *plenty*, of a massively productive economy, as opposed to the "austerity communism" some contemporary radicals advocated.[31] Scare stories, by enemies of change, of a radical leveling down, an equality of poverty, are a thousand miles from the vision in the *Manifesto*.

## REVOLUTION

Marx and Engels were far from indifferent to reforms, as we've seen. Throughout their political lives they celebrated and fought for radical reform. They did so out of commitment to improving working-class lives, and—and this is where their attitude to reforms differs from that of even the most sincere reformist—because they held, as is discussed above, that particular reforms, fought for with strategic nous, potentially strengthened the pressures towards the root-and-branch reconfiguration they saw as only possible with revolution. As we'll see, even those reforms that capitalists may come to accept because they might "lessen the cost, and simplify the administrative work, of bourgeois government" (3.40), and that might thus seem intrinsically limited, the authors would not automatically oppose—though they would fight for them in very particular ways. Because such reforms might still, in certain respects, if demanded in specific political contexts, strengthen the hand of the working class.

Whether, when and how to support reformist measures is a live issue of socialist strategy. Because unlike the "bourgeois socialists" for whom such measures are keystones of a political program designed to prop up an exploitative system, for communists they are worth struggling for insofar as they gesture beyond their own limits. Reform is change, even substantial, *within* an existing social structure: revolution is, to quote Engels from his 1888 introduction to the *Manifesto*, "total social change"—the radical overthrow *of* that system. One later commentator would describe this as "a cataclysmic leap" from one social structure to another.[32] This is what the *Manifesto* calls "rupture" (2.66).

Obviously such revolutionism is predicated on a sense that bourgeois society is inextricable from toxic social problems. But for Marx and Engels it is also a kind of back-handed compliment of the system. There's a certain bleak admiration in their vision of modern capitalism as so voracious, total, and totalizing a system that it cannot be made liveable with. This doesn't imply impregnability or seamlessness—communist political strategy is predicated on working at cracks. But it understands capitalism's logic as *predicated on* exploitation and oppression, such that it can and will never exist without them, such that whatever reforms can be effected will always be inadequate, opposed ferociously by the bourgeoisie, always embattled. This is why capitalism cannot be accommodated.

Capitalism is unbearable and yet, mostly, it's borne. For lifetimes, and by millions. The strongest weapon against revolution, or any hankering for it, isn't positive but negative: it's not any claim that the world in which we live is good enough, but that capitalist-realist common sense that it's impossible, even laughable, to struggle or hope for change. The tenacity of such a view is in part due to a deliberate ruling-class propaganda strategy to discourage any belief in any such possibility. But it's also, at a base level, because it's so difficult to think beyond the reality in which one has been created, lives, and thinks now. The yearned-for social rupture would be a Rubicon towards a repurposing of social totality itself. Conditioned as we are by *existing* reality, we cannot prefigure or simply "imagine" such radical alterity. As such, it's beyond our ken—we can only yearn for it, strain for it, glimpse some sense of betterness out of the corner of the eye.[33]

To oppose revolution not merely as impossible but *undesirable*, a common axis of anxiety is *violence*. This is perfectly understandable, given the violent and repressive history of various moments of various self-proclaimedly leftist revolutions and/or coups—consider Cambodia for a grim example. It's no less understandable that the enemies of change would deploy such histories as cautionary fables. Without question the dominant vision of revolution in the *Manifesto* is of "the *forcible* overthrow of all existing social conditions" (4.11)—the emphasis here is mine, but the adjective is key. But important details give nuance to this.

The first is that, some time after they wrote the *Manifesto* but still standing by it, Marx and Engels would repeatedly moot the possibility of non-violent social transformation in certain circumstances.[34] In a speech in The Hague in 1872, for example, Marx suggested that in countries such as the Netherlands or the US, where the bureaucracy and army did not dominate the state, "the workers may attain their goals by peaceful means."[35] Engels, in 1896, described Marx as wondering if in England "the inevitable social revolution might be effected entirely by peaceful and legal means."[36] Engels himself, five years earlier, had allowed the possibility of a peaceful socialist revolution in such countries as England, America, and France. This is not to deny that either saw force as potentially or likely necessary: in that very Hague speech, Marx said that even if he were right about these exceptions, in most cases "the lever of the revolution will have to be force." But though he did not shun the prospect of an armed struggle for power, neither he nor Engels glorified violence for its own sake, unlike some earlier communists of more conspiratorialist cast—and some later, too.

One reason for this caution, as Engels clarified in 1895, is that in most situations, given the place of the army in modern statecraft, "a real victory of an insurrection over the military in street fighting . . . is one of the rarest exceptions."[37] The best political method, the authors considered, even allowing for the use of force, was to patiently build up social support. Because the stronger that support, the more likely any necessary coercion would be brief, restrained, and lead to victory.[38]

Again, here the partisans of exploitative order often deploy common-sense scorn. Imagine barricades! Imagine fighting the forces of law and order to fundamentally change society! Imagine marching in the streets and waking up to a new world! How *stupid* are these people?! As if, around the globe, throughout history, and now, on our screens and in our streets, people don't stand on barricades. But neither resiling from nor denigrating that vision of revolution as not just possible but a repeated historical experience, it's important to stress that the *Manifesto*'s authors were open-minded about the possibilities of distinct roads to rupture, of various and unforeseen shapes. Including involving the legal capturing of institutions and their reconfiguration.[39] Leftists can and should debate the likelihood of taking any such roads in various combinations, the possibilities of their efficacy—and they are so debating.[40]

The very counterposing of simon-pure anti-state "revolutionism" and a caricature "legal"/"democratic" road is often too stark. The two instead might be variously weighted necessary elements of a broader strategy for rupture. This suggestion is often met with nervousness on the Marxist Left, and not without reason: whatever their initial claims, there's a history of leftists who interrogate such possibilities moving to the right, giving up on ruptural reconfiguration altogether, sometimes even embracing reaction.[41] But that doesn't justify a retreat to the comforts of binarism, according to which there are, as one leftist committed to the Manichean model puts it, necessarily "two positions— one that the shell of the old society must be burst by force; the other, that the existing state can be taken over peacefully by gaining control of bourgeois representative institutions."[42] Particularly when there's a tradition of socialist debate and theorizing that problematises exactly that stark either/or, and all in the service not of aspiration to reform the state or capitalism, but of rupture itself. The brilliant and controversial Greek Marxist Nicos Poulantzas, for example, worked hard to construct a model of the state as a complex knotting of conflictual social forces, precisely "to escape the false dilemmas in which we are presently stuck," to "develop some coordination" between tactics, to stress the necessity of "a struggle within the state . . . to sharpen the internal contradictions of the state, to carry out a deep-seated transformation of the state," and "on the other hand, a parallel struggle, a struggle outside the institutions and apparatuses."[43]

This has been the cause of great debate in the Left—though sometimes it seems there's less distance between the interlocutors than at least one of them seems to think.[44] Poulantzas's isn't a trans-historic claim, but a judgement about a particular moment, and the ruptural strategy appropriate to it. With which, of course, one can reasonably disagree, as with a thousand details, with the direction Poulantzas takes his work, with various of his concrete hypotheses (his thoughts about the possibility for a radical left French government in the 1970s, for example, seem a reach now).[45] But this doesn't in and of itself invalidate the anti-binary approach he advocates. Sometimes parodied as "reformist," Poulantzas's model is one of fidelity to rupture—it's telling that he interrogates precisely that crucial term considerably more than do most radical theorists.[46] If nothing else, his approach is invaluably open to a model that doesn't presume that rupture can be articulated *solely* through mass revolutionary opposition to a state from without its structures—even if one believes that's also key and necessary. It was to such possibilities of complementary "democratic" strategy that Marx and Engels were cautiously open.

Which absolutely should not blind us to the structural opposition to meaningful reform, let alone rupture, baked into bourgeois states in general, and certain states in particular. Such states are not only aggressively anti-anti-capitalist, but very often overtly anti-democratic, too, constraining ruptural or even reformist possibilities from without *and* within. In the UK, for example, the second chamber is wholly unelected, and the constituency-based, first-past-the-post electoral system leads to the profound skewing of representation in parliament, squeezing out smaller parties. And in 1929, 1951, and 1974, the party which won the election with the most seats, to form a government, did so with a lower share of the popular vote than its opposition. Among the other countries where this has also happened is the US, most recently and controversially in 2000 and 2016. And that's only one element of the structural resistance of the US state to democracy. As what's been called the "scholarly gold-standard" work on the US constitution makes clear, the document was framed "with a frankly anti-democratic agenda . . . opposed to a purely democratic system in which the majority would always rule," and was "a vastly more nationalist and democracy-constraining Constitution" than most voters would have chosen.[47] Hence the construction, and development of, the extraordinary anti-democratic power of the Senate, where representatives of roughly 16 percent of the population—overwhelmingly conservative, rural, white—can outvote the other eighty-four; of life membership of the absurd and partisan Supreme Court; of the high hurdles for legislation; of the unbelievably illogical and rigged electoral college; of the deliberately staggered votes for and lengths of tenure of representatives, without simple means of popular recall; of the filibuster that can block Senate bills; and of the byzantine byways that must be negotiated to change any of this. The Constitution cult in the US—deliberately stoked in the early twentieth century in part as a bulwark against socialism[48]—is a nastily brilliant wheeze by capitalism's apologists. In the name of democracy, an avowedly anti-democratic document is lionized, and demands to change it denounced as a threat to democracy.

The question of constitutional reform in the US is abruptly more live than it has been for some time, given the great majority of conservative judges on the Supreme Court, the intransigent and obstructionist hard-right politics of the Senate and the malignant and accelerating programs of voter-suppression underway in Republican districts. The question of how hard the Democratic Party leadership wants or is willing to fight these measures is open: given its history, its right-wing politics, and its commitment to what's euphemistically called "the donor class," it's hardly surprising that many spectators see Biden and the centrist and right-wing leadership of the Democrats as relating to such hurdles as an excuse against actually changing the system itself, with which they are, largely, content.[49] The US state—among others—represents an immensely powerful roadblock to any program of change, no matter how mild. And that situation is worsening.

What that might mean about the relationship of the socialist movement to the state is open to debate. But any such discussions around the complex relationship of rupture, reform, and revolution can be hampered by a strain of showboating machismo within the Left that treats consideration of any revolutionary parameters other than more or less precisely those of St Petersburg October 1917—a model which certainly remains inspirational—as effete perfidy.[50] A rational kernel of such border-guarding is the fact that "revolutionary" is an easy word to throw around and domesticate. In the *Manifesto*'s terms, three elements are key for any social revolution to be worthy of that name. The first is that its aim is rupture. Its point isn't merely amelioration, but the overthrow of the existing order, the start of the instigation of a wholly new social way of being. The second is the certainty that it will provoke political struggle and contestation. This is a project with enemies. It will be opposed, because it means the expropriation and disempowering of those who currently extract profit from and hold power over others. To the ruling class *as a class*, this is an existential threat, to be fought by any means available. And their counter-revolutionary project might win.[51] And thus, the third, no matter how open "revolutionists" might be to a variety of forms of revolution, they cannot shy away from the necessity of struggle.

The relationship between coercion, force, and violence is crucial here. As we've seen, Marx and Engels, unlike the moralist utopian socialists they criticize, were clear that because of their enemies' class interests, the working class would have to exercise some degree of coercion to transform the world. There's no prospect of a revolution without a struggle against those set to lose by it. And the horizon of coercion is force. But depending on how much social weight a movement has, how strategically it deploys it, actual *violence*, in no way a good in itself, can be minimized.

And underpinning all of this, explaining why the possible necessity of force isn't something from which Marx and Engels recoil, is the fact that they hold "so-called civilisation" to be itself a barbarous and violent system. This is not to be relaxed about violence on any side, but to contest the image of revolution as an irruption of violence into a peaceable system. It's to accept, rather, the necessity of violence *against* violence, to fight for the end of the mass death and social violence which underpins capitalism, surrounds us, at a greater scale today even than it did the *Manifesto*'s authors.

## ETHICS OF A HORIZON

A visitor once reported that "the moment that anyone started to talk to Marx about morality, he would roar with laughter."[52] Marxism has been notoriously skeptical of ethical arguments, and the *Manifesto* seems to actively reject any recourse to moral or ethical philosophy: consider, for example, the passage describing not just law and religion but morality itself as "so many bourgeois prejudices, behind which lurk in ambush just as many bourgeois interests" (1.47). In this model, recourse to anything like moral argument appears to be a trap laid by the class enemy. One of the text's attacks on the utopian socialists is precisely that they are moral critics, without a sense of historical grounding.

It's hard to deny that there's a strain in the *Manifesto* according to which communist advocacy is *not at all* a moral question, and is driven purely by other considerations. These considerations include the historical "necessity of total social change" (as Engels put it in the 1888 introduction). This, though, leaves various issues unexamined, as we will see: the—questionable—suggestion of the inevitability of revolution, for one; and, for another, why, even if something is inevitable, support for it should follow.

However, alongside such moral skepticism, "Marx and Engels had the 'highest' moral reasons for abhorring capitalism and seeking to achieve socialism."[53] The *Manifesto* thunders repeatedly with denunciation of bourgeois society. To make sense of the *Manifesto* in terms of ethics means to acknowledge this contradiction.

In a seminal overview of Marx's approach to justice and to normative questions in general, Norman Geras pointed out that for all

> Marx's impatience with the language of norms and values . . . he himself, despite it, does plainly condemn capitalism—for its oppressions and unfreedoms and also . . . for its injustices. Denied publicly, repressed, his own ethical commitments keep returning: the values of freedom, self-development, human well-being and happiness; the ideal of a just society in which these things are decently distributed.[54]

One can see this tendency at play in the *Manifesto*. At one level it does seem clear that the *Manifesto*'s writers were simply wrong to believe that they had superseded morality. This is a real oversight—Marxists, as Geras insists, "must openly take responsibility for their own ethical positions, spell them out, defend, and refine them."[55] But this flaw doesn't necessarily invalidate the *Manifesto*'s analytic vision or even—for all that the text may disavow it—its ethical one.

In their criticisms of the utopian socialists for faint hearts when it comes to anything other than "peaceful means" (3.52), the authors imply that the necessary rupture demands an elasticity of appropriate means. This caution against guiltily limiting "permissible" political methods might seem to be radically anti-ethical. In point of fact, whatever one thinks of the argument and its limits, it isn't an abjuring of ethics but one predicated on *ethical urgency*, the absolute necessity of revolution as speedily as possible.

The text's animus is mostly against *moralising*.[56] The elision of moral and moralising arguments is common, but the two aren't coterminous. It's perfectly reasonable to be sceptical of the latter, the toxic and/or sentimental deployment of, say, shame, to segment people into worthy and unworthy, rather than attempting a grounded analysis of abilities, constraints and concomitant ethics of behavior. Moralizing is also the clearest articulation of the ahistoricism implicit in any recourse to timeless moral precepts. Such a practice is always ideological, and its honored "morality" is rarely congenial to radical change.

Stressing the "freedom" of the "individual," for example, as Steven Lukes puts it, overwhelmingly tends to assume market relationships, and "the very concept of the 'individual' can be given a truncated meaning" implying "self-ownership" and "possessive individualism."[57] Fundamental to the communist project is the opposite approach, the denaturalization of capitalism, the insistence that things can be other than they are. Hence the authors' critique of the supposedly "eternal truths" of "Freedom, Justice, etc." as an expression of, and thrown up by, class society.

But what doesn't follow, as they claim it does, is that communism will oversee the withering of "all religion, and all morality" (2.63). With regard to religion, this *might* be true, but as has already been argued it's in the nature of a radical rupture that one cannot see the other side from here. A post-scarcity communism that doesn't dispense with all thoughts of the divine and numinous can't be precluded. And as regards "all morality," one might defend the formulation with regard to specifically class-partisan morality, but it reads more strongly than that. And this in a book that repeatedly condemns capitalism precisely on ethical grounds, for carrying out "shameless, direct, brutal exploitation" (1.14).

When they defend such formulations, Marx and Engels often beg questions. In a later introduction to Marx's *Poverty of Philosophy*, for example, Engels says his friend "never based his communist demands" on moralizing "but upon the inevitable collapse of the capitalist mode of production."[58] But even if it's inevitable (a questionable claim, even for the *Manifesto* itself, as I'll argue in Chapter 6) why then should it be something for which one hopes, let alone agitates? Why should it be desirable?

And what of the corollary, the implied "good" in the alternative, communism? The proletariat will take power and—what? Free the forces of production. But, as Howard Selsam points out, this is "a circular argument," within which moral judgement is already implicit. "Why is increasing productivity good? . . . Why is man's increasing mastery of nature desirable?"[59] Unfortunately, having raised this excellent question, Selsam, typically for an influential strain of Marxist apologia, immediately brackets it as "irrelevant"—a claim put under strain by his own counterposing of the "crises, war, famine, mass misery" of capitalism to "free men [sic] freely developing their relations with one another and with nature in the interests of all."[60]

We may share the moral intuitions that the latter conditions are more desirable than the former, but they still deserve unpacking. Selsam is exemplary of a particular tradition, according to which this communist ethic is "higher in that it represents a movement in a direction which mankind, in its subsequent historical development, will pronounce good."[61] Communism, that is to say, will define communism as better than capitalism. In point of fact, social ethics are of course often contested within the societies that officially proclaim them, but even as a weaker statement that people will tend to accept the ethical precepts of their society, this is thin to the point of vacuous.

And absent from this position is any sense that history might get *worse*, as in the celebrated later Marxist slogan "Socialism or barbarism,"[62] or that dreaded outcome right there in the *Manifesto* itself, the fear that class conflict might lead to "the common ruin of the contending classes" (1.2). Certainly, neither Selsam nor the *Manifesto*'s authors would, just because it's "subsequent," just because "[f]rom the standpoint of the historical process as a whole it is absolute . . . only in the sense of direction,"[63] celebrate as "higher" whatever brutal survivalist ethics of trash-heap warlordism might pertain after that common ruin—though they might *explain* it and its widespread hold.

Engagements with the ethics of the *Manifesto* often oscillate in like manner, swiftly and uneasily, between common-sense appeals to a better life and then, out of fidelity to the perceived anti-moralism of Marx and Engels, the insistence that there are no standards for judging that "betterness" (other, perhaps, than that supposed inevitability, as if that follows). Nor does it much help to suggest that any moral judgement must be historically "apt," that of a particular revolutionary class when social contradictions open up the possibility of some new ethics and system: that is to say, in another of Selsam's formulations, that "moral judgements reflect reality, and the judgements of the workers today reflect the contradictions in this reality."[64] Not only does this leave unanswered all the questions above, but it's a fact that Marx and Engels did *not* restrict ethical approval to such "favourable" moments. Famously, Marx's historical hero was Spartacus, a slave whose revolt was enormously "premature," and Engels wrote eruditely and respectfully on the sixteenth-century rebel against feudal power, Thomas Müntzer, and other Christian communists, whose programs were "impossible" in their time. As materialists, the authors might well regret the "prematurity" of these positions, but their admiration for such figures is relevant.

For the ruling ideas to be those of the ruling class, as *The German Ideology* has it, doesn't imply unanimity of opinion, including within a class. It's the ethical and ideological *terrain* that's historically conditioned. Not only is contestation over specific ideas common, but, as with the case of Spartacus, it certainly doesn't follow that such systems of ideas and agendas only contain ethical alternatives when "the time is right," as Engels can be read to have implied: "When the moral consciousness of the master declares this, that or the other economic phenomenon to be wrong, as happened at one time in the case of slavery and at another in the case of serfdom, this means that the phenomenon in question has *already* outlived its time, that new economic conditions have arisen, thanks to which the old ones have become intolerable, and must be swept along."[65]

It's clearly true—more or less tautologous—that a *mass* shift in consciousness implies that societal moral norms are changing. But any such shift is a matter of such contestation. And new mass consciousness doesn't simply appear *ex nihilo*: it may have been a minority position, vociferously argued for, for a long time, before becoming adopted by a wider mass of people. The point at which a majority considers a phenomenon "wrong" may mark the point at which there's a good chance to sweep that phenomenon away, but it cannot, with any ethical seriousness, be the point at which that phenomenon *becomes* ethically problematic.

History is crucial, and this isn't a binary question: to condemn slavery in the ancient world would certainly be considerably more abstract, as well as unusual, than to condemn it in 1866. But for all that, certain precepts of the "higher" ethics which Engels himself considers, as we'll see, are at least, and repeatedly, implied in the *Manifesto*.

Ethical contestation occurs precisely because "the ideas of the ruling class" aren't seamless. And sometimes there occur contexts in which certain categories of even ruling-class thought may operate as standards for a tribunal by which that class and even those very ideas are found wanting. Just as a new society emerges out of the cradle of an old society, dissident political ethics can arise—even in "premature" material circumstances in which they cannot realistically succeed—out of ideas and standards that condemn them. Recall, for example, that those liberal, capitalist clarion calls of "freedom," "justice" and "equality" are strictly limited in their application and content, and actively countervailed, under capitalism itself, where they come into conflict with structures of capitalist power. They are capitalist promises—which capitalism is often structurally incapable of delivering.[66] Thus the deployment of liberal promises can, in part, square a circle: conditioned by the ethics and morals of an existing society, they can be deployed against that society, looking towards a different—better—future. For materialist communists, even such desirable ethical precepts don't provide evidence of an "eternal truth." But nor does it follow that they are entirely contingent to the communist program. They are, rather, *part* of what makes communism ethically desirable. They are an implicit end.

And a sense of a "higher morals" as such a human good isn't absent from the corpus of the *Manifesto* writers. For all that, in *Anti-Dühring*, Engels diagnoses morality as having "always been class morality" and rejects "moral dogma . . . as an eternal, ultimate, and forever immutable ethical law," he does *not* reject a hierarchy of ethics *in terms of the fulfilment of human need and freedom*. He allows that "on the whole" (an important, anti-teleological qualification) there has "been progress in morality," and there may come a future of a "really human morality which stands above class antagonisms."[67] Human, rather than "eternal"; this is an ethics predicated on plenty, on the freedom from necessity, on that anti-austerity communism of the *Manifesto*. The specifics of ethics in a communist future we, by definition, cannot know. But the *direction*, an implicit emancipatory ethics, foreshadows it, and can be uncovered.

For Marx and Engels, the commitment to the free development of each person is inextricable from that of all people, at a collective level, the one the grounds and condition for the other. They are committed to this as an ethics of freedom—though one that, precisely in that co-constitutive totality, is very far removed from the impoverished, atomized notion of bourgeois "freedom" that defines our society. The freedom to which Marx and Engels are committed is distinguished from that which is available under capitalism, given the stunting, stultifying and impoverishing dynamic of commodification.

As communists, Marx and Engels saw "rights" as an expression of the atomized individual thrown up by capitalism and its subjectivity in "civil society." They stressed, in *The German Ideology*, "the opposition of communism to *Recht* [German for 'right'], both political and private." Their rejection of *Recht* is a rejection of the reality of commodification that is the condition and expression *of Recht*—let alone of the implication that it's intrinsic and definitional to human society.[68] It's rather a product of circumstances of "antagonism of people against one another" due to class struggle. By contrast, to quote the authors' legendary communist principle from the later *Critique of the Gotha Programme*, in the "realm of freedom" beyond such conflict, beyond systematic material scarcity, "the narrow horizon of bourgeois right [can] be crossed in its entirety and society inscribe on its banner: From each according to their ability, to each according to their need."[69]

The breach with any equivalence principle, any calculation, is here total. And in that free development of one is the free development of all. Perhaps not so explicitly as in later works, but even the *Manifesto* is structured by such an ethics of freedom, what Steven Lukes calls "a morality of emancipation," according to which the iniquities of the present are criticized "from the (truly human) standpoint of a future beyond class antagonisms."[70]

Thus the final exhortation to the proletariat to lose its chains. Thus the yearning invocation of "an association in which the free development of each is the condition for the free development of all." Capitalism repeatedly, obsessively, promises freedom. And, inevitably, it fails to provide it. Crushes it.

It is towards freedom, a freedom worthy of the name, that communism cleaves.

# 5

# Criticisms of the *Manifesto*

---

Perfection is a stick with which to beat the possible.

Rebecca Solnit, *Hope in the Dark*

We've already touched on various criticisms of the *Manifesto*: those are now the focus. I start with quick dismissal of a few exhausted anticommunist bromides. Thereafter it's more serious lines of criticism that are given the engagement they deserve.

## THREE COMMONPLACES

As I've indicated, the most common, and historically an extremely effective, line of attack on the *Manifesto* is capitalist realism, the common sense according to which fundamental social change, desirable or not, is obviously impossible. It's a paradox that this in particular requires next to no substantive engagement—indeed, it's deeply resistant to it, because it is empty. Common sense is, by definition, generally very powerful; it's also very often wrong, and not infrequently swept aside by history. It was common sense to many that women should not be given the vote. It was obvious that slavery was eternal and desirable. Whatever the merits or otherwise of the *Manifesto*, attacks on it predicated on the obviousness of its absurdity are obviously absurd.

A closely related line of attack—often, in fact, the epistemology underlining such common-sense capitalist realism—is that human nature itself is the problem for radical change, for social collectivity. "Wonderful theory," the biologist E. O. Wilson once said of Marxism, "Wrong species."[1] It should be clear from the *Manifesto*'s repeated stress on the changes that the revolutionary process would work on the people carrying them out—that "alteration of men [sic] on a mass scale"—that the authors were under no illusions about the anti-social tendencies currently present on a mass scale. Their model, however, is predicated simply on the plasticity of humanity, how much people change in different social contexts. This is a vision of totality, a dialectical model of the interaction of individual and society, in which the social context is enormously influential on, rather than merely constrained by, human nature.

Stephen Jay Gould, the evolutionary biologist, cheerfully allows that "general nastiness" is a biological reality and "represent[s] one subset of a possible range of behaviours. But peacefulness, equality, and kindness are just as biological—and we may see their influence increase if we can create social structures that permit them to flourish."[2] A sense that communism is a wager worth making doesn't imply the end of all individual "bad behaviour," nor does it presume the innate goodness of humans: only their variability and changeability. And it's not, or should not be, controversial that selflessness and social solidarity exist as well as their opposites, that human behavior is anything but rigid. The "human nature" critics of the *Manifesto*, for all their cherished self-image as hard-headed realists, are negative sentimentalists who must pathologize vast ranges of actually existing human behavior— kindness, unselfishness, decency—or at the very least dismiss them as epiphenomenal, on the basis of nothing but belief.

Third in this troika of objections is that the *Manifesto*'s program has been disproved by history: specifically, by the dismal Stalinist experiments.

The unedifying stories of these regimes can't be license for a complete lack of empathy with those through history with illusions in them, or committed to the Communist parties loyal to them, as a counterweight to the depredations of capitalism and history. The ideological lip service those institutions paid to socialism and liberation; the real, often major advances in healthcare, literacy, and so on, they enabled; the material—if partial and often inadequate, cynical, and conditional—support they offered to some anti-colonial and anti-racist struggles in the twentieth century; the uneven and ambiguous but powerful social and cultural networks they developed: all this goes some way to explain why thousands of people, including sincere and courageous activists, put their faith in "official" (here capitalized) Communism. But the history of those regimes is a history of the betrayal of the workers' and other radical movements, of oppressive, profoundly anti-democratic, creatively dead-handed, murderous politics. We're now at a point in history when whole political generations have been born and come to adulthood without their glowering presence. This may be one reason there is even, today, a new small cadre of voluble online hipster Stalinists, poised, to be generous, somewhere in a liminal zone between adolescent provocation and political illiteracy.[3]

It's impossible to touch more than briefly on the rise, nature, fall, and disgrace of these institutions. For all their great differences, they originated in the state model that emerged from the international isolation of the Bolshevik regime in Russia in the 1920s. The revolutionaries who fought for the 1917 socialist revolution always insisted that—as per the *Manifesto* which inspired it—the workers' state which arose from it could only survive as part of an international revolutionary wave. In the wake of the failure of the German revolution, on which the Russian activists pinned their hopes, and after intense and contested internal debate, in

1925 the official line of the Bolsheviks shifted from an insistence on the necessarily international nature of socialism to the disastrous position of "Socialism In One Country."[4] From this defensive theoretical volte-face, in the context of the collapse of the working class and the working-class movement, and of civil war, emerged a top-down and authoritarian politics diametrically opposed to the grassroots democracy of socialism.

To build up domestic production and international power, these regimes of "socialism from above" relied on brutal and moralizing exhortations backed up by repression and violence, and networks of secret police and surveillance. Figures are fiercely contested, but certainly a million or more died in Stalin's prison camps, and millions more due to famine induced by forced collectivization of agriculture in the early 1930s. Other regimes on similar models deployed similar methods. When mass mobilisation shook them, these bureaucratic states crushed them by force—in 1956 in Hungary, in 1968 in Czechoslovakia, in 1970 and 1980 in Poland. Imbricated as competitors in the international system of imperialism, such regimes were far more invested in maximizing their own power than in independent workers' movements, and were perfectly willing, where they could not control them, to betray, attack, or destroy them. Hence the role of the Stalinist parties in helping to undermine the revolutionary regime in Barcelona thrown up to defend against a far-right revolt against democracy in 1936, famously outlined by Orwell in *Homage to Catalonia*.[5] Competing in an international capitalist system, these state-controlled economies had to exploit their workers no less, and often more, brutally than did their explicitly capitalist competitors. Hence the—to be sure, extremely variable degrees of—totalitarianism and authoritarianism of such regimes, ranging from the relative openness of Cuba to the grotesque mandatory cult of North Korea.

And hence, too, for the most part, the fall of these regimes, which, combining brutality with sclerosis, could not ultimately keep pace with neoliberalism, and collapsed soon after 1989, to be replaced with variously piratical capitalism. With what might seem the exception of China. After various see-sawing of political lines, and a similar history of authoritarianism and death, today that vast power combines a discourse and ideology of socialist kitsch and the authoritarian and top-down state politics inherited from Stalinism (notwithstanding the historic antagonism between the Chinese and Soviet regimes), with aggressive free-market economics. Even the libertarian ideologues of the Cato Institute allow that it's a capitalist country,[6] though one disavowing the fact, and overtly authoritarian in the name of something it calls socialism.

Both the rise and fall of the Stalinist regimes can be adduced against the *Manifesto*: the former, because what came into being was so inimical to human liberation; the latter because whether one supported or opposed it, it failed. It's enough that these states called themselves communist to denounce any communism, without the slightest serious investigation as to whether they deserved the name, or how they related to Marx's stated program. Marx and Engels saw socialism as workers running society, and communism as the end of all classes and states. The Stalinist regimes created societies run by a centralized state, not controlled by workers but by an apparatus claiming to represent them, ruled by a privileged elite, under conditions of global military and economic competition. If the status of these regimes as "socialist" is even up for debate—and it should be that and more, as the merest intellectual curiosity should demand—this line of pre-emptive retaliation is spent. The fact that those dead-handed regimes claimed fidelity to Marxism and the *Manifesto* isn't irrelevant, and is the focus of much critical investigation on the left—not that one would know that from most anticommunists. But it isn't reason enough to take their word for it, any more than we should believe that the US is Number One, or a shining city on a hill, just because it says so.[7]

## INEVITABILISM

"It is," A. J. P. Taylor writes in his lauded introduction to the *Manifesto*, "a grave upset to the Marxist system that the proletariat has not become the ruling class in the community and shows no sign of doing so."[8] And it's true that the *Manifesto* repeatedly expresses certainty about particular outcomes.[9] Such "inevitabilism" is misplaced. As we've seen, the *Manifesto*'s argument for the ineluctable impoverishment of the working class under capitalism, for example, has not been borne out. And ultimately, its claim that the bourgeoisie's "fall and the victory of the proletariat are equally inevitable" (1.53) clearly cannot stand, either as a matter of historical reality (at least so far), or philosophically.

But for all that, and conceding that such formulations can do more harm than good, matters aren't so simple as that triumphant conclusion of Runciman that "[n]o rereading can alter or circumvent" the fact that the *Manifesto* predicted the "inevitable self-destruction of capitalism, and its consequent replacement by a system in which private property, and therefore exploitation, would be abolished."[10] To expand on an earlier point, there are several problems with seeing this as the end of the matter.

Even that notorious claim that this fall and rise are *unvermeidlich*—unavoidable, inevitable—"appears," in the words of one scholar, "as neither scientific prediction nor determinist doctrine" but "counterintuitive *prophecy*," to evoke in readers "a sense of destiny and imperative."[11] And, crucially, more contingent and anti-teleological models exist alongside such seeming certainties, right there in the same document.

Here, a degree of good-faith rigor, and the acknowledgement of ambiguities, are vital for any reading. The final argument cannot be what Marx and Engels "really meant": this is unfalsifiable, and in any case it's hardly news that motivations change, or are contradictory, or opaque to the motivated, or that writers can be wrong about their own work. Whatever Marx and Engels believed that they believed, they argue here that the triumph of the proletariat is inevitable and certain—what's less remarked upon, however, is that they also imply and even state the opposite.

Class conflict, for example, can lead, rather than to triumph, to that "common ruin of the contending classes" (1.2). Here, rather than the triumphalism of doubtlessness, is an abrupt minatory sense that the working class in which the *Manifesto* vests its faith might *not* win, that things might get even worse. And the celebrated rhetorical power of the text, too, complicates its own statements of inevitabilism. "We will win!": prediction in the course of an exhortatory text is not of the same kind as prediction that water will boil at 100°C, which complicates much of this line of attack on the *Manifesto*.

In fact, an *absence* of belief in the inevitability of triumph is implied in the very tenor of exhortation itself, the "explosive imagery of a theatre of catastrophe and redemption."[12] The fervent recruitment drive—Workers of the world, unite!—expresses the opposite of that supposed certainty of a desired outcome. That an outcome is perfectly assured is a strange argument for the urgent necessity of bending oneself to a movement for it. That urgency suggests, rather, that nothing is so written in the stars.[13]

The common claim that "Marx unequivocally embraced a teleological perspective" is thus far too simple.[14] The point isn't that the *Manifesto* does *not* embrace such a perspective at times—it's that it also does the obverse.

Especially with regard to inevitabilist readings of history, it's telling how strong capitalist realism remains: strong enough to act as petard with which plenty of attackers of the *Manifesto* hoist themselves. For many critics attacking the document on these grounds, for example, an alternative teleology is given or implied—one of stasis, of the inevitable continuance of a capitalist status quo. This is not analysis but its failure.

I've argued that the resilience of capitalist ideologies, and the widespread non-transformation of the working class *in* itself into a class *for* itself—a self-conscious agent of political transformation—would indeed be an unpleasant wake-up call to Marx and Engels. For all they are countervailed in their own work, their fervent prophecies of triumph are not irrelevant. Even those of us sympathetic to the *Manifesto* can deepen our understanding of it, and its limitations, by taking such formulations in the text seriously. They may not add up to a simple and unequivocal statement of certainty, but without question they express not only urgency but an excessive political optimism about the likelihood of change.

It has been very common on the Left to relate to such optimism as a model, a perspective to be emulated, even, in the words of one sympathetic scholar, as a "gift."[15] By this point in history, however, that should be far from certain.

Marx and Engels are hardly alone in such optimism: as the great Marxist writer Lucien Goldmann puts it, "[n]early all thinkers actively engaged in trying to achieve a particular set of values tend in fact to suffer from an illusion . . . From the medieval masters of the spiritual life to Marx [and] Engels . . . all such thinkers tend to overestimate the chances of success and to underestimate the opposition of reality."[16] At the same time, Michael Harrington shrewdly discerns conflicting pulls in Marx and Engels, and, with reference to their other words, describes "[t]his contradiction between a sense of imminent proletarian revolution on the one hand, and the sober knowledge that the coming battle would seek only democratic freedoms on the other,"[17] in the *Manifesto*. To which would very soon be added the depressing revelation that even that latter battle the proletariat would wage without its intended class ally.

Rather than seeing in the *Manifesto* a mortally wounding certainty about inevitable outcomes, we should diagnose in it a poignant example of a political tendency towards pathological optimism—and one that's undercut by clear anxiety that such optimism isn't warranted. An anxiety that is correct.

## CLASS AND REDUCTION

The changes in the productive forces of capitalism of course change the nature of work itself. This, the fact that the working class of today doesn't, mostly, look like the working class of 1848, is enough for the least interested and least interesting critics of the *Manifesto* to consider it outdated. At what one might call the *haute* end of such vulgarity, Runciman counts as evidence against the text the fact that "industrialization brought into being whole new categories of clerical and administrative occupations which came to form a growing rather than a diminishing proportion of the employed population."[18] Clerical workers, then, aren't, well, workers. And yet it's Marx and Engels who, their critics often hold, have reductive, simplistic views on what sort of work makes the working class. Pot, kettle.

It's uncontroversial, including among Marxists, that with historical change in the structure of capitalism, the specifics of work, and the complexities and balance of class structure itself, change. Thus, for example, important debates over the recent—if often substantially exaggerated, in terms of its role in fundamentally reshaping industrial relations—rise of the "gig economy" as an arena in which workers can sell their labor-power.[19] However, it should be clear by now that for all the real impact and importance of such changes, the power relations and profit-generating role of work performed are what determine class position. As Engels put it in the "Communist Confession of Faith," a key layer in the palimpsest that is the *Manifesto*, "[t]he proletariat is that class of society which lives exclusively by its labour and not on the profit of any kind of capital; that class whose weal and woe, whose life and death, therefore, depend on the alternation of times of good and bad business; in a word, on the fluctuations of competition."[20] That "classes are never frozen and fixed, they are constantly changing,"[21] that the proletariat is not static, is no argument at all against proletarianisation. Nor are such changes any reason to suggest that workers will not "continue to organise on the basis of their own necessary, if sporadic, conflict with the system."[22]

It's obvious that the *Manifesto* unapologetically foregrounds class. Does it do so, however, in an illegitimate, reductive way? Do Marx and Engels see class where there's another phenomenon at work, or nothing at all?

Sometimes such a suspicion might be confusion over terminology. When an eminent introducer of the *Manifesto* argues that history is not the history of class struggle because "[o]ften there has been class cooperation," and "[m]ore often still men [sic] have gone on with their work and not thought about the class struggle one way or another,"[23] this is, to put it generously, a startling misunderstanding of what the text means. Never do the authors imply a state of constant, *conscious* class war. Rather, their claim is that a fundamental motor of social history—whatever people's ideas, however they feel about their "betters" or those over whom they hold sway—is the existence of structural and conflictual class interests. To deny *this*, one must deny that there are those with power, able to control the lives and work of those without, and to appropriate the product of their labor. Even so hostile a critic as Runciman is more accurate when he describes the model as of a "sometimes hidden and sometimes open *Kampf* [struggle] between oppressors and oppressed."[24]

Implicit in most such criticism is the view that the *Manifesto* collapses everything into class, in a simplistic and illegitimate way. In fact, the vision of the *Manifesto*—rightly or wrongly, and with a brevity and polemic that can certainly blunt nuance—projects an image of the modern world as defined *at a fundamental level* by the conflicting interests of capitalists and those who must work for them.

This doesn't, as we've seen, imply the permanent disappearance of all other classes, let alone other social groups, nor has it ever precluded acknowledging and analyzing the changing role and relative weight of, and contradictory pulls on, managerial layers between bosses and workers.[25] Still less does this model deny the complexity of human experience, the overlapping of individual histories, drives, desires, wants, allegiances and antipathies, rational, irrational, and other. What it *does* suggest is that individuals in their uniqueness will not have infinitely elastic opportunities to act on and in the world, but will be enabled and constrained by their positions within their societies, which societies are themselves expressions of class conflict. Whatever actions people take will occur in such conflictual history. It isn't that all struggles are necessarily class struggles, even "ultimately," but that all actions occur in the defining context of class, and will be part of that structure.

A common corollary of that accusation that the *Manifesto* depicts a too-simple opposition between workers and capitalists is that it also moots a too-simple unity within them, as when Runciman chastises the *Manifesto* for underestimating systemic conflicts other than those between exploiter and exploited, of "violent redistribution of power within the ruling class."[26] This misses the facts that i) such intra-class conflicts, though not its focus, are explicitly discussed in the *Manifesto* ("The bourgeoisie" is in "a constant battle" not only with opposing classes but with other "portions of the bourgeoisie" and the "bourgeoisie of foreign countries" (1.41)); and ii) such tensions as Runciman describes are products of something, interests he doesn't investigate, but that the *Manifesto*—again, rightly or wrongly—analyses in terms of regimes of accumulation which make class struggle an inevitable context.

To read class and class struggle as fundamental doesn't imply that no other phenomena are real or of interest. It isn't to suggest that no dynamics other than class exist at a structural level, or impact the world or the individuals who live in it. It's to make a claim about certain driving forces, the motor of society as a whole. It's this, rather than any sentimentality about workers—not that the Left has always avoided that temptation—that lies behind the focus. As Ben Davis puts it, "as a socialist, I support struggles against oppression on all fronts—but I think that struggle rooted in the workplace is key."[27] Not that the others are irrelevant, epiphenomenal, unimportant, or unrelated. This is to suggest, rather, that the importance of who controls society's productive processes, and how, and who produces, and how, and what conflictual relations this portends, is key to understanding society *as a whole*, and to identifying the axes by which it might be changed.

## GENDER

The *Manifesto* excoriates capitalism's oppression of women in ferocious terms.[28] Its discussion of the bourgeois family, of its hypocrisy and sexual oppression, of the moralist preaching of "purity," its punitive monogamy coextensive with widespread infidelity, the structural cruelty of poverty-inflected prostitution, is vitriolic. The *Manifesto* has not much truck with the stated precepts of the patriarchal bourgeois family. If key problems with the liberal notion of "freedom," say, relate to the fact that under capitalism it will always fall short of its promise, in the case of these patriarchal notions, by contrast, social oppression lies not only in quite how the gendered "promises" are transgressed, as they are, but also in the promises themselves.

For all this, as well as exhibiting personal hypocrisy on such issues, the authors did not develop their critical views on sex and gendered oppression as far as they could have. Engels would return to this question elsewhere, producing in *The Origin of the Family, Private Property and the State* a work that, flaws notwithstanding, remains a seminal and vital analysis of women's oppression. There's nothing nearly so penetrating in the *Manifesto*.

Nor can one exonerate the text for its lacunae on the grounds that it was "of its time." Sheila Rowbotham elegantly and wittily made this clear on the *Manifesto*'s 150th anniversary, criticizing Marx in comradely fashion for neglecting the politics around women's suffrage, conditions of life, and resistance as workers, writing in the persona of a socialist feminist of the 1850s, and using citations of figures, events, or literature from that moment. She includes eloquent testimonials, such as an 1850 letter from the French radicals Pauline Roland and Jeanne Deroin to an American women's convention: "your socialist sisters in France are united with you in the vindication of the rights of women to civil and political equality. We have, moreover, the profound conviction that only by the power of association based on solidarity—by the union of the working-classes of both sexes to organise labour—can be acquired, completely and pacifically, the civil and political equality of women, and the social right of all."[29] Clearly the *Manifesto* authors neglected a body of theory and a lively political tendency.

This is all the more frustrating, given that they did not always do so, having read another figure Rowbotham cites, Flora Tristan, for example, and defended her in *The Holy Family*.[30] The text of the *Manifesto* would have benefited from an engagement with this current. Not least because, as the quote from Roland and Deroin illustrates, beyond the mere fact that feminists were writing on such topics, some of this literature suggests interrelations of the dynamics of class struggle and women's liberation that would have substantially enriched its theses.

Many modern editions of the *Manifesto*, even those derived from Moore's authorized translation, including the one reproduced as an appendix here, shift from "working men" to "workers," or "proletarians"— as, it should be stressed, Macfarlane originally translated the German. But how much does this address a more fundamental issue? To what extent is the proletarian of the *Manifesto* implied to be *intrinsically* male, and the text itself thereby deep-structured with gendered blind spots and/or sexism? Is this at base a manifesto for and about working men?

Of course, the book addresses the expansion of women into waged employment, becoming the very proletariat it addresses. But one can read an ambiguity in the text. Alongside the call for and faith in radical grassroots change, and that awareness of the degree to which "the more is the labour of men superseded by that of women" (1.33) it has been argued that in the *Manifesto*'s language is an implication that capitalism's iniquity inheres partly *in* bringing women into this sphere. That working women are *casualties* of bourgeois society not merely in that they are workers, but as *women* forced into an alien realm of work, less the subject of history than of its pathologies. The *Manifesto* claims, for example, that the family only exists for the bourgeoisie, is predicated on "public [that is to say, *de jure*] prostitution," noting "the practical absence of the family among the proletarians" because of that expansion of women into the workforce (2.40). In point of fact the family has proved tenacious, for good and/or ill, but even some sympathetic critics read in those words a sentimental and sexist regret that the "security" of the traditional patriarchal family is denied the proletarian. For Joan Tronto, for example, this is a "lament for traditional families among the working class," an exhortation that the "working men had to be able to protect their women and children."[31]

This is arguably too harsh a reading, certainly if presented as if it occurs without ambivalence.[32] The *Manifesto* is clear that the "traditional" patriarchal family is a structure predicated on the oppression of women, and its ending necessary for women's liberation. This doesn't mean there are no gendered nostrums in the *Manifesto*, nor that the specific contributions of women activists and thinkers aren't neglected, nor that they wouldn't have strengthened the *Manifesto*'s analysis of class. The missed opportunity for the project isn't one of merely *adding* gender to class, but, to use a useful and increasingly common verb form, of *gendering class*, of understanding class as a relation from which gender is inextricable, precisely to better understand class, gender and capitalism.

Here, for example, is one of the most important paragraphs in the *Manifesto*:

The less the skill and exertion of strength implied in manual labour, in other words, the more modern industry becomes developed, the more is the labour of men superseded by that of women. Differences of age and sex have no longer any distinctive social validity for the working class. All are instruments of labour, more or less expensive to use, according to their age and sex. (1.33)

The true paradoxes of capitalist modernity are visible here, in the simultaneity, for example, of the observation that "[d]ifferences of age and sex have no longer any distinctive social validity for the working class" with the gendered experience noted in the very next sentence, that women are underpaid compared to men. And if a certain elegiac regret is discernible in the sentence, it isn't at all clear that it is the *authors'* regret. Indeed, it was the opposition of some socialists to women entering industry, "this traditional attitude of conservative workingmen," Hal Draper glosses it, "that the Manifesto was rejecting."[33]

In pointing out as uncontroversial that male and female workers are "more or less expensive" to capitalism, the *Manifesto* implicitly acknowledges the instrumentality of sexist norms *for* capitalism, the potential for lowering the cost of labor-power by employing women, or at one remove, by using their labor to maintain downward competition on the rates for male workers. Here, a relationship between capitalist exploitation and women's oppression suggests how the latter—an axis of oppression that pre-exists capitalism—can be deployed for the benefit of the former. But this insight isn't developed.

An insufficiently gendered theory underlies the *Manifesto*'s claim that the family is likely moribund, and its false theory of the inevitable absolute impoverishment of the worker. Because it's in part the maintenance and support of the wage worker *outside* of the immediate sphere of commodification by what's often called "social reproduction," the unpaid domestic labor, and sexual reproduction in the household, that the *Manifesto* fails to address.[34] That support is a crucial countervailing element on the downward pressure on the value of wage labor, on the tendency to absolute immiseration.

The *Manifesto* doesn't neglect women's oppression in the family, including that of bourgeois women as women, nor women's exploitation as workers, nor as women workers. It sees their social power and leverage lying above all *in* their position as workers. With the overturning of capitalism, the bourgeois family, too, will be swept away, so ending the oppression of bourgeois women, as women, within its structures. It's as workers that women can effect such change. But it is true that the text doesn't rigorously question the relation between gender and class. In neglecting to interrogate how the latter is constitutively imbricated with the former, it doesn't gender class. Nor does it engage adequately with the crucial question of social reproduction, developed by generations of socialists, feminists, and socialist feminists.[35] Those questions underline the central importance not of gender-blind politics, but of class politics that, being gendered, are more powerful.

## Nationalism, Imperialism, and Race

The *Manifesto*'s rhetorical instability, both productive and unproductive, is vivid in its assertion that working people "have no country" (2.53). This notorious claim is regularly cited as evidence that the text underestimates the tenacity of nationalism.

What's particularly at stake here, and not so simple as is sometimes averred, is the question of how much that is a moment of preaching, how much it is a prediction and how much it is a portrayal.[36] Not only that: turning the usual criticism on its head, to the extent that this is preaching, as in some part it unquestionably is, it's a sermon predicated not on a sense of the withering of nationalism, but precisely on an understanding of its *resilience*, its pernicious effects on the workers' movement. This understanding the authors would develop more clearly in years to come, outlining how racism and supremacism, particularly in a dominant nation, is inimical to the class consciousness for which they strove, finding as it does scapegoats for social problems in "outsiders," rather than in the system and its partisans.[37]

To an extent, then, this section should be read as a suggestion about what loyalty is due from workers to "their" country: none.[38] But this doesn't stop even Draper, a pioneer of such a nuanced reading, agreeing that this section is "one-sided" in its vision, "stating tendencies as accomplished facts, without also investigating countervailing forces."

These forces include, importantly, the "effort to propagate nationalism by ruling classes to promote their own interests."[39]

The literature on nationalism is notoriously, "unsurveyably vast"[40]— far beyond us here. What's needed, and is often lacking, is a theory that doesn't take its subject for granted. It must be able to suggest certain processes by which sectoral political interests combine or are reconciled into "national" interests, in the context of overarching political-economic systems, and of fissures and possible hierarchies on ethnic, religious, and/or racial grounds. How "imagined communities," in the seminal formulation of Benedict Anderson,[41] emerge and/or develop in the social, political and cultural context of modernity itself.

In 1939, the erstwhile leftist-turned-anticommunist Franz Borkenau announced that "nationalism is the fact against which Marxist theory breaks itself."[42] And it's commonly held, even on the Left, that the tenacity of the nation and nationalism isn't just underestimated in *The Communist Manifesto*, nor even in Marx's theory in general, but, in the words of the distinguished leftist writer Tom Nairn, that "the theory of nationalism represents Marxism's greatest historical failure."[43]

Certainly, some actually existing Marxism has failed to wrestle seriously with nationalism. The cliché whereby the Left insists that nationalism not only must but will be overcome relatively straightforwardly through class solidarity isn't wholly fair, but nor is it wholly calumny. For tradition(s) of Leninist politics, international solidarity is promoted by the insistence on the right of oppressed nations to self-determination. This is honorable in principle and tactically persuasive as far as it goes, but i) the latter only at a fairly abstract level, and ii) right or not, it has little to say about the origin and sheer tenacity of the nationalism it opposes.

However, the philosopher Erica Benner, among others, has put forward a bravura argument for a rich and subtle theory of nationalism in Marx, and, to a lesser extent, Engels, even early in their careers—if you know where and how to look. "[T]he simple class-*versus*-nation thesis . .

. reflects a tendency to reconstruct Marx and Engels' views on national issues from their most abstract statements of theory, while overlooking the concrete strategies they recommended in specific political contexts."[44]

Drawing in particular from their immediately political writings on contemporary events, though elsewhere, too, Benner sees alongside a long-term diagnosis of the tendencies of history a more grounded *strategic* theory of nationalism of remarkable suppleness. Her agenda-changing work demands a rethinking of the standard dismissal of Marxist "crudeness" on nationalism.[45] Even with regard to the *Manifesto*, which Benner herself sees as more "theoretical and polemical" than the political interventions in which she sees a strategic theory of nationalism more clearly, Benner reads paragraphs 2.52–2.53, wherein the workers are declared to "have no country", with exactly the critical generosity needed, to argue brilliantly against the common interpretation that this is a vague appeal to a transnational class interest only. Even here, she starts to pick apart national society from national state, opening up the vexed and peculiar formulation of 2.53 that the proletariat "must rise to be the leading class of the nation, must constitute itself *the* nation, it is so far, itself national, though not in the bourgeois sense of the word." Benner insists that "while Marx and Engels saw class as the principal basis of collective action at both national and international levels, they did not belittle the role of nationality in shaping the parameters of class-based movements," the different temporalities and pace of radical change, nationally and internationally.[46]

Benner's is a salutary insistence that the internationalism of the *Manifesto* doesn't imply the "downgrade" of nationalism and "national 'consciousness'" for Marx and Engels, as their critics suggest.[47] But whatever the nuances of their approach to nationalism across their oeuvres—and Marx's work on France in the late 1840s, for example, is vividly subtle on the relations of class and nation[48]—and though even the *Manifesto* itself has been unfairly judged on this axis, it's hardly beyond reproach. Benner allows that the authors "did expect the cultural differences between national societies to be greatly diluted in the capitalist era," and that they "prematurely" imagined that world capitalism would "render the nation-state increasingly moribund."[49] For all that the *Manifesto* isn't nearly so obtuse as is generally claimed, Marx and Engels do understate the difficulty in overcoming nationalism.

Something of an underestimation of the mesh of cultural, political, economic relations imbricating class and nation can also be seen in that inadequately textured, too-flat vision of globalization that we've seen the *Manifesto* can express. As Aijaz Ahmad puts it, in vital correction "[f]or all the globalizing tendency inherent in capitalism, the bourgeoisie has always had a profound connection with its national origin and nation-state ... The British bourgeoisie set out to win for itself a world empire not as a universal class but as a doggedly British one, in mortal competition with other national bourgeoisies."[50] Here, again, with regard to the working class and its increasingly transnational subjectivity, we see that surplus political optimism diagnosed by Goldmann, and its deleterious impact.

Inextricable from the questions of nation and nationalism are those of racism and race. Marxism has been a profound inspiration to countless anti-racist and anti-colonial activists, "from Fidel Castro in Cuba to Frantz Fanon in Algeria, from Kwame Nkrumah in Ghana to Julius Nyerere in Tanzania, and from the Indian National Congress in India to the African National Congress in South Africa," and to the wider traditions of Afrosocialism.[51] For all that, it has, too, been accused of systemic blind spots on race.[52] Some critics see in the *Manifesto* a centring of European experience—implicitly or explicitly, whiteness—at the expense of non-European subjects.

There are certain formulations of the anti-racist critique of Marx and Marxism in general that are flatly false. In an introduction to his celebrated book *Black Marxism*, for example, Cedric Robinson claims that "Marx consigned race, gender, culture, and history to the dustbin."[53] Even allowing for polemic and generous interpretation, this is misleadingly unhelpful to the point of calumny. In all the good-faith debate that should ensue on this topic, and without obscuring the fact that the details of Marx and Engels's positions on these issues developed and grew more subtle and thoughtful over their lifetimes, as we'll see, what shouldn't be forgotten is their anti-racist commitment, and their awareness of racism as a factor impacting the world and the workers' movement, as part of a commitment to radical change. In 1866, Marx wrote in a letter to François Lafargue that "[l]abour in white skin cannot emancipate itself where the black skin is branded,"[54] a line he would reuse in *Capital*. Nor is it the case that even so early a work as the *Manifesto* underestimates the centrality of colonial relations to capitalist exploitation. Quite the opposite: in its pages, "[t]he discovery of America, the rounding of the Cape . . . [t]he East Indian and Chinese markets, the colonisation of America, trade with the colonies" (1.7) are absolutely central to capitalism's development. As Robin Kelley puts it, though the text "has the shortcomings of its time, place, authors, even the character of the revolution that spawned it," "it is startling that young Marx recognised the interdependency of 'barbarian and semi-barbarian countries' with workers in Europe."[55]

It's true that in the 1840s Marx's view of history was somewhat unilinear, "tinged," in one author's words, "with an ethnocentrism in which non-western and pre-capitalist societies would be integrated and modernised through colonialism and the world market."[56] But his positions would evolve. The *Manifesto* does tend to depict non-western societies as ineluctably and violently dragged into "modernity" by the vigors of (western) capitalism—battering down those "Chinese walls."

Gilbert Achcar and Vishwas Satger usefully distinguish between *epistemic* and *supremacist* Eurocentrism: that is, the construction of knowledge based on partial, limited and Eurocentric positions and notions, versus a sense of the *intrinsic superiority* of Europe. These two can blur into each other, and neither is innocent, but the two aren't coeval. Even in the 1840s the Eurocentrism in the *Manifesto* was—in contrast to that of countless writers—"epistemic" rather than "supremacist." In fact, in Marx and Engels's depiction of supposed capitalist dynamism is a deep cynicism about the violence of, as they rendered it, "so-called civilisation," rather than a supremacist mode.[57] For all this, it's true that in the text agency is largely absent from the depicted colonized subject: "the colonized and subjugated peoples remained shadowy, hardly visible ghosts on the periphery of the brilliantly lit European stage."[58]

By the time of the Russian introduction and its examination of the *obshchina*, along with that more developed analysis of the structural role of racism, Marx and Engels had come to a less reductive understanding of non-western societies. But the *Manifesto*'s earlier formulations about modernist capitalism destroying local specificities flattered capitalism with regard to its transformative vigor and neglected the extent to which local traditions and conditions might persist in, and/or adapt to, and perhaps even operate against the dynamic of capitalism. On its ninetieth anniversary, the great Russian revolutionary Leon Trotsky insisted that the *Manifesto*'s declaration that the workers have no country and that communists "support every revolutionary movement against the existing social and political order" means that "[t]he movement of the coloured [sic] races against their imperialist oppressors is one of the most important and powerful movements against the existing order and therefore calls for the complete, unconditional and unlimited support on the part of the proletariat of the white race."[59] What this represented was not so much a break with as an improvement of the *Manifesto* itself, on its own terms.

On the question of the relationship of the *Manifesto*'s project to the specific, most pressing and epochally barbarous question of racism at the time of writing, the transatlantic slave trade and slave labor, Marx's own investment in US abolitionism is well attested. Less well known is the nexus of Marxism and abolitionist politics in the nineteenth century in the context of the working-class group known as the First International, leading to the *Manifesto*'s translation and publication in the weekly paper of the unorthodox radical sisters Victoria Woodhull and Tennessee Claflin in 1871, the year before Woodhull ran for president with the great abolitionist and escaped slave Frederick Douglass as her running mate.[60]

The rich, comradely, contentious history of radical debates over Marxism and race fills many bookshelves. For all the power of such history, for some black nationalist writers Marxism is indelibly white politics, and black capitalism more desirable than socialism. There are also so-called "class-first" writers, for whom relations between racism and capitalism are ultimately "circumstantial," because capital itself is "color-blind."[61] For others, racism predates capitalism, and/or is informed by a specific, irreducible social dynamic which modern class politics, however just and vital, cannot explain, nor, ultimately, overcome.[62] Then there are radical critics of such an "antiquity of racism" arguments.[63] And there are those for whom the heuristic should be neither class versus race, nor class plus race, but to see class as indelibly inflected by race. That is, again to verb a noun, a "racing" of class.*

---

* At the time of writing, the emerging mainstream norm is to render "Black" thus, in upper case. The *New York Times* laid out its case for shifting its house style in this direction in 2020 here: <https://www.nytimes.com/2020/07/05/insider/capitalized-black.html> (accessed June 17, 2021), describing it as a move from "color" to "culture," and the *Huffington Post* laid out the thinking behind the practice here: <https://www.huffingtonpost.co.uk/entry/why-capitalize-word-black_l_5f342ca1c5b6960c066fa ea5> (accessed June 17, 2021). These explanations deserve to be taken very seriously. At the same time, it is important to acknowledge that this is a long-standing and still live debate, with regard to which reasonable people, including of course people of color, can and do disagree, in comradely fashion. See for example Salami, 2021, for a thoughtful discussion on the topic, Whittaker, 2021, for a radical and skeptical take on capitalization, and Olaloku-Teriba, 2018, for recent use of the lower-case "b" in a radical discussion of race. At the time of writing, I am swayed by the approach of the black radical writer Samuel Delany, in his seminal and outstanding 1998 essay, "Racism and Science Fiction" (Delany, 1998). Readers should not be misled by the seemingly narrow title: the essay expands into a brilliant outlining of the structural nature of racism and the lived reality of its aggressions, and, in particular, those of "liberal," "non-racist" racism. As regards the issue under discussion, as part of his argument Delany glosses his own lower-casing of black thus: "the small 'b' on 'black' is a very significant letter, an attempt to ironize and de-transcendentalize the whole concept of race, to render it provisional and contingent, a significance that many young people today, white and black, who lackadaisically capitalize it, have lost track of."

In this conception, a key, constitutive contradiction of capitalism is that between the law of value that underpins it, and the hierarchical dynamics by which it must operate. The former is abstract and abstracting, universalizing and articulated in part through the tendency towards the abstract equality of individuals. The latter is characterized by brutally maintained, and systematically necessary, real and concrete inequality. At a structural level, as part of capitalism's exploitative dynamics, subjects aren't differentiated only as individuals but as groups—crucially including, of course, groups considered "races"—and socially and politically differentiated as such. The fact that the concrete historical reality is of gross inequality of various degrees and kinds doesn't mean that a tendency towards the assertion of abstract equality is merely a lie. Rather, i) it's a tendency that is always contested; and crucially ii) under capitalism abstract equality and concrete inequality can co-exist.

An extreme and mass-murderous example of the former fact, the non-universality of abstract equality under capitalist accumulation, is plantation slavery, the existence of juridically unfree labor deployed for purposes of profit maximization in the context of a capitalist world market. But the end of that *formal* unfreedom and inequality did not, of course, see the end of racism. To understand this, point ii), in particular, is key to the "racing" of class. Not that logical rigor is necessary to capitalist apologia, but still, that co-extensiveness of abstract equality and concrete inequality—which is to say brutal hierarchy—is something of a conundrum for capitalist ideology, begging explanations, justifications and questions. And ideology will answer its own questions. Hence the variety of racist explanations to square the circle in capitalism's terms. The idea of the intrinsic inequality of races is vastly more congenial to it than that its nature is intrinsically generative and sustaining of hierarchy and oppression—that its "equality" is predicated on structural inequality.

Capitalism may work its inequalities through certain already extant categories of social differentiation thrown up in other historical contexts, changing and crystallizing them into essentialised hierarchies, and/or it may translate its inevitable differentiation of working conditions and wage and profit rates into new group terms. This is to generate racisms, and race.[64] This is why "multi-racial working-class unity will not be produced spontaneously," but "must include *anti-racism*," that "race specific struggles" in industry as well as "non-workplace movements against racist police killing, for residential and educational integration and inclusion and the like are also necessary."[65]

The particular boundaries of concretely oppressed groups shift through history, according to context. That is to say that not only is "race" a sociological and ideological category rather than a biological one, but that what comprises a particular "race," as well as the hierarchies of "races," isn't static. This is why it's more accurate to think in terms of "racialised people" than of race. Such categoric movement may occur for reasons of class mobility, of historic shifts in regimes of accumulation, and/or of changing strategies for ruling-class hegemony. In any case, a previously defined minority group can go from a position of being structurally oppressed within society to being granted "normal" citizen-status. In a capitalism wherein the oppression of a group is inextricable from categories of race, defined in opposition to an implied "norm" that has come to be understood as "whiteness," such a shift is one of racialization. To quote the title of a famous and seminal book on this topic by Noel Ignatiev, one celebrated example of this is "how the Irish became white."[66]

Not that promotion to "whiteness" might not be withdrawn, or diluted. There's certainly a danger, in the words of one radical scholar, that as with much theoretical terminology, "[t]he promiscuity of the concept of whiteness" can make it slippery and hard to engage with.[67] But the fact that it can be unhelpfully evasive doesn't mean that it isn't an important axis at play in popular consciousness—and the unconscious—and politics. It's not, for example, a binary category, nor one that precludes internal differentiation. The aftermath of the Brexit vote saw a substantial spike in hate crimes against Eastern Europeans (and others), particularly

Poles, in the UK, including the murder of the factory worker Arkadiusz Jóźwik when he was heard speaking Polish.[68] To be sure, given years of Polish "whiteness," various nuances have been suggested to describe this phenomenon at the edges of whiteness, so to speak, such as "xeno-racism."[69] But whether xeno- or not, this is a form of racism: indeed, "[r]acialisation does not require putative phenotypical or biological difference," and "the nominal absence of somatic difference does not get in the way of xenophobic racism; it turns out racialised difference can be invented in situ."[70] Race, after all, is a function of racism, not the other way around.

And this abruptly energized "ethnic" animus was inextricable from class, and the shifts in racialized class anxiety. Though it's certainly true that some portrayals of Poles as "criminals and welfare spongers" dates from the accession of Poland to the EU (European Union), and the concomitant arrival in the UK of a substantial number of Polish workers,[71] what's more striking is a later shift away from the initially widespread cultural depiction of the community as a "desirable minority," with a salutary impact on the British labor force. With the economic crisis of 2008–09 this began to alter, towards an image of Poles "as an economic threat responsible for society's malaise: job shortages, unemployment and the strain on social services."[72] This turn accelerated with the run-up to and aftermath of the Brexit vote.

Race, as the history of laboring populations and their rulers makes immediately clear, even allowing for historical contingency, is inextricable from, articulated by, and articulates class. That's why while racialized lines and particular racisms may change, "the notion of 'racial capitalism' is redundant—there is no "non-racial" capitalism."[73]

As he came to learn more about the processes of international capitalism and colonialism, even Marx's epistemic Eurocentrism shifted, the agency of the oppressed grew in his model and he began ever more urgently to stress anti-racism for the sake of the oppressed group *and* for the sake of unity with the working class of the oppressor nation. "For a long time, I believed it would be possible to overthrow the Irish regime by English working-class ascendency," he wrote to Engels in 1869. "Deeper study has now convinced me of the opposite. The English working class will *never accomplish anything* before it has got rid of Ireland."[74] The next year he wrote that racism against the Irish meant the "ordinary English worker hates the Irish worker as a competitor ... In relation to the Irish worker he regards himself as a member of the ruling nation, and consequently he becomes a tool of the English aristocrats and capitalists against Ireland, thus strengthening this domination over himself."[75] To "race" class, then, is also to understand how such a condition props up capitalism.

And it isn't just a condition of hatred. With that powerful affective drive come others. The great W. E. B. Du Bois, in his towering 1935 work *Black Reconstruction*, expanded brilliantly and seminally on the affective rewards of racism for the racist. Arguing against any optimistic faith in an ineluctable tendency towards working-class unity—such as the *Manifesto* can be read as evincing at times, and which remains tenacious—Du Bois sternly diagnosed racism as a key and powerful countervailing pressure.

The theory of laboring class unity rests upon the assumption that laborers, despite internal jealousies, will unite because of their opposition to exploitation by the capitalists. According to this, even after a part of the poor white laboring class became identified with the planters [in the US South after the Civil War] and eventually displaced them, their interests would be diametrically opposed to those of the mass of white labor, and of course to those of the black laborers. This would throw white and black labor into one class, and precipitate a united fight for higher wage and better working conditions.

Most persons do not realize how far this failed to work in the South, and it failed to work because the theory of race was supplemented by a carefully planned and slowly evolved method, which drove such a wedge between the white and black workers that there probably are not today in the world two groups of workers with practically identical interests who hate and fear each other so deeply and persistently and who are kept so far apart that neither sees anything of common interest.

It must be remembered that the white group of laborers, while they received a low wage, were compensated in part by a sort of public and psychological wage. They were given public deference and titles of courtesy because they were white. They were admitted freely [to various restricted amenities and milieu] with all classes of white people . . ."[76]

The focus, in discussions of this passage, is often on the "psychological wage" for white workers. And race clearly does operate at a level of ideology, including as conscious ideas of white supremacy, discouraging solidarity between black and white. But ideology is made real and concrete in lived reality, and in powerful affective structures and drives, rather than merely in ideas. No less important than "psychological" is Du Bois's first adjective for the wage: "public." He describes the real concrete relative advantages accruing to white workers, inextricable from but not reducible to those racist ideas: better access to public goods such as education and leisure. And, crucially, the poorest whites were given access alongside "all classes" of white people. It's worth noting that in contrast to many of the more common deployments of notions of "white privilege" now, in the analyses that would develop out of this Du Boisian perspective in the 1960s, the term "privilege" was "ironic and bitter," because as in Du Bois, while those relative privileges offered to break working-class solidarity were certainly real, they were "crumbs from masters' tables being pitiable and fully worth rejecting."[77]

For Du Bois, then, racism wasn't merely an encouragement to spite against a scapegoated other, nor only "compensation" to a poor white that there was someone "lower" (which begs the bleak question of why that would be compensation at all). It was, crucially, a project of generating cross-class solidarity among whites to the overwhelming benefit of the (white) ruling class, and for the downgrading of class itself as a perceived social schism, and its replacement with "the color line." Such dynamics, in some cases somewhat more decorously dressed up, are hardly unfamiliar today.

Du Bois stresses the constant reassurance of ideology and the culture industry that, *as* white, poor whites were superior to black people— "newspapers specialized on news that flattered the poor whites."[78] The other side of which flattery was that they "almost utterly ignored the Negro except in crime and ridicule." And should black people visibly improve their own lives? "White labor saw in every advance of Negroes a threat to their racial prerogatives, so that in many districts Negroes were afraid to build decent homes or dress well, or own carriages, bicycles or automobiles, because of possible retaliation on the part of the whites."[79] He describes an "inferiority complex" that, unsurprisingly, could afflict some black Americans in this context of the material exclusion from, and the sadism of, culture.[80]

Nearly 100 years later, circumstances are perhaps not so different in their underlying dynamics as we might wish. On the first point, *mutatis mutandis*, there's no shortage of examples of such racialized cross-class identification, as the preposterous elevation of the commodity trader Nigel Farage into a man of the people demonstrates. And on the second, echoing that "complex" that Du Bois describes, in 2019 the activist Akala, as just one element of a brilliant, systematic and much longer demolition of the racist discourse about "black knife crime" in the UK, described how in the context of British racism with its very particular pathologisation of them as a group, "[y]ou could argue that only a very particular demographic of young black boys, only at a very particular stage in their lives, feel a degree of psychological self-hatred or contempt for themselves."[81]

The "public and psychological wage" of racism props up capitalism by uniting sections of the working class with the ruling class, setting them in opposition to other members of their own class, demoting class as a concept and inflating the imaginary category of "race" to a set of explanations, rather than something that should be explained. Race—which is to say racism—inheres in ideas, perhaps, and certainly in lived realities that structure our affective and psychic drives. And it is, as these examples show, inextricable from and co-constitutive with class, impacted by and impacting economic systems and capital accumulation itself.

There is nothing so developed as any of this in the *Manifesto*. There is, though, soil in its pages in which such understandings could grow.

Race and racism, in turn, of course, are historically and theoretically inextricable from imperialism. In the sympathetic critique of Utsa Patnaik, "the single greatest weakness of Marxist theory to date" has been to focus on the contradiction between capital and labor "without a corresponding theoretical focus on and understanding of" the conflict between "the capital of metropoles and people of the colonies and otherwise subjugated nations."[82] It isn't merely that there's a lacuna to be filled. The point is that the imperialism-shaped gap makes for a flawed and inadequate understanding of capitalism as a world system, exaggerating its seeming dynamism, the supposed "Promethean vision" of the bourgeoisie, the potential limitlessness of its expansion—as well as underestimating how, through imperialism, capitalism is able to endure. This shortcoming is visible in the *Manifesto*.

It's unfortunately true that in the history of actually existing communist movements, specific issues of racial oppression have been overlooked or underestimated, cynically and instrumentally deployed, and/or even, in the worst cases, justified, explicitly or implicitly, according to some bastard "socialism" or other. For which the "civilising mission" ideologeme of imperialism is generally key. There have long been battles for the soul of the Left with regard to its position on race, which have included a few shocking and explicit racist positions, particularly relatively early in the movement.

In 1901—in, it should be stressed, a contested response to an admirable and sensitive US Socialist Party resolution recognizing the oppression of black people—Victor Berger, leader of the organization's right wing, insisted in the party press that "[t]here can be no doubt that the negroes and mulattoes constitute a lower race" and that "free contact with the whites has led to the further degeneration of the negroes, as of all other inferior races."[83] Such overt white supremacism among self-styled socialists has been rare, and is vanishingly so today. Less so has been an authoritarian and racist recourse to some sentimentalised "nation," often combined with patronizing attitudes towards people of color. In 1956, in a shameful example, the powerful French Communist Party supported the French prime minister Guy Mollet granting himself "special powers" to send conscripts to Algeria, more than doubling the number of French troops fighting against the struggle for independence for this brutally oppressed nation. In justification, the CP glossed and excused colonialism, declaring itself "to be in favour of the existence of political, economic and cultural ties between France and Algeria."[84]

More common still on the Left have been formal commitments to equality enshrined in theories that nonetheless reify race in reactionary fashion. In the 1950s, for example, the British Communist Party's literature on discrimination against "colonial workers" in the UK suggested that dealing with problems of housing and employment was linked to "righting the wrongs of British imperialism with the colonies themselves."[85] In the broadest sense, given that everything is connected to everything else, this wasn't untrue. Concretely, though, the claim was made as the party was "explaining" that black workers in Britain did not emigrate "for fun" but "because there's no work in their own country," and that thus "the real solution to the problem [of race relations] is to free the colonies and end imperialist exploitation, so that colonial workers can freely build up their own countries and reap the benefits of the wealth which they produce." Not only does this implicitly posit homegrown racism as an essentially epiphenomenal response to immigration, but, worse, implies that that immigration is a cause of the problem, and the ultimate solution the end not (only) of colonialism but of that immigration itself. This isn't to say that the party didn't contain many sterling fighters against racism, including many militants of color, nor that the theoretical perspective was unchanging, nor uncontested within its ranks.[86] Whatever the intentions and beliefs of individual members, however, this is an implicitly racist model.

A more current example of that "class-first" Marxism—or Marxish-ism—has been the German organization Aufstehen, set up in 2018 on an anti-immigration platform. Aufstehen claims a basis, as one founder, Bernd Stegemann, had it, on "the materialist left, not the moral left." "When people live in social conditions that make them feel secure, they are usually prepared to act generously and tolerantly," he said. "When they live in increasingly precarious and atomised conditions, however, they are also likely to react to challenges in a tougher and colder manner. Brecht summarised it wonderfully. Grub comes first, then ethics."[87]

Thus far the argument, as is typical with left appeals to patriotism and the nation, is primarily predicated on an idea of *other people's racism*. To pull voters away from the hard-right Alternative für Deutschland, Aufstehen would accommodate their supposedly—and, to be sure, in some cases actually—intransigent attitudes with regard to immigration. But, as is also typical, that supposed "strategic realism" segues into an opposition to immigration on principle.

As Richard Seymour has lucidly laid out in his engagement with Wolfgang Streeck, another Aufstehen advocate, in even the radical social-democratic counterpositioning of global capitalism and the nation-state, that state is "the key strategic locus" allowing for glimmers of democratic control and regulation of labor markets and wage inequality, to distribute social goods and encourage the social solidarity for which Stegemann understandably pines. This becomes a *moral* argument for tough borders, according to which concern for immigration doesn't (necessarily) bespeak explicit racism but a concern about goods financed by taxation being, in Streeck's words, "declared morally liable to being expropriated." As Seymour stresses, "[i]t is not clear whom the expropriators are supposed to be here, if not migrants"[88]—thus given as in opposition to "locals," a reification of racialized competition.

Even bracketing principles of solidarity, even if one posits the nation-state as the best hope for democracy and social solidarity—by no means a given, nor something the Left has always taken as such—the implicit model whereby immigration undermines the power and wages of labor ineluctably and overall is, for all its extraordinarily tenacious hold, quite false, as repeated research has made clear.[89] This cannot be stressed often enough, though the necessity to keep doing so can make one despair. Here yet again, analysis that counterposes class and race, rather than investigating their complex co-constitution, at a minimum, opens the door to positions that minimize or even exculpate the us–them dynamic of modern racism.

But all such positions have always been opposed by vastly more persuasive, nuanced, and inspiring currents within Marxism—often within the same organizations. In the 1930s, whatever just criticisms could be made of its increasingly monolithic orientation towards an ossifying Russian regime, the US Communist Party's militant, non-sectarian civil rights campaigning in the South, as well as in Harlem in New York City, at the heart of the intellectual, creative, and political foment of the Harlem Renaissance and during the Depression, forged extraordinary links between black and white workers and intellectuals, with a radicalism in contrast to the liberal caution of the NAACP (The National Association for the Advancement of Colored People). The dancer and activist Howard "Stretch" Johnson would only slightly exaggerate when he later claimed that in Harlem, "75% of black cultural figures had Party membership or maintained regular meaningful contact with the Party."[90] Working within the US Workers' Party in the 1940s, the great Russian and Trinidadian activists Raya Dunayevskaya and C. L .R. James, writing as the "Johnson–Forrest Tendency," distinguished themselves from activists who saw anti-racist struggles of black Americans as fundamentally reformist, secondary, and ancillary demands, insisting that they were independently valid, and pivotal in the fight against capitalism itself.[91] At their best, such traditions could be both personally psychically empowering and politically radical: that is, in the words of the Jamaican sociologist Erna Brodber, they could represent "[t]he union between definition of self as blackman [sic—she also uses 'blackwoman'] and the acceptance and work within the alternative [to capitalism], universal socialism."[92]

The dead-handed dogmatism of class reductionism has not stopped radical anti-racist movements from finding resources in the Marxist tradition—even if it has sometimes been "a creative appropriation of 'mainstream' communist discourse and dogma for black people's liberation projects."[93] Even quitting such dogmatic organizations in disgust did not necessarily mean breaking with the Marxist tradition. That tradition, it cannot be stressed enough, even with all due cautions and caveats about that early text, is rooted in the *Manifesto*.

The great poet and radical Aimé Césaire, resigning from the French Communist Party in 1956, cited among other factors the CP's support for Mollett as evidence for the party leaders' "inveterate assimilationism; their unconscious chauvinism; their fairly simplistic faith, which they share with bourgeois Europeans, in the omnilateral superiority of the West." He stressed, however, that "it is neither Marxism nor communism that I am renouncing," that his desire was "that Marxism and communism be placed in the service of black peoples, and not black peoples in the service of Marxism and communism."[94]

Rather than dispensed with, Marx's analysis must, in the words of the Combahee River Collective of radical queer black women, be "extended";[95] it must, as Fanon insisted, be "stretched."[96] As, in the hands of the great anti-racist and anti-colonial movements, it has been.

# 6

# *The Communist Manifesto* Today

To love, I hate.

Mira Mattar, *Yes, I Am A Destroyer*

## RENDING THE VEIL

"[T]he secret history of the *Communist Manifesto* is not its conscious materialism and Marx's own opinion of it, but the religious spirit of prophetism."[1] Few anticommunist accusations are more trite than that Marxism is a religion, the *Manifesto* a religious tract and Marx himself, in the words of one right-wing libertarian critic, Murray Rothbard, a "religious eschatologist."[2] At a banal level, to many of the accusers can be said in retort: I am rubber, you are glue. In the case of Rothbard, for example, crusader's faith in the efficiency and liberatory potential of the invisible hand is resolutely resistant to the piled-up evidence that it's catastrophe for the many.

In any case, *qua* accusation, this is predicated on an empty theory of what religion is or does. Religion isn't just intellectual error or the eclipse of reason. Though it can certainly partake of that, so, too, can it of solace, inspiration, justifications, insights, and countless other roles. So what, then, if the critics have a point?

Incant the *Manifesto*, as its catechism-derived rhythms and techniques plead for you to do. Here are mesmeric repetitions—litanies of ambivalent but deeply admiring description of the enemy, opening five, six paragraphs in a row with the rat-tat-tat staccato "The bourgeoisie [*Die Bourgeoisie*] . . ." (1.20–1.24, 1.13–1.18); here a single short sentence punctuated thrice with "everywhere," a word denoting its own ubiquity, form, and content in synergy: "It [capital] must nestle everywhere [*überall*], settle everywhere, establish connexions everywhere" (1.19). Here is a sudden interruption of remorseless, detailed exposition with a triple-punch of one-sentence paragraphs of self-identification (2.1–2.4), and of an apophatic, negative kind, statements of what communists are *not*, have *not*, do *not*—"a special party," "interests separate and apart from those of the proletariat," "set up any sectarian principles of their own"—so building up tense impatience to learn what they *are*, *have* and *do*. Here the interspersal of sinuous exposition with abrupt one-line summation, an insistent rhetorical rhythm demanding caesuras between the two: "To be a capitalist is to have not only a purely personal, but a social position in production. Capital is a collective product, and only by the united action of many members, nay, in the last resort, only by the united action of all members of society, can it be set in motion." *Beat.* "Capital is, therefore, not only a personal, it is a social power" (2.18, 2.19). Here is that gush, vatic visions of those "fixed, fast-frozen relations" melting (1.18—in the English translation this passage is particularly insistent, given the frenetic triple F rendered from the "*Alle festen, eingerosteten Verhältnisse*" in the German). Consider through the chant that both Marx and, particularly, Engels were interested in religion, heresy and faith, religious communism.[3] Does not the *Manifesto* repeatedly describe its aim as rupture?

Rothbard is right. This is an eschatological moment.

Marshall Berman describes a reminiscence from the (non-Marxist) intellectual Hans Morgenthau, about his childhood in Bavaria before the First World War.

> Morgenthau's father, a doctor in a working-class neighbourhood of the town of Coburg . . . had begun to take his son along on house calls. Many of his patients were dying of TB; a doctor in those years couldn't do much to save their lives, but might help them die with dignity. Coburg was a place where many people who were dying asked to have the Bible buried with them. But when Morgenthau's father asked his workers for last requests, many said they wanted to be buried with the *Manifesto* instead. They implored the doctor to see that they got fresh copies of the book, and that priests didn't sneak in and make last-minute switches. Morgenthau was too young to "get" the book, he said. But it became his first political task to make sure that the workers' families should get it. He wanted to be sure we would get it, too.[4]

To hear of such yearning at the end of a hard life, and to see in it mere fallacy, mere foolishness, merely the abnegation of rigor, is a breathtaking empathetic and epistemological miserliness. No, the concrete content of the desired book is not irrelevant, and one should not celebrate all books with which a person might beg to be buried merely because of the request. But the plea was for *this* book, and it should not be beyond sensitivity to understand something of the longing behind *this* wish for *this* book, this book that cleaves unremittingly to liberation, that burns with fury at injustice, so bright that even as it abjures religion it represents to those wanting a dignity in death denied them in life a presence so strong that, whether or not they believed they would rise again, it brought them comfort to bring it with them across that ultimate divide, on their own rupture, that moment of private eschatology. Rather than grounds for scorn, why would this not just as well, and more productively, be grounds for admiration?

The *Manifesto* was built atop a catechism, a confession of communist faith.

In this form, and in the deathbed yearning, the sheer individual and social solace of faith—in the sense not of uncritical brainwashedness but of *committed fidelity*—is inextricable from the vision presented: the social and historical horizon. Though he intends it destructively, Rothbard is right that there are relations between the millennial hope for justice he archly calls KGE—the Kingdom of God on Earth—and communism.[5]

As a witty online meme points out, critics of Marx are keen to zero in on his 1843 description of religion as "the opium of the masses," but far less to acknowledge his reading of the same phenomenon, in the same paragraph of the same piece, as "the sigh of the oppressed," the "heart of a heartless world," "the soul of soulless conditions," or of religious suffering as "the expression of real suffering and also a protest against it."[6]

That protest against the suffering of class society is predicated, for the *Manifesto*'s authors, on an intuition that *the world need not be so*. An intuition that is correct. And that is not mere guesswork but a reknitting—what, in the rich but obscure language Marx inherited from Hegel might be called "sublation"—of the rational and the affective.

The latter, to be clear, isn't the *ir*rational, but that particular human quality that, while irreducible to narrow "rationality," is not simply wrong, either, nor category error, but something other: the *non*-rational.[7] Such an intuition, rendering inextricable the rational and the non-rational into a political program that's both rigorous and affectively compelling, can be understood as an irreligious example of, and evidence for, a certain heritage of dissent. Of, as one scholar of heresies has shrewdly described it, "that strange connection between bizarre religious notions and incipient rationalism," and more particularly, the passage from specifically *eschatological* eccentricities to political radicalism.[8]

In many such theories—and certainly in Marxism—the "transcendent" moment of apocalypse, that extra-temporality, is already embedded in the everyday. As potentiality, at least, the schism between oppressive present and the promised future is overcome, the latter being implicit and brimming up within the former. To make sense of this means a new understanding of time and agency is necessary. The contradiction, implicit in so much philosophy, between social totality in the abstract, and the atomized individual, will not do: social agency is both constrained and enabling, conditioned by and potentially transformative of, social structures. This interconnection implies a new, specifically *social* concept of time.[9]

Rightly or wrongly, the *Manifesto* has a materialist analysis of why the world need not be as it is, that it draws on and develops from earlier yearnings for emancipation. Even when it offers a sympathetic explanation for why they were precipitate, that hardly invalidates the yearning itself. "When Adam delved and Eve span / Who was then the Gentleman?," demanded the radical priest John Ball in 1381.[10] One doesn't have to share the naturalized gendered division of labor, here, nor the theology through which he asks his fundamental question, to find that question perspicacious and wrenching: why is it a given that some should expropriate and control the fruits of the labor of others?

For all his anti-clerical scorn, his anti-idealist theory of causality, and his "strong demarcation" of his thought from other socialisms and communisms,[11] Marx clearly did trace elective affinities between certain religious structures of ideas and certain relations of production: for example, between English Puritanism or Dutch Protestantism and moneymaking.[12] For Marx, the relationship is obviously not merely a matter of chance, of the random co-existence of ideas and productive relations: how could that make sense, in a social totality? Nor, of course, can it be understood as one of idealist cause and effect, in which the religious notions *produce* the economic and social reality. But despite the often crude models of some of Marx's followers, in which ideas "express" or "reflect" "underlying" reality in a startlingly direct and analogic way, and often with the implication that they could not have been other than they were, as per Engels's irritated corrective about materialism quoted in endnote 15 to Chapter 2, the nature of the relation is vastly more mediated and subtle. And, though not reducible to it, that relationship can certainly be importantly inflected by contingency. Societal notions, including religion, can be considered a kind of constrained iteration of the real abstractions of social relations—that is, a heavily mediated expression, in particular social conditions, of fundamental productive (economic) relations. But, of course, those relations are never uncontested—and neither are those ideas. The connections between dominant religious notions and historical modes and relations of production raises the question of those between *dissenting* notions, on those axes.

All of which is to say that in this Marxian model, alongside the imbrication of powerful social norms and structures must be added the question of another, concomitant and connected relation, though one definitionally less socially dominant: that between certain heresies and social protest, oppositional bottom-up political strategies.

So, what does it mean to find inspiration in—to have fidelity to—the *Manifesto* today? To read generously enough to gain what we can from its pages, critically enough to see its blind spots and failures, to criticise it rigorously and sensitively?

And if we are pulled by even a trace of something like that *Sehnsucht*, that intense and melancholy longing for otherness, if we are moved by the book's condemnation of a world wounded by exploitation, where the drive for profit hobbles the mass of humanity, bolsters vast integuments of oppression and repression, and if we are even in one held breath inspired by the urgent and vivid vision of liberation in this old book, by the rupture, the transformation of society by those whose work enriches and empowers others, by the aspiration for a new democracy, an equality that doesn't efface but nurtures the individual, in and inextricable from a new collectivity, and if we relate to the *Manifesto* as a flawed and partial product of its time and yet as something vital, still, reading it in this new time, in our time, without blinkers, with empathy and yearning, what is it, then, that we read? What might it teach us?

## Neoliberalism, Adaptation, Universalism, and Tenacity

The iteration of capitalism that has defined the last four decades, neoliberalism, is characterized by a ruthless prioritization of fast-moving financial and rentier capital, and a brutal intensification of class struggle—overwhelmingly one-sided in the ruling class's favor—and exploitation. The neoliberal approach to capitalism's complex balancing act with regard to capitalist realism, of judging how much reform to offer when, and how and when to insist that no change is possible, has been characterized by an aggressive campaign to collapse the boundaries of the possible, an ideology of eternal exploitation most vividly expressed in Margaret Thatcher's notorious formulation: There is no alternative—TINA.

The TINA nostrum has recently come, to various extents, to be challenged. Though the anglophone Left's most exciting and vibrant projects for years—the Corbyn and Sanders campaigns in the UK and US—have been soundly defeated, the horizon of social possibility isn't quite so constrained as it recently was. Such questioning has also occurred from the other pole of politics, with the profound crisis into which the Covid-19 pandemic has pushed it, forcing capitalism's partisans to hurriedly offer the kind of massive, systemic support they scoffed at as impossible scant weeks earlier. It's increasingly whispered that neoliberalism is over.

In fact, the chaotic jostling for strategy by the managers of global capitalism, particularly in the UK and US, have often represented an attempt to square neoliberalism with new realities. But the scale of transformation necessary in capitalism's accumulation regime, in the new reality dictated by Covid in the context of weak underlying economies, is such that whatever shape of economy the British state (and others) cobble together will likely not be recognizable as the neoliberalism that has defined the last four decades.[13] But even for those of us sickened by the system of brutality neoliberalism has installed, this in itself isn't ground for optimism. There's no particular reason to hope that the most cruel specificities of recent capitalism will be lessened. They are at least as likely to be made worse.[14]

US capitalism, one of neoliberalism's playgrounds, having grown without a mass reformist movement, a workers' party or a welfare state, is unusual for the savagery of its exploitation among "advanced" countries. It has been resistant even to these social reforms that might stave off the social collapse or upheaval unconducive to capital accumulation. The country has been increasingly marked by the structural power of its short-termist and narrowly venal bourgeoisie, and, concomitantly, the overtly barbarous sadisms and vulgarities of its ideology. Along with which, of course, come its realities, such as its vicious, racialized, carceral regime, for example, with more (poor) people in jails than in any other country in recorded history.[15] These aren't "imperfections" or pathologies of late capitalism: they are its excrescences and symptoms. They bring advantages—in capital's terms—such as a weak working-class movement. But such structural rigidity comes with disadvantages, too. Cracks in the ideological edifice can have more shattering effects than they would in a more flexible version of capitalism, for example. As we've seen in the abrupt social upheaval in the US in 2020. Those flowerings of consciousness could call into wider question capitalism's dynamics of exploitation and social control.

After decades of TINA, it's extraordinary to witness the rise of a wave of mostly young activists for whom it's no longer the desire for transformation that's denounced as absurd, cowardly, unreal, or an excuse for barbarism, but the scorning of that desire.

Which isn't, of course, to suggest that socialism is just around the corner.

Even allowing for the unusual brittleness of US capitalism, we read the *Manifesto* now considerably more aware than were its authors of capitalism's sheer adaptability. Perhaps above all else, the key lesson we must learn from the decades of brutality since the *Manifesto*'s publication is the one Trotsky learnt more than eighty years ago, when he stressed the document's "underestimation of future possibilities latent in capitalism."[16]

Capitalism is no less crisis-ridden than Marx and Engels depict it: but it's vastly more tenacious, not least due to "the unprecedented economic and military flexibility of the bourgeoisie, operating on a world scale," and "the unprecedented development of bourgeois resources to maintain cultural hegemony."[17]

And the system has shown itself to be more adaptive not only with regard to unforeseen events, but to *pre-existing* circumstances and social formulations, accommodating not only a wider variety of futures than the authors anticipated, but "pasts," too, sometimes maintaining certain appearances, even if radically altering their essence.

There are no shortage of stories of capitalism utterly transforming the societies into which it crashes, very often in desolating ways, as, say, in the degradation of the autonomous and relatively egalitarian Semai society in Malaysia from the 1950s on through the predatory interventions of state and merchant capital on their subsistence-based way of life.[18] But the complex reality of the real universalizing drive towards the exploitation of abstract labor, inextricable from capitalism, isn't necessarily coterminous with the idea, present in the *Manifesto*, that capitalism itself "universalises," especially not in terms of the flatter image of "universalism" also present in the text.[19] It can destroy in various ways, and it can also change even through encouraging a certain seeming stasis.

At one level, such a history has, for example, seen the maintaining of "traditional" family units and the subsistence modes of that domestic economy in certain sub-Saharan and West African societies, in the context of imperialism and capitalism. These have not survived "against the odds" as atavisms or throwbacks, but, as the anthropologist Claude Meillassoux explains, *as part of* a process of capital-driven change, the conservation of the subsistence sector meeting the needs of biological and social reproduction, allowing for capitalism to pay wages lower than it otherwise could.

> Initially, contact is obviously between two modes of production, and one of them dominates and begins to change the other. As long as the domestic *relations* of production and reproduction persist, rural communities, although in a process of change, remain qualitatively different from the capitalist mode of production. However, in the long run the general conditions for reproducing the social whole resulting from this interpretation no longer depend on determinations inherent in the domestic mode of production [that is, of the social group interacting with capitalism], but on decisions taken in the capitalist sector. By this process, contradictory in essence, the domestic mode is simultaneously maintained and destroyed—maintained as a means of social organisation which produces value from which imperialism benefits, and destroyed because it is deprived in the end of its means of reproduction, under the impact of exploitation. Under the circumstances the domestic mode of production both exists and does not exist.[20]

At a very different scale, and at the heart of "advanced" capitalism, consider the British royal family. There could hardly be an institution more definitional to pre-capitalist society than a monarchy. But after a brief foray into republicanism in the aftermath of the English Civil War, Britain was graced with a restoration, and a monarchy which has survived and, in its own peculiar terms, thrived for over three and a half centuries. Very clearly the role of the British royal family in 2022 is utterly different from what it was in 1660, never mind in 1500. Where once it was an organizing hub of national accumulation and a center of political power, now—as well, of course, as a congeries of extraordinarily wealthy rentiers—it's a farcical and profitable commodity for the culture industry, and an invaluable component of authoritarian national mythology. All of which is perfectly functional to British capitalism.

In Peter Osborne's outstanding formulation: "The social forms that Marx would have capitalism destroy live on within it, transfigured, as both points of identification and functioning relations, suffused with fantasy in ways which cannot be fully comprehended apart from their 'non-capitalist dimensions.'"[21]

So it is that to correct the *Manifesto*'s breathless descriptions of capitalism reshaping the world in a single social image is also to be mindful of the possible tenacity of capitalism, in the face of future challenges, not to succumb to that misplaced inevitabilism of change. Capitalism's logic—contested and countervailed—is of a tendency towards abstracting away from socially particular relations, including of hierarchy, into abstract equality; from socially embedded particular roles towards abstract wage labor; towards commodification and concomitant sets of contractual juridical relations; towards the money form that dissolves all those fixed, fast-frozen relations, and so on. But none of this is the same as "homogenising." Capital's "differentiating" drives are also crucial—its deployment and articulation of previously existing social distinctions, and/or its encouragement of new ones, for the ends of capital accumulation.[22] Capitalism can be awesomely elastic and adaptable. And that will include metabolizing aspects of society that were there before capitalism and even seem to stand against it, as well as those newly thrown up, even seemingly in opposition to it and its predatory tendencies.

Even an adaptable capitalism cannot guarantee the recuperation of such tendencies to its ends, of course—but it has a far, far better shot at it than its critics might wish. Mild reforms and radical moments are proposed and contested and opposed and co-opted and deployed, sometimes simultaneously, by those committed to capitalism's maintenance, as well as by its enemies.

The histories of capitalism are full of examples. Perhaps most famously, in the context of Marx's writings, are the Factory Acts, British legislation dating particularly between 1833 and 1878, regulating and slowly reducing the length and conditions of the working day, limiting child labor, and so on, particularly for textile workers. The push for such measures, in particular for the ten-hour day, was key to the agitation of various working-class groups, such as the Chartists, the Ten Hours Movement, and what were known as "Short Time Committees." Such struggles redoubled in the 1850s and 1860s, after the severe setback of the defeat of the Chartists, increasing to the point where, in the words of the official factory inspectors' reports, "the antagonism of classes had arrived at an incredible tension."[23] Initially, these reforms were, predictably, stoutly opposed by the leaders of the two main parties, the Conservatives and the Whigs, as well as by the manufacturers, who insisted that limiting child labor would be an "invasion of the rights of the parent over the child," and that restricting working hours would destroy England's competitive advantages. The manufacturers organized an early business lobby, the Anti-Corn Law League, which by 1843 employed more than 800 people to push its anti-reform arguments.[24]

But the story isn't quite so simple as it may appear. Supporters of the legislation always included certain paternalist Tory politicians, as well as various reformism-inclined factory owners such as Robert Owen. For some, this was a question of humanitarian ethics. But, crucially for understanding the underlying dynamics of capitalism, Marx himself, in *Capital*, went further, in seeing the Acts' limitations on the working day as simultaneously against the inclinations and immediate profits of individual capitalist concerns, while also being *in capital's collective interest*.[25] On the one hand, "[c]apital . . . takes no account of the health and the length of life of the worker, unless society forces it to do so" and "[i]ts answer to the outcry about the physical and mental degradation, the premature death, the torture of over-work, is this: Should that pain trouble us, since it increases our pleasure (profit)?" This isn't simply sociopathic sadism but a rational and inevitable result of the economic pressures of capitalism itself. "[T]his does not depend on the will . . . of the individual capitalist.

Under free competition, the immanent laws of capitalist production confront the individual capitalist as a coercive force external to him."[26] But on the other hand, unlimited expansions of the working day will ultimately exhaust—literally—the labor force, and lead to a deterioration in the amount and quality of the labor-power available to capitalism.

> If . . . the unnatural extension of the working day, which capital necessarily strives for in its unmeasured drive for self-valorization, shortens the life of the individual worker, and therefore the duration of his labour-power, the forces used up have to be replaced more rapidly, and it will be more expensive to reproduce labour-power . . . It would seem therefore that the interest of capital itself points in the direction of a normal working day.[27]

Because the interests of individual capitals and of the system of capital in general are very often directly counterposed, for Marx, not only could capitalism *in toto* adapt to the Factory Acts, but such acts were in the long run invaluable for the growth and stability of the economy.[28]

However, further to the discussion in Chapter 4, it doesn't follow that, being recuperable or domesticated or defanged, all such demands are always unworthy of support from the workers' movement or the radical Left. To suggest otherwise is a form of "ultraleftism," which is another kind of inevitabilism, according to which nothing short of an explicit push for the destruction of capitalism itself can do anything other than feed into or strengthen that system. The truth is more complex and ambivalent. Marx himself, for all his clear-sighted analysis that the Factory Acts were ultimately a stabilizing force for capitalism, full-throatedly supported them as measures to improve the lives and well-being of the working class. Thus his inaugural address to the First International in 1864:

After a 30 years' struggle, fought with almost admirable perseverance, the English working classes, improving a momentaneous split between the landlords and money lords, succeeded in carrying the Ten Hours' Bill. The immense physical, moral, and intellectual benefits hence accruing to the factory operatives, half-yearly chronicled in the reports of the inspectors of factories, are now acknowledged on all sides. Most of the continental governments had to accept the English Factory Act in more or less modified forms, and the English Parliament itself is every year compelled to enlarge its sphere of action. But besides its practical import, there was something else to exalt the marvellous success of this workingmen's measure. . . . [T]he middle class had predicted, and to their heart's content proved, that any legal restriction of the hours of labour must sound the death knell of British industry, which, vampirelike, could but live by sucking blood, and children's blood, too. . . . This struggle about the legal restriction of the hours of labour raged the more fiercely since, apart from frightened avarice, it told indeed upon the great contest between the blind rule of the supply and demand laws which form the political economy of the middle class, and social production controlled by social foresight, which forms the political economy of the working class. Hence the Ten Hours' Bill was not only a great practical success; it was the victory of a principle; it was the first time that in broad daylight the political economy of the middle class succumbed to the political economy of the working class.[29]

Marx is clear that the calculus with regard to how and how hard to support such measures isn't only that the day-to-day lives of the working class and/or exploited and oppressed peoples are made better, vital though that is. It's also the extent to which certain measures—even those capitalism can recuperate—can be understood as increasing working-class power and room for maneuvers overall.

We can apply similar standards to new epochs and new demands— welfare state provision, minimum wage, universal healthcare, as well as a plethora of less grand-scale reforms. And, inevitably, good-faith debate will arise on the Left about such measures—whether, for example, they do in fact strengthen the working class, or whether the cost of a short-term improvement might be a medium- or long-term diminution of political power.

But in any case, supporters of insurgent demands must not be in denial about capitalism's ability to assimilate them. For all that such denial is understandable from a Left desperate for heroes and victories. Take even so transformative a demand as the historic shift from restrictive, property-based voting rights to universal suffrage itself. In 1839, the dashing *enfant terrible* of Chartism, George Julian Harney, gave a blistering speech in Derby telling the audience that "we demand universal [male] suffrage because it is our right, and not only because it is our right but because we believe it will bring freedom to our country, and happiness to our homesteads; we believe it will give us bread and beef and beer."[30] Three years later, Harney's class enemy Thomas Babington Macaulay spoke in the House of Commons, eloquently agreeing, from the opposing political perspective, that

> universal suffrage is incompatible . . . with all forms of government, and with everything for the sake of which forms of government exist . . . it is incompatible with property, and . . . consequently incompatible with civilization . . . On the security of property civilization depends . . . If it be admitted that on the institution of property the well-being of society depends, it follows surely that it would be madness to give supreme power in the state to a class which would not be likely to respect that institution.[31]

In fact the transformative impact of any such measure isn't reducible to the demand's particular *content*, but is also a function of the context in which it's made, and how it's fought for. Marx made this point in 1852, when, on the one hand, he stressed that "the carrying of universal suffrage in England would . . . be a far more socialistic measure than anything which has been honoured with that name on the Content," while that same year averring that "[u]niversal suffrage in France did not possess the magical power attributed to it by republicans of the old school."[32] The point being, in the words of Paul Foot, in his magisterial history of the vote, that given the particular class and political context in which the vote had recently been won for all men in France, versus what the situation in Britain would have been *had* the vote been won under those contested conditions in which it was demanded, Marx saw "universal [male] suffrage in France as something very different from what universal suffrage would have been if it had been introduced in England at the point of a Chartist pike."[33]

In point of fact, as we know, the miserable truth is that Macaulay's concerns itself turned out to be vastly overstated, and Harney's magnificent furious hopes not met. Whatever bread, beef, and beer have followed, decades of universal suffrage in Britain have brought neither freedom nor happiness.

Though it emphatically doesn't follow, of course, that it wasn't therefore worth fighting for, this sense of capitalism's recuperative power is a key lesson in reading the *Manifesto* now. It's one that, in the years after the *Manifesto*, the authors themselves came to learn. Engels, in 1885, two years after Marx died, described 1848 as "a new industrial epoch" characterized by capitalist control, but said that capitalists had learned that they could not fully grasp social and political control "except by the help of the working class"—hence their initially grudging toleration of, for example, those Factory Acts, trade unions and an extended franchise. Adaptation.[34]

The situation is always complex, even ambiguous. Opposed as the extraordinary recent upheavals against violence directed at women and against racism are by ruthless bigots and partisans of oppressive order, and transformative as to some extent and in some contexts they are, the Left's support for and excitement about them is wholly justified. But that cannot mean myopia that such protests and movements cannot be co-opted. Quite the opposite: examples of pro-capitalist and right-wing appropriation of their conception of woke idioms are already widespread, including as explicit attacks on more radical dissent.[35]

Consider, for example, the hawkish right-Democrat Hillary Clinton's 2016 attack on her vastly more principled and radical opponent for the party nomination, Bernie Sanders, with the sardonic question, "If we broke up the big banks tomorrow, would that end racism?" At face value this was absurd—as Matt Taibbi among many others pointed out, "lots of things worth doing, even political things, won't 'end racism'"[36]—but the point was to deploy certain language and concepts of "intersectionality"—a term for the indispensable task of considering the reality of overlapping oppressions, but one so increasingly nebulous in its usage that, absent definition and clarification, it can be used to mean almost anything—against a once-in-a-generation redistributive and relatively transformative social-democratic agenda, in favor of her ruthless and cynical neoliberal program.

Not much less worthy of piss and vinegar are declarations of solidarity with, for example, Black Lives Matter protests by capitalist companies. The culture-war elements of this, according to which, again, partisans of more "traditional" cultural reaction attack such formulations, might tempt some radicals into a defence of so-called "woke capitalism." This would be to implicitly mistake certain conservative ideologies for structuring ideologies of capitalism *tout court*.

Consider the achingly hip US vegan foods producer No Evil Foods, for example: it has ostentatiously declared its support for Black Lives Matter, donated to the Black Trans Travel Fund, denounced excessive plastic packaging (not unpersuasively) as environmental racism, and declared its intent to go "beyond making and selling products" to "building deep community partnerships and speaking out on subjects that we believe in."[37] Since 2020, it has also been granted the nickname Mo Evil Foods by labor activists, due to its extensive, systematic, and successful campaign of union-busting among its workforce, including laying off pro-union activists.[38]

Nor, importantly, has this been at all incidental to its talking of a politically right-on talk: the anti-union drive itself has been articulated through precisely the kind of unreflexive "progressive" language which is no less the company's product than its fake meat. One of the company's founders can be heard in the leaked audio of an anti-union meeting (mandatory for employees), referring disparagingly to the "old white guys" in high ranks at the United Food and Commercial Workers union, which the company described as "a business," comparing its dues-based income to turnover. "I think a lot of these points are being made to draw a contrast between the culture we are trying to build at No Evil Foods," said her co-founder, "and the culture and atmosphere that sometimes is built around unions."

Here, the conflict is depicted not as between capital and workers' representatives, but progressive pro-BLM vegans and old white guys.[39] Not that the founders shied away from that underlying dynamic: having a union, one stressed, could mean that investors would "run the other way." No Evil Foods' future as a profit-making business was at stake.

As Asad Haider implies, a logical extension of that liberal position according to which the good of "political correctness" outweighs the bad of capitalism, implies that "society would be fair if 1% of the population controlled 90% of the resources so long as the dominant 1% were 13% Black, 17% Latino, 50% female, 4% or whatever LGBTQ, etc," leaving "the very fact that there is a dominant 1% of the population . . . unquestioned."[40]

The point is that capitalism doesn't win by taking one side or another in such battles in "culture wars"—it has always been a system of "warring siblings"—but by dictating the terms of the debate. It gets you coming or going. Hashtag-deploying, notionally right-on capitalism is capitalism, and no friend of liberation.

A modern reading of the *Manifesto*, predicated on understanding capitalism's flexibility and adaptability, demands a position that isn't so much paradoxical as it is attuned to the prevailing contradictions, including those between "reactionary" and "progressive" liberal politics, that constitute capitalism—and that must therefore be nimble about negotiating, even deploying, such contradictions itself. One must understand previously existing systems of oppression, such as differentiation by ethnicity and the oppression of women, as subsumed into the logic of capital; not caused by it, necessarily, but certainly coming to be inextricable from it, and constitutively part of it. Simultaneously, one must walk a line between celebrating and building resistance to such dynamics, and understanding that certain iterations *of that very resistance* might be appropriated by the system of barbarity itself.

The struggle against racism, for example, is a liberatory struggle that cuts against the grain of the history of capitalism, and it's vital that it wins. But whatever improvements come, to the extent that whatever else they do, they are deployed to prop up capitalism—as they have been in the past, and can and may still be—violence, exploitation, and oppression will not end.

To be attuned to capitalism's potential for adaptation is to be both more and less hopeful than the *Manifesto*, both more and less pessimistic.

## CLIMATE AND CATASTROPHE

Today, the urgent danger of climate catastrophe is appallingly clear. In the ruthless pursuit of profit over the needs of the biome or humanity, capital accumulation has led to cataclysmic upheaval and death. Whatever the desires of any individual capitalists, whatever the pious declarations about "corporate responsibility," at a social level that fundamental dynamic towards accumulation is definitional, and will always be stronger than any other tendency—including the cost of the liveable reproduction of capital and society itself. This is hardly hyperbole: it's nothing other than the same dynamic by which capitalist concerns have often been vectors driving towards war.

This is why appeals to "corporate responsibility" or green capitalism are utopian in the worst sense. And because of this, it's overwhelmingly likely that this capitalist dynamic will fail to adequately address the climate crisis.

It is true that capitalism, as we've just underlined, is adaptable. Given that the crisis itself incentivises certain sections of capital to address it, and given that climate disaster threatens their very existence, it would be a hostage to fortune to claim that no such patch-up amelioration could *possibly* occur. However, the mainstream pro-capitalist position, especially as flat-out climate-change denialism becomes less common in the ruling class, is that the invisible hand and mighty forces of "entrepreneurialism" will definitely lead to the "fixing" of the problem. This is the fallacious inevitabilism of, and a cultish faith in, a rapacious system.

And should such development even occur, it will be competing against established "dirty" industries, and with whatever capitalist tears, the competitive advantage may very well allow dirtier technology to outcompete the less so, because that driving dynamic is profit, not need, as the healthy sales of torture implements and weapons of mass destruction prove. (On the day these words are written, the COP26 climate summit watered down proposals to end the ecocidal use of coal power in what *The Sydney Morning Herald* described as a "major backdown" after intensive lobbying.)[41] No such progress is inevitable, or even likely. Socialism, wherein the astonishing scientific and technical powers of humanity are harnessed to need, for all the uncertainties and errors that would occur, would give an infinitely greater likelihood of sustaining a habitable world than more of the same system that got us here.

In its brief discussion of environmental problems, the *Manifesto* proposes a democratic social plan to address them. But its suggestion is for "the bringing into cultivation of waste-lands" (2.72). Though such a fervent admirer of the *Manifesto* as Lenin, when in a position of power, had a more judicious view, and was concerned for the protection, rather than eager cultivation, of so-called wildernesses, the grotesquerie of

Stalinism dispensed with any such nuance for an ugly and disastrous cult of industrial production for its own sake, strands feeding into which are visible in the *Manifesto*.[42] Any such vulgar Prometheanism is countervailed, though, also in the *Manifesto*, by the insistence on the development of humanity and democracy. It's those human drives in the pages that deserve fidelity, rather than any celebration of productive capacity per se.

From which follows a warning. We've seen that the *Manifesto* views liberation, equality and the free development of individuals as arising when the productive capacities of society have reached a certain degree of red plenty. There's a beauty to this vision of development growing, stalling, then unfurling under mass control. There's a poignancy, too. Because to read the *Manifesto* today is to have to acknowledge that after centuries of exploitation and planetary degradation, the rupture is more urgent than ever—and is unlikely to be into a realm of freedom and plenty, but of necessary slow *repair*.[43]

There is a world to win: won, it must be fixed. This is "ruin communism," or "salvage communism." As part of such project, naive dreams of profligacy have to be set aside.

This is in no way to advocate a new utopian asceticism. But, increasingly, ecosocialists are questioning the productivity paradigm, acknowledging that we are at a pass such that, after a break from capitalism, some constraints on production may be necessary to allow the fullest development of humanity itself.[44] If the liberation of the productive forces of humanity under democratic control means imposing these, it will be as a stage in the salvaging of the world, and for our own liberation.

## On Humility

The necessity or otherwise of a "party" in the fight for socialist revolution is a long-standing dispute on the Left.

There are trends of radical and revolutionary thought that place their faith in the spontaneous activity and consciousness of workers. For others, the sorry history of working-class division, the hold of reactionary ideology on large numbers of the oppressed and exploited, are strong evidence for the *Manifesto*'s claim that "the ruling ideas" tend to be "the ideas of the ruling class" (2.59). And accordingly, that an organized party is an indispensable organ to intervene, argue, agitate, to help mobilize and radicalize others. This, however, might raise at least as many problems as it solves, given the litany of infighting, toxic cultures, blinkered loyalties, and unedifying hostilities that is an integral part of the history of left-wing parties—though not, it should be stressed, all of it, nor of the Left alone.

Some on the Left have raised the question of how much these excrescences have been intrinsic to traditional leftist party-forms themselves, and what to do about it.[45] The question of communism's relationship to a party is as much as anything a theory of political consciousness, and is not and cannot be divorced from questions of political activity more generally. But, not least given the unhappy history of many self-styled Marxist parties in and out of power, three important caveats must be part of any conviction of the necessity of a revolutionary party for a ruptural politics.

First, what exactly a party *is* must start as an open question. We've seen that at the time of writing the term did not portend what we would mean by it now; "only at the end of . . . [Marx and Engels'] lives were [parties] beginning to assume the forms that we know today."[46] It would be satisfying to offer here an outline of a habitable organisation adequate and appropriate to ruptural politics under capitalism. But this is an epoch of political shock, of the breakdown of bromides and certainties, the de- and recomposition of traditional mass parties of the right, center and center-left, as well as of small radical groupuscules, and even for those of us on the Left for whom a wager on some kind of party seems necessary, and worth it, the appropriate party form is currently an urgent and ongoing debate.

Secondly, for all the unedifying elitism of some activists, a party model doesn't imply a hierarchical top-down model of persuasion. Without question the party attempts to forge the most rigorous position on relevant questions, but to be healthy this is a feedback process, one of learning no less than of persuading, in which a party is not so much an imparter of, as an arena for, political development.[47]

Relatedly necessary is a puncturing of any sense of a clear-eyed Elect teaching the masses. From theoretical developments from long after the *Manifesto*, we can stress the importance of contingency to insight (no less than to politics, as Lenin always stressed). If the wager is correct that a party's analysis is persuasive to people, this certainly isn't because its intellectuals and activists are innately smarter. We all come to ideas for countless complex reasons. In the psychoanalytical terms used by Tad DeLay, "[w]e are not subjects who desire to know, we are subjects who desire full stop. And only occasionally does that desire attach to a desire for knowledge. . . . [S]ometimes people will educate themselves out of certain perspectives. More often people have a crisis that . . . creates the certain mental conditions by which they can transition into a different way of thinking."[48]

DeLay is very explicit that this doesn't mean argument is pointless: far from it. But his model introduces a humane sense of contingency that answers, without contempt, the liberal question "What's the matter with Kansas?" and retorts, "What's the matter with Hampstead?"—and indeed everywhere? Why do intelligent people across classes and geographies hold fast to ideas that are absurd and/or that work against their interests?

This is also an invaluable reminder of the limits—which is very far from the same thing as uselessness—of "rational debate." "I ask again," as DeLay has it elsewhere, "do you believe you will be able to fact-check your [racist] relatives into the light?"[49] You *might*—people do change their minds—but not, or not only, because of the power of your arguments.

Which, in part, takes us right back to conventional socialist, indeed trade-unionist, wisdom, that activism alongside the exploited and oppressed irrespective of whether they agree with you isn't just an important principle, but also strategically sensible. After all, those "crises" that DeLay describes will or have come to many of us—what's capitalism but a system of crisis, including psychic?—and with ideas up for grabs, it isn't just ideas in the abstract that will shape them, but experiences, including of solidarity. "Revolutionary practice is a laboratory," as Susan Buck-Morss has it.[50]

And finally, when it comes to those ideas that communists do forge and defend, as thoughtfully and empathetically as we can, a degree of humility is urgently required.

The cliché of the Left—though not the Left alone—is of a movement doggedly certain of "the line," the established party position on any particular issue, bulldozing over nuance, scepticism and counter-evidence. Whatever its qualities, one would be hard-pressed to discern in such a Left much theoretical humility.

In fact, some of the appeal of a radical movement can be, sometimes, for some people, precisely that it *does* seem to have an answer to most questions, in a world which disempowers in part through a sense of ignorance and shame therein. But political disaffection can and should set in not only when those answers prove inadequate, but when the absence of a pause before their expounding is evidence not of thought but of its absence. To suggest that a new humility is necessary for the Left is to insist that our texts are indispensable but not sacred. A first step is to not assume what we know, and fall prey to dogmatism. To be very frank about the limits of our prognostication: "[T]here is no point in denying that, at the present time, we can see humanity's historical prospects, even in the fairly short term, through a glass at best only very darkly."[51] Another step is to admit, including to ourselves, that at times we've been very wrong. And will be again.

Not that we should make a counter-fetish of uncertainty. To have fidelity at all to the project of this *Manifesto*, no matter how critically, is to be convinced of certain claims of which capitalism and its ideologues demand we remain unsure: that inequality and oppression aren't states of nature; that our social reality is controlled by the few; that it's so controlled in opposition to the needs and rights of the many; that we have the capability, at the very least, to make it worth attempting to change the world. That if we succeed, it will be better for the vast majority. There are minimum grounds for agreement without which comradely activity and radical analysis are functionally impossible. Some certainties and what we might call humilophobia can be liabilities for radical change, but not all.

The Left can hamstring itself precisely by combining a hunt for that political "line" by which to approach the world with a binary politics of either/or with regard to it. More fruitful would be a degree of comfort with contradiction. Both on principle—even where we are confident of some positions, necessary humility demands accommodating the possibility that we are wrong—and tactically. The concept of a "party line" might productively be replaced with that of a "band" or "zone" of reasonable understandings and approaches, certainly not infinitely wide, but more elastic than that notion of a single line to which everyone should conform. Comradeship might inhere in shared commitment to positions within that band, even when those positions themselves aren't identical, so long as they trend in the same direction. Even if sometimes, within that bandwidth, they are directly opposed. Not merely out of some nebulous "tolerance," but because there are contexts in which it's precisely out of such comradely opposition, rather than the precipitous foreclosure into "a" or "the" line, that nuanced and rigorous political progress might be made. Rather than allergy to factions and stern correction of minoritarian positions, "in politics there must be an opposition," wrote the great Congolese revolutionary Andrée Blouin. "How else can one learn one's errors?"[52]

The key to embracing a qualified uncertainty is that it improves, rather than diluting, the efficacy of activism, and should increase the traction, for all within that band, towards rupture.

The organised Left has tended to act as if certainty, the line, and, very often, a host of associated attitudinal positions—"optimism," the stress on activity instead of, rather than as well as, personal or organizational introspection—are the best or only ways to recruit to an ethics of liberation. Sometimes our duty as radicals should be to acknowledge our ignorance, and our failure, and that we have much to learn. As a matter of honesty, and because while such humility may still be anathema to some, it can also be a *radicalizing factor* to others. For too many of us, for too long, uncertainty has been disavowed. A reading of, an approach to, *The Communist Manifesto*—a fidelity to its horizon—that learns from history must put aside any shame of such communist frailty. Not because it doesn't exist, but because it's nothing to be ashamed of.

## On Hate

We have no reason to succumb to the complex comfort of despair, a retreat to lugubriousness by which failure is foreordained. But to stress the repeated failures of the Left is a necessary corrective, given its history of boosterism and bullshit, and to stress quite how appalling and terrible these days are, even if we can also find in them hope. To take the liberal approach and see Johnson, Bolsonaro, Modi, Duterte, the recently defenestrated Trump, Berlusconi and his aftermaths, violent and intricate "conspiracism," the rise of the alt-right, the growing volubility of racism and fascism, as *deviations,* is exoneration of the system of which they are expressions. Trump is gone, but Trumpism remains strong.

But even for all this, and for the recent defeat and smearing of left movements in the UK and US, a cause of profound depression and demoralization on the Left, this has also been, as it's important to keep stressing, a moment of unprecedented insurgency in American cities (and elsewhere). History, and the present, are up for debate.

Capitalism cannot exist without relentless punishment of those who transgress its often petty and heartless prohibitions, and indeed of those the punishment of whom it deems functional to its survival, irrespective of their notional "transgression." It increasingly deploys not just bureaucratic repression but an invested, overt, supererogatory sadism. The claim, in one thirty-year-old book on carceral politics, that "'punitiveness", as such, has come to be a rather shameful sentiment during twentieth century . . . so that arguments . . . tend to be couched in utilitarian terms', now reads as painfully naive:[53] it was only five years after those words were written that Alabama reintroduced the chain gang for inmates, for the first time in forty years. In Georgia, the "Tier Step Down" prison program involves the deliberate malnourishment of prisoners, the denial of access to education—and the inability to flush toilets. In 2014, an Ohio judge ruled that, in the words of the state's Attorney General, "You're not entitled to a pain-free execution"—and the man subsequently executed by experimental cocktail of drugs, Dennis McGuire, did indeed visibly experience intense pain. In response to the horror, one public commentator writes: "Who says that cold-blooded killers have a right to be executed like a worn-out puppy being put down?"[54]

The separation of families at the borders of the US; the deliberate malnourishment of Palestinians in Gaza through blockade—"putting them on a diet," per Israeli official Dov Weissglas; the erstwhile US President's encouraging the police to acts of brutality in 2017 ("Don't be too nice"[55]); the sale of hoodies commemorating the slow death of black men like Eric Garner at police hands ("Breathe Easy: Don't break the law," and "I CAN BREATHE"[56]). There are countless ghastly examples of the rehabilitation and celebration of cruelty, in the carceral sphere, in politics and culture. Spectacles like this aren't new, but they have not always been so "unabashed," as Philip Mirowski puts it, "made to seem so unexceptional"—and they are not only distraction but part of "teaching techniques optimised to reinforce the neoliberal self."[57]

Such social sadisms have always been opposed and fought over, and officially disavowed—particularly "at home," rather than where deployed against subjects of colonial rule—by structures that depict themselves as rational and just, even merciful. That's changing. These are more and more openly sadistic and apocalyptic times—and not without some popular support.[58] And nor is the Left, in its various virtue-signalling iterations, immune to the addictive pull of a related, if vastly less powerful, *Schwarmerei*—purulent, swarm-like sentiment, and authoritarian sentimentality, visible, for example, in certain online shitstorms, in-group anathematisation, moralistic bullying.[59]

This is a system that thrives on and encourages such sadism, despair, and disempowerment. Alongside which are thrown up species of authoritarian notional "happiness," an obligatory drab "enjoyment" of life,[60] a ruthless insistence on cheerfulness, such as Barbara Ehrenreich describes in her book *Smile or Die*.[61] Such mandatory positivity is not the opposite, but the co-constitutive other, of such miseries. This bullying is a version of what Lauren Berlant calls "cruel optimism,"[62] including on the Left: no judicious earned hope but a browbeating insistence on the necessity of positive thinking, at the cost not only of emotional autonomy but the inevitable crash when the world fails to live up to such strictures.

In a social system of mass cruelty, which celebrates only such miserable, commodified, and ultimately impoverishing "pleasures," it's perfectly understandable that the Left should be eager to stress a different kind and depth of positive emotion, to find potential radical opposition in socially destabilizing infections of *joy*, as an iteration of the opposite of sadism. To see in *love* a shattering, reconfiguring event, a key revolutionary motivation. After all, the ethics underpinning socialism, says Terry Eagleton in his wonderful *Why Marx Was Right*, resolves a contradiction of liberalism "in which your freedom may flourish only at the expense of mine," as "[o]nly through others can we finally come into our own," which "means an enrichment of individual freedom, not a diminishing of it. It is hard to think of a finer ethics. On a personal level, it is known as love."[63]

This sense, to love, of a certain political prefiguration, has inspired radicals for a century. In her seminal "Make Way for Winged Eros," the great revolutionary Alexandra Kollontai described love as "a profoundly social emotion," insisted that "[f]or a social system to be built on solidarity and cooperation it is essential that people should be capable of love," and encouraged education to that end.[64] How can we not, to quote the title of one fascinating and provocative recent book, consider "the communism of love?" Be drawn by its claim that "[w]hat is called 'love' by the best thinkers who have approached the subject is the beating heart of communism?"[65]

By all means let us take love seriously.

But we must take our enemies seriously, too, and learn from them. In what is an epoch of great hate. What aspects of the *Manifesto* does such barbarism bring into sharp focus?

In 1989, Donald Trump suggested that "maybe hate is what we need if we're going to get something done."[66] His hatred was then, and remains, a vicious deployment of racist class spite: a demand for the judicial murder of the Central Park Five, black teenagers falsely accused of rape. The concrete content of this hate is everything against which we should stand. But how best to counter hate? Is such hate as this itself not worthy of hatred?

Trump is shrewd. If not his initial aim, his hate certainly got something done. Perhaps, negatively inspired, our own hate should get something *else* done, and urgently. Something very different. The hatred of such systemic hate.

The philosopher and Anglican priest Steven Shakespeare warns that a focus on hate as anything other than a force to be rejected is "fraught," and "dangerous territory."[67] How could it be otherwise? Hatred, after all, is an emotion that can short-circuit thought and analysis, can segue into violence, and not necessarily with any discrimination.

But, duly careful, Shakespeare then attempts exactly the focus about which he warns, precisely to be "more discriminatory about hate, where it comes from, where it should be directed, and how it gets captured for the purposes of others." And a key point he makes is that hatred "which assumes no founding truth or harmony, but . . . knows itself to be against the dominating other" is "a constituent part of the singularity of every created being."

The claim, then, in the face of human history, is that hatred, particularly by the oppressed, is *inevitable*.

This isn't to say that it's inevitable that all people, even all oppressed people, will experience hate. It's to claim that, hate being neither contingent nor alien to the human soul, some, likely many, will. That, particularly in the contexts of societies that pit people against each other individually and en masse, hate will certainly exist. People will hate. As many of us know personally.

Hate is part of humanity. There's no guarantee of the direction of such inevitable hate, of course. It can be internalized, into the deadening self-hatred that, under capitalism, is so widespread. So often so validated by the system itself. Who, ground down by capitalism, does not feel, in the closing words of Rae Armantrout's poem "Hate," that "[t]he market hates you / even more / than you hate yourself"?[68] Hate can be externalized, without any justice: it has often been turned against those who least deserve it. But, though it has become a cliché, Marx's favorite maxim is richly pertinent here: *Nihil humani a me alienum puto*—nothing human is alien to me. It's hardly productive to pathologize hate per se, not least when it's natural that it arises, let alone to make it cause for shame.

Sophie Lewis puts the point with customary trenchant clarity. "Hate is almost never talked about as appropriate, healthy, or necessary in liberal-democratic society. For conservatives, liberals, and socialists alike, hate itself is the thing to reject, uproot, defeat, and cast out of the soul. Yet anti-hate ideology doesn't seem to involve targeting its root causes and points of production, nor does it address the inevitability of or the demand—the need—for hate in a class society."[69] To raise this issue, not only of the existence of hatred but, for some at least, of its potential rigorous necessity, is, to put it in Kenneth Surin's terms, what lies behind "deploying a deliberate hate as a rational category."[70]

Hate should never be trusted, nor treated as safe, nor celebrated for its own sake. But, inevitable, it should not be ignored. Nor is it automatically undeserved. Nor, perhaps, can we do without it, not if we are to remain human, in a hateful epoch that pathologizes radical hate and encourages outrage fatigue.

And nor is careful hate necessarily an enemy of liberation. It might be its ally.

In 1837, membership of the radical left group of the great pre-Marxian socialist Auguste Blanqui, known as the "Seasons," made such socially informed hate central. Standing against the degradation of the revolutionary tradition, for freedom, acolytes swore an oath: "In the name of the Republic, I swear eternal hatred to all kings, aristocrats and all oppressors of humanity."[71] In 1889, the radical Australian poet Francis Adams wrote that he had destroyed his health in the pursuit of working-class struggle in London. "It seemed a failure," he wrote. "But I never despaired, or saw cause to despair. There was a splendid foundation of hate there. With hate, all things are possible."[72] In 1957, Dorothy Counts desegregated a school in North Carolina. Writing of the photograph of her walking past the vicious jeering mob of demonstrators, James Baldwin wrote that "[i]t made me furious. It filled me with both hatred and pity."[73] The latter for Counts; the former for what he saw in the faces of her attackers. It would be an astonishing and priggish piety to suggest that hatred such as this was unbecoming, or that it did not work for emancipation.

Crucially, as Francis Adams wrote, *all* things are possible with hate—not only good things. That's the danger. But some good things, surely, in terms, for example, of activist vigor. Raging, too, certainly, but raging *against* something, wishing its eradication. The very absence of a critical mass of hatred may militate against resistance: Walter Benjamin, in his extraordinary, prophetic, controversial 1940 essay "Theses on the Philosophy of History," took social democracy, as opposed to militant socialism, to task for its focus on the future and on the working class as "redeemer," thus actively weakening that class by directing its eyes away from the iniquities of the past and present, to "forget both its hatred and its spirit of sacrifice."[74] It was in part in this hatred that he thought there might be strength.

And hate may help not only with strength but intellectual rigor, and of analysis, too. The very flat abstractions of capital can generate their own seemingly implacable logic, against which an emotionally invested, a *hating* contrary eye, might prove necessary not only ethically but epistemologically. "What will never function is the cold logic of reason," Mario Tronti writes, "when it is not moved by class hatred." Because "knowledge is connected to the struggle. Whoever has true hatred has truly understood." Tronti goes so far as to describe a radical antinomianism, that is, opposition to "the entire world of bourgeois society, as well as deadly class hatred against it" as "the simplest form of Marx's working-class science." Even in Marx's early political writings, from 1848–9, wrong as they were in various particulars, Tronti finds "a clear-sightedness in foreseeing future development such as only class hatred could provide."[75]

*Class* hatred. Hatred by a social force, of an opposing social force, of that "dominating other" Steven Shakespeare identifies. Such a hate is just, indicated and necessary: "not a personal, psychological or pathological hate, but a radical structural hate for what the world has become."[76]

Such radical structural hate, carefully deployed, might even give productive shape to the more protean forms of hate that are also inevitable, and more dangerous. "The proposed melding here of hate with a strategic logic is essential if hate is not to descend into rage or a mindless apocalypticism."[77] Hate will arise, and though shame should not attach to it, it must be urgently directed. "*Radical* hate," in Mike Neary's description, "is the critical concept on which absolute negativity"—that antinomian rupture—"is based."[78]

What has all this to do with the *Manifesto*? Even so subtle and hate-curious a Marxologist as Tronti focuses on and finds his material in other of Marx's writings. But those texts precisely come *after* the *Manifesto*, and can be seen in part as responses to it and to its failures, the failures of its prophecies, its hopes. The class hatred those later writings express doesn't emerge out of nowhere.

In the rhetoric of the *Manifesto* itself, Bosmajian sees "not only attempts to arouse anger . . . but . . . to arouse hatred which is directed not only against an individual, but also against a class." Quoting Aristotle that where anger provokes a desire for revenge, "'hatred wishes its object not to exist,'" for Bosmajian Marx's "goal was to arouse his listeners to that state in which they would wish the bourgeoisie eradicated."[79] This is ambiguous: the point for Marx and Engels isn't the "eradication" of individuals, but of the bourgeoisie *as a class*—which is to say, of capitalism. To suggest that the text evokes "hatred" of bourgeois individuals is to misrepresent the ambivalence in its passages, as well as its focus on the class system of capitalism. To go further and claim, as does Leo Kuper, that the "thoroughgoing dehumanization of the bourgeoisie" has "relevance" for the problem of *genocide*, implying a teleology of "the inevitable violent extinction of a dehumanized class of people" is absurd.[80]

On the one hand, this is simply to deploy the question-begging liberal nostrum that Stalin is the inevitable outcome and end of Marxism, and is thus not particularly interesting or surprising. It should, of course, be acknowledged that there are those who have used such arguments as are in the *Manifesto* to commit appalling acts. Still, though, describing this imaginary terror sententiously as one meted out on the basis of guilt ascribed to people "for what they are, rather than for what they do"[81] is precisely wrong. In the *Manifesto*, in Marxism in general, the relation between classes is definitionally not on the basis of static, given identities, but relations, which include things done. And the "eradication" necessary is of those relations, not of specific people. The

*Manifesto* is clear: "To be a capitalist is to have not only a purely personal but a social position in production" (2.18). And not by essence of self, either, as the *Manifesto*'s description of class renegacy among some of the bourgeoisie attests, but by virtue of taking "positions that reflect tendencies, a tendency toward capital concentration and a tendency toward dependency and immiseration," in Dean's gloss—that is to say, actively perpetuating these structures and dynamics.[82] It's precisely the pressing need for rupture in the *Manifesto* that expresses what radical hatred it contains.

But in any case, in fact, as much of the reading of the *Manifesto* here has argued, for all their magnificent spleen against the system, Marx and Engels were too generous in their eulogy to its transformation and energetic properties, and to the bourgeoisie itself, as well as about the likelihood of its collapse. The *Manifesto* is a call to arms, but those real traces of a sense of inevitable collapse pull against that drive to *eradicate* the system. The *Manifesto* hopes to be a "swan song" of the system, but it is, too, a "hymn to the glory of capitalist modernity."[83] "Never, I repeat, and in particular by no modern defender of the bourgeois civilization has anything like this been penned, never has a brief been composed on behalf of the business class from so profound and so wide a comprehension of what its achievement is and of what it means to humanity." If this, from the conservative economist Joseph Schumpeter, is an exaggeration, it isn't by much.[84]

The *Manifesto*, for all its fire, its anger and indignation, admires capitalism and bourgeois society and the bourgeoisie. It admires the bourgeois class too much.

It's telling that Gareth Stedman Jones, a relentlessly disillusioned biographer of Marx, describes the tone of the *Manifesto*'s most well-known passage as one of "playful sadism."[85] One might well contest the noun, but not the adjective. And to be playful, to play, implies a playmate. The very scintillation and swaggering provocation that makes the *Manifesto* so brilliant implies, for all its antagonism, something ludic, that pulls against any eliminationist hatred in the text.

This is not to imply that the *Manifesto* is hate-free. It admires the bourgeoisie, plays roughly with them, and hates them, too, no doubt. Of course, hatred of the system is clear throughout. But at its most combative, how hard does it hate the bourgeoisie as a class? The most antagonistic section is paragraph 2.15 to 2.67, wherein the bourgeoisie are argued with directly. That switch to second person locates what hatred there is in, or at least inextricable from, the admiration. 2.34 implies that they are lazy; 2.38 selfish; 2.45–2.51 accuses them of hypocrisy. These are about all, as far as direct attacks go. And the sincere fury here sits atop that play, the enjoyment of winning an argument, rhetorical roughhousing. But is the direct scorn here greater than in the ferocious attacks on various left-wing opponents? If anything, the palpable vituperation against, say, the True Socialists, is greater, precisely because it has none of that ambivalence in attitude that the *Manifesto* has towards the bourgeoisie.

To borrow a phrase from Neary, in another context, *The Communist Manifesto*'s "negativity is not negative enough."[86] It does not hate enough.

Against the rolling eyes of the know-all cynic, we should retain our shock at those litanies of iniquity capitalism throws up. That they provoke in us an appropriate, human, humane response, the fury of solidarity, the loathing of such unnecessary suffering. Who would we be not to hate this system, and its partisans? If we don't, the hate of those who hate on its behalf will not ebb. "[T]here's a splendid foundation of hate today, too—and if we don't build something positive from it, the edifices that will inevitably emerge will be very ugly indeed."[87] We should feel hate beyond words, and bring it to bear. This is a system that, whatever else, deserves implacable hatred for its countless and escalating cruelties.

The ruling class needs the working class. Its various fantasies of getting rid of them[88] can only *be* fantasies, because as a class it has no power without those beneath it. Thus wider ruling-class contempt for the working class ("chavs"), thus class loathing, thus social sadism, thus the constant entitlement from the ruling class, that sense that they are special and that rules don't apply, thus the deranged eulogising of cruelty and inequality. Vile as all this is, what it is not is *hate*, certainly not Aristotelian hate—because its object absolutely cannot be eradicated.

For the working class, the situation is different. The eradication of the bourgeoisie *as a class* is the eradication of bourgeois rule, of capitalism, of exploitation, of the boot on the neck of humanity. This is why the working class doesn't need sadism, nor even revenge—and why it not only can, but must, hate.[89] It must hate its class enemy, and capitalism itself.

There is a model for a better hatred in one of the key texts from which the *Manifesto* was born: Engels's *The Condition of the Working Class in England*. Hate, of the most class-rigorous kind, recurs and recurs repeatedly, runs through that unendingly shocked and blistering work. It recognizes in the bourgeoisie, for its part, "hatred towards these associations" of the working class, of course: those *associations* the bourgeoisie could certainly do with eradicating. But not only does Engels not shy from the hate of the working class for its oppressors in turn, but he repeatedly invokes it, and more.[90]

He sees it as necessary and central to working-class politics. Workers, for Engels, "shall live like human beings, shall think and feel like men [sic]" "only under glowing hatred towards their oppressors, and towards that order of things which places them in such a position, which degrades them to machines." Hatred is necessary for dignity, which means for political agency. He doesn't celebrate hate *tout court*, all too aware of the dangers of "hatred wrought to the pitch of despair" and manifesting in individual attacks by workers on capitalists. "Class hatred," by contrast, is "the only moral incentive by which the worker can be brought nearer the goal." This stands in direct opposition to individualised hatred: "in proportion as the proletarian absorbs socialistic and communistic elements, will the revolution diminish in bloodshed, revenge, and savagery . . . [I]t does not occur to any Communist to wish to revenge himself upon individuals."

It would admittedly be a prim and pious socialism which failed at least to empathize with individualized hate, or simply denounced it wholesale as an ethical failure. This is particularly so in our modern epoch, when sadism and trolling have become central to political method, especially among the ruling class. It would take an unreasonable amount of saintliness for no one on the left to feel any hate for, say, hedge fund founder, pharmaceuticals CEO, and convicted fraudster Martin Shkreli, for example, not only because of his ostentatious profiteering from human misery, but given his repeated, performative, stringent efforts precisely to be hated.[91] And, of course, there's the race-baiting, disability-mocking, sexual-assault-celebrating Trump.

The point, though, is that to fully and uncritically surrender to such agon against individuals is to invite one's own ethical degeneration; to implicitly give a pass to those others in the ruling class more inclined to decorously veil the misery from which they profit; and to lose focus on the system of which such turpitudinous figures are symptoms. Which is to risk exonerating it.

The history of the revolutionary movement is, among other things, a history of organized radicals attempting to *restrain* individualized class hate.[92] Hatred must be class hatred, with "communistic ideas," precisely to obviate "the present bitterness." But that *class* hate is glowing and must glow, and only by "cherishing the most glowing hatred," in Engels's vivid formulation, can those at the sharp end of history keep self-respect alive. Herein lies the "purity" of which the radical journalist Alexander Cockburn enquired when he famously asked of his interns, "Is your hate pure?"[93] This is a political iteration of the תַּכְלִית שִׂנְאָה, the *taklit sinah*, the "utmost" or "perfect hatred" of the Psalms for those who rise up against the Lord—that is to say, to translate into political eschatology, the enemies of justice. Psalm 139:22: "I hate them with a perfect hatred."

We must hate harder than did the *Manifesto*, for the sake of humanity.[94] Such class hate is constitutive with and inextricable from solidarity, the drive for human liberty, for the full development of the human, the ethic of emancipation implicit throughout the *Manifesto* and beyond. We should hate this world, with and through and beyond and even more than does the *Manifesto*. We should hate this hateful and hating and hatemongering system of cruelty, that exhausts and withers and kills us, that stunts our care, makes it so embattled and constrained and local in its scale and effects, where we have the capacity to be greater.

Hate is not and cannot be the only or main drive to renewal. That would be deeply dangerous. We should neither celebrate nor trust our hate. But nor should we deny it. It's not our enemy, and we cannot do without it. "At the risk of seeming ridiculous," said Che Guevara, "let me say that the true revolutionary is guided by a great feeling of love."[95] It's for the sake of love that, reading it today, we must hate more and better than even *The Communist Manifesto* knew how.

# Afterword

# A Communist Catechism
## (after Engels)

---

the Revolution aint dead
its tired,
and jest resting

Carolyn Rodgers, "The Revolution Is Resting"


**Question 1:** Are you a Communist?

Yes, we are communists.

**Question 2:** What is the aim of the Communists?

To organize society in such a way that every member of it can
develop and use all their capabilities and powers in complete
freedom and without thereby infringing the basic conditions of
this society. Wait, let us ask you a question in turn: what is it to
be "left"? It is to say that we deserve better, and that betterness is

not impossible. The US Supreme Court has ruled—8 to 1—that Nestlé has no responsibility, no guilt, for the use of child slavery in its supply chain (2021, Nestlé USA, Inc. v. Doe). No, not because it didn't know, as the activists who've pushed this case and won to this degraded point have shouted; Nestlé knew or should have known, and if you don't know when you should know that's a very knowing kind of un-knowing, isn't it? They're not responsible because that's beyond the court's jurisdiction, going on overseas, it says. Which is, then, authority from the highest court in the most powerful state in human history to outsource slavery. Welcome to capitalism. No, before you say that that's a terrible anomaly, or a questionable ruling, or a regrettable side effect of a flawed but otherwise decent system, or anything, ask yourself, how many such does it take before you can diagnose a fundamental dynamic? A way of things? Welcome to capitalism, where in the heart of "civilisation" outsourced child slavery is acceptable. To be a communist is to say not just that this is a world of systematic barbarism and cruelty, not just that this is what it is to always prioritize profits over people, but that the system that does this is strong, and adaptable, and seeps into every area of our political and economic and cultural and psychic lives, and so whatever bulwarks and defences and counter-attacks we make against it, as we have done and will again, they will always be embattled, strained, constrained, rowed back, pushing against the fundamental tide of a society in which the vast majority of people are expendable for the profits controlled and sought by a very few. To be on the right is, at base, to say at very minimum that nothing can change, nothing can be done, systematically, to alter that system—if not that such a system is desirable, and that it's more important that some have the power to control the world, even if that means others in vast numbers suffering and being without power. To be on the Right is even, increasingly, to say that that suffering is a good in itself. And

for all that there are those who've made their peace with power
or enjoyed the cruelty of the moment, this isn't, moralistically, to
separate people into Good and Bad. Capitalism implicates us all.
We can't live outside of it, we can't think outside of it. No wonder
the circuses that increasingly take the place of bread appeal, even
against our own better angels. But the system isn't seamless, and
we can all change our minds, and the world. None of us is born
a communist, any more than we're born capitalists, or sadists.
And is it any wonder that for whatever knowable and unknowable
reasons individual minds change, they change en masse when
history changes? How many times has the utter impossibility of
change been proved, only for change to rock the world and throw
up everything we thought we knew? Open up a glimmer to a life
worth living, is it not possible, likely, that millions of people who
now see no prospect of any fight ever making this a habitable
world, who've been encouraged by our rulers to believe absolutely
that the sum total of their input in the grand decisions of history
is at best ten to fifteen crosses on a ballot paper for parties they
don't control and which betray them at every turn, might suddenly
decide that in fact the fight is worth it, not only in principle, but
because it might, just possibly, win? And those who don't? Who,
in the face of a prospective crack in history, push back and fight
for this regime? They won't be the enemies of the communists,
then, they'll be the enemies of humanity, a humanity changing
and liberating itself, and that's no license for cruelty or spite, but
it's legitimate to struggle as hard as you must against the enemies
of a better world. Yes, we know that even many who love us are
bewildered by our "unrealism," our la-la land dreamwork, our
utopian foolishness, in striving for what we strive for; but can you
understand how unrealistic their beliefs are to us? Their wager that
this system, this carnival of predatory rapacity, will ever be fit to
live in? Their sad certainty that we can do no better?

**Question 3:** How do you wish to achieve this aim?

By the elimination of private property and its replacement by
community of property. By rupture. Yes, we will change the
existing state of things. Not "we" communists: "we" all of us who
come to believe through the slow accretion of tiny victories and
of defeats, too, by experiencing the solidarity of others directed
at us and ours at them; we who change our minds when the
blared lie that "Nothing can ever be different" is heard for the lie
it is, whether or not difference follows; we who reach the tipping
point where this unliveable disempowering tawdry ugly violent
murderous world can no longer be lived; we who don't believe the
barked insistence that the best targets for the exhausted rage that
follows are black people or brown people or Jews or Muslims or
queers or trans people or migrants or children in cages; we who
for whatever reasons don't succumb to or who recover from the
sadism that is inculcated and encouraged by this same system that
endlessly hoses down true sentiment with caustic sentimentality;
we who come to believe not only that we deserve better, but that
there is a chance, a chance that we can build that betterness. Yes.
Yes we will change the existing state of things. Not *we will* in the
sense of *it is inevitable* but in the sense of *it is not impossible,* in
the sense that *it is necessary,* that *it is utterly worth the wager and
the fight.* In the sense that living with that *Yes* smouldering at the
core of you, next to, as strong as, ultimately stronger than the also
smouldering *No* of necessary hate, is the only way to come close
to existing, to living as a human, in so foul and monstrous and
in- and anti-human a system. Yes. Yes we will change the existing
state of things.

## Appendix A

# MANIFESTO OF THE COMMUNIST PARTY

by Karl Marx and
Frederick Engels

Published February 1848

*Translated: Samuel Moore in cooperation with Frederick Engels, 1888*

The canonical 1888 translation is here very fractionally adjusted, and numbered by section and paragraph, drawing on the version in Gasper, 1995, and the insights of other translators including Carver and Draper.

0.1)  A spectre is haunting Europe—the spectre of communism. All the powers of old Europe have entered into a holy alliance to exorcise this spectre: Pope and Tsar, Metternich and Guizot, French Radicals and German police-spies.

0.2)  Where is the party in opposition that has not been decried as communistic by its opponents in power? Where is the opposition that has not hurled back the branding reproach of communism, against the more advanced opposition parties, as well as against its reactionary adversaries?

0.3)  Two things result from this fact:

I.  Communism is already acknowledged by all European powers to be itself a power.
II.  It is high time that Communists should openly, in the face of the whole world, publish their views, their aims, their tendencies, and meet this nursery tale of the Spectre of Communism with a manifesto of the party itself.

0.4)  To this end, Communists of various nationalities have assembled in London and sketched the following manifesto, to be published in the English, French, German, Italian, Flemish and Danish languages.

# 1. Bourgeois and Proletarians*

1.1)  The history of all hitherto existing society† is the history of class struggles.

1.2)  Freeman and slave, patrician and plebeian, lord and serf, guild-master‡ and journeyman, in a word, oppressor and oppressed, stood in constant opposition to one another, carried on an uninterrupted, now hidden, now open fight, a fight that each time ended, either in a revolutionary reconstitution of society at large, or in the common ruin of the contending classes.

1.3)  In the earlier epochs of history, we find almost everywhere a complicated arrangement of society into various orders, a manifold gradation of social rank. In ancient Rome we have patricians, knights, plebeians, slaves; in the Middle Ages, feudal lords, vassals, guild-masters, journeymen, apprentices, serfs; in almost all of these classes, again, subordinate gradations.

1.4)  The modern bourgeois society that has sprouted from the ruins of feudal society has not done away with class antagonisms. It

---

* By bourgeoisie is meant the class of modern capitalists, owners of the means of social production and employers of wage labour. By proletariat, the class of modern wage labourers who, having no means of production of their own, are reduced to selling their labour power in order to live. [Engels, 1888 English edition]

† That is, all *written* history. In 1847, the pre-history of society, the social organisation existing previous to recorded history, all but unknown. Since then, August von Haxthausen (1792–1866) discovered common ownership of land in Russia, Georg Ludwig von Maurer proved it to be the social foundation from which all Teutonic races started in history, and, by and by, village communities were found to be, or to have been, the primitive form of society everywhere from India to Ireland. The inner organisation of this primitive communistic society was laid bare, in its typical form, by Lewis Henry Morgan's (1818–1861) crowning discovery of the true nature of the gens and its relation to the tribe. With the dissolution of the primeval communities, society begins to be differentiated into separate and finally antagonistic classes. I have attempted to retrace this dissolution in *The Origin of the Family, Private Property, and the State*, second edition, Stuttgart, 1886. [Engels, 1888 English Edition and 1890 German Edition (with the last sentence omitted)]

‡ Guild-master, that is, a full member of a guild, a master within, not a head of a guild. [Engels, 1888 English Edition]

has but established new classes, new conditions of oppression, new forms of struggle in place of the old ones.

1.5) Our epoch, the epoch of the bourgeoisie, possesses, however, this distinct feature: it has simplified class antagonisms. Society as a whole is more and more splitting up into two great hostile camps, into two great classes directly facing each other— Bourgeoisie and Proletariat.

1.6) From the serfs of the Middle Ages sprang the chartered burghers of the earliest towns. From these burgesses the first elements of the bourgeoisie were developed.

1.7) The discovery of America, the rounding of the Cape, opened up fresh ground for the rising bourgeoisie. The East-Indian and Chinese markets, the colonisation of America, trade with the colonies, the increase in the means of exchange and in commodities generally, gave to commerce, to navigation, to industry, an impulse never before known, and thereby, to the revolutionary element in the tottering feudal society, a rapid development.

1.8) The feudal system of industry, in which industrial production was monopolised by closed guilds, now no longer sufficed for the growing wants of the new markets. The manufacturing system took its place. The guild-masters were pushed on one side by the manufacturing middle class; division of labour between the different corporate guilds vanished in the face of division of labour in each single workshop.

1.9) Meantime the markets kept ever growing, the demand ever rising. Even manufacturer no longer sufficed. Thereupon, steam and machinery revolutionised industrial production. The place of manufacture was taken by the giant, Modern Industry; the place of the industrial middle class by industrial millionaires, the leaders of the whole industrial armies, the modern bourgeois.

1.10) Modern industry has established the world market, for which the discovery of America paved the way. This market has given an immense development to commerce, to navigation, to communication by land. This development has, in its turn, reacted on the extension of industry; and in proportion as industry, commerce, navigation, railways extended, in the same proportion the bourgeoisie developed, increased its capital, and pushed into the background every class handed down from the Middle Ages.

1.11) We see, therefore, how the modern bourgeoisie is itself the product of a long course of development, of a series of revolutions in the modes of production and of exchange.

1.12) Each step in the development of the bourgeoisie was accompanied by a corresponding political advance of that class. An oppressed class under the sway of the feudal nobility, an armed and self-governing association in the medieval commune:* here independent urban republic (as in Italy and Germany); there taxable 'third estate' of the monarchy (as in France); afterwards, in the period of manufacturing proper, serving either the semi-feudal or the absolute monarchy as a counterpoise against the nobility, and, in fact, cornerstone of the great monarchies in general, the bourgeoisie has at last, since the establishment of Modern Industry and of the world market, conquered for itself, in the modern representative State, exclusive political sway. The executive of the modern state is but a committee for managing the common affairs of the whole bourgeoisie.

---

* This was the name given their urban communities by the townsmen of Italy and France, after they had purchased or conquered their initial rights of self-government from their feudal lords. [Engels, 1890 German edition] 'Commune' was the name taken in France by the nascent towns even before they had conquered from their feudal lords and masters local self-government and political rights as the 'Third Estate'. Generally speaking, for the economical development of the bourgeoisie, England is here taken as the typical country, for its political development, France. [Engels, 1888 English Edition]

1.13)    The bourgeoisie, historically, has played a most revolutionary part.

1.14)    The bourgeoisie, wherever it has got the upper hand, has put an end to all feudal, patriarchal, idyllic relations. It has pitilessly torn asunder the motley feudal ties that bound man to his 'natural superiors', and has left remaining no other nexus between man and man than naked self-interest, than callous 'cash payment'. It has drowned the most heavenly ecstasies of religious fervour, of chivalrous enthusiasm, of philistine sentimentalism, in the icy water of egotistical calculation. It has resolved personal worth into exchange value, and in place of the numberless indefeasible chartered freedoms, has set up that single, unconscionable freedom—Free Trade. In one word, for exploitation, veiled by religious and political illusions, it has substituted naked, shameless, direct, brutal exploitation.

1.15)    The bourgeoisie has stripped of its halo every occupation hitherto honoured and looked up to with reverent awe. It has converted the physician, the lawyer, the priest, the poet, the man of science, into its paid wage labourers.

1.16)    The bourgeoisie has torn away from the family its sentimental veil, and has reduced the family relation to a mere money relation.

1.17)    The bourgeoisie has disclosed how it came to pass that the brutal display of vigour in the Middle Ages, which reactionaries so much admire, found its fitting complement in the most slothful indolence. It has been the first to show what man's activity can bring about. It has accomplished wonders far surpassing Egyptian pyramids, Roman aqueducts, and Gothic cathedrals; it has conducted expeditions that put in the shade all former Exoduses of nations and crusades.

1.18)    The bourgeoisie cannot exist without constantly revolutionising the instruments of production, and thereby the relations of production, and with them the whole relations of society. Conservation of the old modes of production in unaltered form, was, on the contrary, the first condition of existence for all earlier industrial classes. Constant revolutionising of production, uninterrupted disturbance of all social conditions, everlasting uncertainty and agitation distinguish the bourgeois epoch from all earlier ones. All fixed, fast-frozen relations, with their train of ancient and venerable prejudices and opinions, are swept away, all new-formed ones become antiquated before they can ossify. All that is solid melts into air, all that is holy is profaned, and man is at last compelled to face with sober senses his real conditions of life, and his relations with his kind.

1.19)    The need of a constantly expanding market for its products chases the bourgeoisie over the entire surface of the globe. It must nestle everywhere, settle everywhere, establish connexions everywhere.

1.20)    The bourgeoisie has through its exploitation of the world market given a cosmopolitan character to production and consumption in every country. To the great chagrin of reactionaries, it has drawn from under the feet of industry the national ground on which it stood. All old-established national industries have been destroyed or are daily being destroyed. They are dislodged by new industries, whose introduction becomes a life and death question for all civilised nations, by industries that no longer work up indigenous raw material, but raw material drawn from the remotest zones; industries whose products are consumed, not only at home, but in every quarter of the globe. In place of the old wants, satisfied by the production of the country, we find new wants, requiring for their satisfaction the products of distant lands and climes. In place of the old local and national seclusion and self-sufficiency, we have intercourse in every direction, universal inter-dependence of nations. And as in material, so also in intellectual production. The intellectual creations of individual nations become common property. National one-sidedness and narrow-mindedness become more and more impossible, and from the numerous national and local literatures, there arises a world literature.

I.21)  The bourgeoisie, by the rapid improvement of all instruments of production, by the immensely facilitated means of communication, draws all, even the most barbarian, nations into civilisation. The cheap prices of commodities are the heavy artillery with which it batters down all Chinese walls, with which it forces the barbarians' intensely obstinate hatred of foreigners to capitulate. It compels all nations, on pain of extinction,* to adopt the bourgeois mode of production; it compels them to introduce what it calls civilisation into their midst, i.e., to become bourgeois themselves. In one word, it creates a world after its own image.

I.22)  The bourgeoisie has subjected the country to the rule of the towns. It has created enormous cities, has greatly increased the urban population as compared with the rural, and has thus rescued a considerable part of the population from the isolation of rural life.† Just as it has made the country dependent on the towns, so it has made barbarian and semi-barbarian countries dependent on the civilised ones, nations of peasants on nations of bourgeois, the East on the West.

I.23)  The bourgeoisie keeps more and more doing away with the scattered state of the population, of the means of production, and of property. It has agglomerated population, centralised the means of production, and has concentrated property in a few hands. The necessary consequence of this was political centralisation. Independent, or but loosely connected provinces,

---

* The sense in 'extinction' could arguably better be rendered 'ruin' or 'going under'. CM.
† Notoriously, Moore translates the German *Idiotismus*, rather, and less accurately, as 'the idiocy of rural life'. CM.

with separate interests, laws, governments, and systems of taxation, became lumped together into one nation, with one government, one code of laws, one national class-interest, one frontier, and one customs-tariff.

I.24) The bourgeoisie, during its rule of scarce one hundred years, has created more massive and more colossal productive forces than have all preceding generations together. Subjection of Nature's forces to man, machinery, application of chemistry to industry and agriculture, steam-navigation, railways, electric telegraphs, clearing of whole continents for cultivation, canalisation of rivers, whole populations conjured out of the ground—what earlier century had even a presentiment that such productive forces slumbered in the lap of social labour?

I.25) We see then: the means of production and of exchange, on whose foundation the bourgeoisie built itself up, were generated in feudal society. At a certain stage in the development of these means of production and of exchange, the conditions under which feudal society produced and exchanged, the feudal organisation of agriculture and manufacturing industry, in one word, the feudal relations of property became no longer compatible with the already developed productive forces; they became so many fetters. They had to be burst asunder; they were burst asunder.

I.26) Into their place stepped free competition, accompanied by a social and political constitution adapted in it, and the economic and political sway of the bourgeois class.

I.27) A similar movement is going on before our own eyes. Modern bourgeois society, with its relations of production, of exchange and of property, a society that has conjured up such gigantic means of production and of exchange, is like the sorcerer who is no longer able to control the powers of the nether world whom he has called up by his spells. For many a decade past the history of industry and commerce is but the history of the revolt of modern productive forces against modern conditions of production, against the property relations that are the conditions for the existence of the bourgeois and of its rule. It is enough to mention the commercial crises that by their periodical return put the existence of the entire bourgeois society on its trial, each time more threateningly. In these crises, a great part not only of the existing products, but also of the previously created productive forces, are periodically destroyed. In these crises, there breaks out an epidemic that, in all earlier epochs, would have seemed an absurdity—the epidemic of over-production. Society suddenly finds itself put back into a state of momentary barbarism; it appears as if a famine, a universal war of devastation, had cut off the supply of every means of subsistence; industry and commerce seem to be destroyed; and why? Because there is too much civilisation, too much means of subsistence, too much industry, too much commerce. The productive forces at the disposal of society no longer tend to further the development of the conditions of bourgeois property; on the contrary, they have become too powerful for these conditions, by which they are fettered, and so soon as they overcome these fetters, they bring disorder into the whole of bourgeois society, endanger the existence of bourgeois property. The conditions of bourgeois society are too narrow to comprise the wealth created by them. And how does the bourgeoisie get over these crises? On the one hand by enforced destruction of a mass of productive forces; on the other, by the conquest of new markets, and by the more thorough exploitation of the old ones. That is to say, by paving the way for more extensive and more destructive crises, and by diminishing the means whereby crises are prevented.

1.28) The weapons with which the bourgeoisie felled feudalism to the ground are now turned against the bourgeoisie itself.

1.29) But not only has the bourgeoisie forged the weapons that bring death to itself; it has also called into existence the men who are to wield those weapons—the modern working class—the proletarians.

1.30) In proportion as the bourgeoisie, i.e., capital, is developed, in the same proportion is the proletariat, the modern working class, developed—a class of labourers, who live only so long as they find work, and who find work only so long as their labour increases capital. These labourers, who must sell themselves piecemeal, are a commodity, like every other article of commerce, and are consequently exposed to all the vicissitudes of competition, to all the fluctuations of the market.

1.31) Owing to the extensive use of machinery, and to the division of labour, the work of the proletarians has lost all individual character, and, consequently, all charm for the workman. He becomes an appendage of the machine, and it is only the most simple, most monotonous, and most easily acquired knack, that is required of him. Hence, the cost of production of a workman is restricted, almost entirely, to the means of subsistence that he requires for maintenance, and for the propagation of his race. But the price of a commodity, and therefore also of labour, is equal to its cost of production. In proportion, therefore, as the repulsiveness of the work increases, the wage decreases. Nay more, in proportion as the use of machinery and division of labour increases, in the same proportion the burden of toil also increases, whether by prolongation of the working hours, by the increase of the work exacted in a given time or by increased speed of machinery, etc.

1.32) Modern Industry has converted the little workshop of the patriarchal master into the great factory of the industrial capitalist. Masses of labourers, crowded into the factory, are organised like soldiers. As privates of the industrial army they are placed under the command of a perfect hierarchy of officers and sergeants. Not only are they slaves of the bourgeois class, and of the bourgeois State; they are daily and hourly enslaved by the machine, by the overlooker, and, above all, by the individual bourgeois manufacturer himself. The more openly this despotism proclaims gain to be its end and aim, the more petty, the more hateful and the more embittering it is.

1.33) The less the skill and exertion of strength implied in manual labour, in other words, the more modern industry becomes developed, the more is the labour of men superseded by that of women. Differences of age and sex have no longer any distinctive social validity for the working class. All are instruments of labour, more or less expensive to use, according to their age and sex.

1.34) No sooner is the exploitation of the labourer by the manufacturer, so far, at an end, that he receives his wages in cash, than he is set upon by the other portions of the bourgeoisie, the landlord, the shopkeeper, the pawnbroker, etc.

1.35) The lower strata of the middle class—the small tradespeople, shopkeepers, and retired tradesmen generally, the handicraftsmen and peasants—all these sink gradually into the proletariat, partly because their diminutive capital does not suffice for the scale on which Modern Industry is carried on, and is swamped in the competition with the large capitalists, partly because their specialised skill is rendered worthless by new methods of production. Thus the proletariat is recruited from all classes of the population.

1.36) The proletariat goes through various stages of development. With its birth begins its struggle with the bourgeoisie. At first the contest is carried on by individual labourers, then by the workpeople of a factory, then by the operative of one trade, in one locality, against the individual bourgeois who directly exploits them. They direct their attacks not against the bourgeois conditions of production, but against the instruments of production themselves; they destroy imported wares that compete with their labour, they smash to pieces machinery, they set factories ablaze, they seek to restore by force the vanished status of the workman of the Middle Ages.

1.37)  At this stage, the labourers still form an incoherent mass scattered over the whole country, and broken up by their mutual competition. If anywhere they unite to form more compact bodies, this is not yet the consequence of their own active union, but of the union of the bourgeoisie, which class, in order to attain its own political ends, is compelled to set the whole proletariat in motion, and is moreover yet, for a time, able to do so. At this stage, therefore, the proletarians do not fight their enemies, but the enemies of their enemies, the remnants of absolute monarchy, the landowners, the non-industrial bourgeois, the petty bourgeois. Thus, the whole historical movement is concentrated in the hands of the bourgeoisie; every victory so obtained is a victory for the bourgeoisie.

1.38)  But with the development of industry, the proletariat not only increases in number; it becomes concentrated in greater masses, its strength grows, and it feels that strength more. The various interests and conditions of life within the ranks of the proletariat are more and more equalised, in proportion as machinery obliterates all distinctions of labour, and nearly everywhere reduces wages to the same low level. The growing competition among the bourgeois, and the resulting commercial crises, make the wages of the workers ever more fluctuating. The increasing improvement of machinery, ever more rapidly developing, makes their livelihood more and more precarious; the collisions between individual workmen and individual bourgeois take more and more the character of collisions between two classes. Thereupon, the workers begin to form combinations (Trades' Unions) against the bourgeois; they club together in order to keep up the rate of wages; they found permanent associations in order to make provision beforehand for these occasional revolts. Here and there, the contest breaks out into riots.

1.39)     Now and then the workers are victorious, but only for a time. The real fruit of their battles lies, not in the immediate result, but in the ever expanding union of the workers. This union is helped on by the improved means of communication that are created by modern industry, and that place the workers of different localities in contact with one another. It was just this contact that was needed to centralise the numerous local struggles, all of the same character, into one national struggle between classes. But every class struggle is a political struggle. And that union, to attain which the burghers of the Middle Ages, with their miserable highways, required centuries, the modern proletarian, thanks to railways, achieve in a few years.

1.40)     This organisation of the proletarians into a class, and, consequently into a political party, is continually being upset again by the competition between the workers themselves. But it ever rises up again, stronger, firmer, mightier. It compels legislative recognition of particular interests of the workers, by taking advantage of the divisions among the bourgeoisie itself. Thus, the ten-hours' bill in England was carried.

1.41)     Altogether collisions between the classes of the old society further, in many ways, the course of development of the proletariat. The bourgeoisie finds itself involved in a constant battle. At first with the aristocracy; later on, with those portions of the bourgeoisie itself, whose interests have become antagonistic to the progress of industry; at all time with the bourgeoisie of foreign countries. In all these battles, it sees itself compelled to appeal to the proletariat, to ask for help, and thus, to drag it into the political arena. The bourgeoisie itself, therefore, supplies the proletariat with its own elements of political and general education, in other words, it furnishes the proletariat with weapons for fighting the bourgeoisie.

1.42)  Further, as we have already seen, entire sections of the ruling class are, by the advance of industry, precipitated into the proletariat, or are at least threatened in their conditions of existence. These also supply the proletariat with fresh elements of enlightenment and progress.

1.43)  Finally, in times when the class struggle nears the decisive hour, the progress of dissolution going on within the ruling class, in fact within the whole range of old society, assumes such a violent, glaring character, that a small section of the ruling class cuts itself adrift, and joins the revolutionary class, the class that holds the future in its hands. Just as, therefore, at an earlier period, a section of the nobility went over to the bourgeoisie, so now a portion of the bourgeoisie goes over to the proletariat, and in particular, a portion of the bourgeois ideologists, who have raised themselves to the level of comprehending theoretically the historical movement as a whole.

1.44)  Of all the classes that stand face to face with the bourgeoisie today, the proletariat alone is a really revolutionary class. The other classes decay and go under* in the face of Modern Industry; the proletariat is its special and essential product.

1.45)  The lower middle class, the small manufacturer, the shopkeeper, the artisan, the peasant, all these fight against the bourgeoisie, to save from extinction their existence as fractions of the middle class. They are therefore not revolutionary, but conservative. Nay more, they are reactionary, for they try to roll back the wheel of history. If by chance, they are revolutionary, they are only so in view of their impending transfer into the proletariat; they thus defend not their present, but their future interests, they desert their own standpoint to place themselves at that of the proletariat.

---

* Moore renders 'vernommen' not as 'go under' but as 'finally disappear', giving credence to the misleading belief that Marx and Engels believed that only two classes would ultimately exist under capitalism. CM.

1.46)    The 'dangerous class', [*lumpenproletariat*] the social scum, that passively rotting mass thrown off by the lowest layers of the old society, may, here and there, be swept into the movement by a proletarian revolution; its conditions of life, however, prepare it far more for the part of a bribed tool of reactionary intrigue.

1.47)    In the condition of the proletariat, those of old society at large are already virtually swamped. The proletarian is without property; his relation to his wife and children has no longer anything in common with the bourgeois family relations; modern industry labour, modern subjection to capital, the same in England as in France, in America as in Germany, has stripped him of every trace of national character. Law, morality, religion, are to him so many bourgeois prejudices, behind which lurk in ambush just as many bourgeois interests.

1.48)    All the preceding classes that got the upper hand sought to fortify their already acquired status by subjecting society at large to their conditions of appropriation. The proletarians cannot become masters of the productive forces of society, except by abolishing their own previous mode of appropriation, and thereby also every other previous mode of appropriation. They have nothing of their own to secure and to fortify; their mission is to destroy all previous securities for, and insurances of, individual property.

1.49)    All previous historical movements were movements of minorities, or in the interest of minorities. The proletarian movement is the self-conscious, independent movement of the immense majority, in the interest of the immense majority. The proletariat, the lowest stratum of our present society, cannot stir, cannot raise itself up, without the whole superincumbent strata of official society being sprung into the air.

1.50)    Though not in substance, yet in form, the struggle of the proletariat with the bourgeoisie is at first a national struggle.

The proletariat of each country must, of course, first of all settle matters with its own bourgeoisie.

1.51) In depicting the most general phases of the development of the proletariat, we traced the more or less veiled civil war, raging within existing society, up to the point where that war breaks out into open revolution, and where the forcible overthrow of the bourgeoisie lays the foundation for the sway of the proletariat.

1.52) Hitherto, every form of society has been based, as we have already seen, on the antagonism of oppressing and oppressed classes. But in order to oppress a class, certain conditions must be assured to it under which it can, at least, continue its slavish existence. The serf, in the period of serfdom, raised himself to membership in the commune, just as the petty bourgeois, under the yoke of the feudal absolutism, managed to develop into a bourgeois. The modern labourer, on the contrary, instead of rising with the process of industry, sinks deeper and deeper below the conditions of existence of his own class. He becomes a pauper, and pauperism develops more rapidly than population and wealth. And here it becomes evident, that the bourgeoisie is unfit any longer to be the ruling class in society, and to impose its conditions of existence upon society as an over-riding law. It is unfit to rule because it is incompetent to assure an existence to its slave within his slavery, because it cannot help letting him sink into such a state, that it has to feed him, instead of being fed by him. Society can no longer live under this bourgeoisie, in other words, its existence is no longer compatible with society.

1.53) The essential conditions for the existence and for the sway of the bourgeois class is the formation and augmentation of capital; the condition for capital is wage labour. Wage labour rests exclusively on competition between the labourers. The advance of industry, whose involuntary promoter is the bourgeoisie, replaces the isolation of the labourers, due to competition, by the revolutionary combination, due to association. The development of Modern Industry, therefore, cuts from under its feet the very foundation on which the bourgeoisie produces and appropriates products. What the bourgeoisie therefore produces, above all, are its own grave-diggers. Its fall and the victory of the proletariat are equally inevitable.

## 2. Proletarians and Communists

2.1)    In what relation do the Communists stand to the proletarians as a whole?

2.2)    The Communists are not a special party in relation to the other working-class parties.

2.3)    They have no interests separate and apart from those of the proletariat as a whole.

2.4)    They do not set up any sectarian principles of their own, by which to shape and mould the proletarian movement.

2.5)    The Communists are distinguished from the other working-class parties by this only:

1.  In the national struggles of the proletarians of the different countries, they point out and bring to the front the common interests of the entire proletariat, independently of all nationality.
2.  In the various stages of development which the struggle of the working class against the bourgeoisie has to pass through, they always and everywhere represent the interests of the movement as a whole.

2.6)  The Communists, therefore, are on the one hand, practically, the most advanced and resolute section of the working-class parties of every country, that section which pushes forward all others; on the other hand, theoretically, they have over the great mass of the proletariat the advantage of clearly understanding the line of march, the conditions, and the ultimate general results of the proletarian movement.

2.7)  The immediate aim of the Communists is the same as that of all other proletarian parties: formation of the proletariat into a class, overthrow of the bourgeois supremacy, conquest of political power by the proletariat.

2.8)  The theoretical conclusions of the Communists are in no way based on ideas or principles that have been invented, or discovered, by this or that would-be universal reformer.

2.9)  They merely express, in general terms, actual relations springing from an existing class struggle, from a historical movement going on under our very eyes. The abolition of existing property relations is not at all a distinctive feature of communism.

2.10)  All property relations in the past have continually been subject to historical change consequent upon the change in historical conditions.

2.11)  The French Revolution, for example, abolished feudal property in favour of bourgeois property.

2.12)  The distinguishing feature of Communism is not the abolition of property generally, but the abolition of bourgeois property. But modern bourgeois private property is the final and most complete expression of the system of producing and appropriating products, that is based on class antagonisms, on the exploitation of the many by the few.

2.13)    In this sense, the theory of the Communists may be summed up in the single sentence: Abolition of private property.

2.14)    We Communists have been reproached with the desire of abolishing the right of personally acquiring property as the fruit of a man's own labour, which property is alleged to be the groundwork of all personal freedom, activity and independence.

2.15)    Hard-won, self-acquired, self-earned property! Do you mean the property of petty artisan and of the small peasant, a form of property that preceded the bourgeois form? There is no need to abolish that; the development of industry has to a great extent already destroyed it, and is still destroying it daily.

2.16)    Or do you mean the modern bourgeois private property?

2.17)    But does wage labour create any property for the labourer? Not a bit. It creates capital, *i.e.*, that kind of property which exploits wage labour, and which cannot increase except upon condition of begetting a new supply of wage labour for fresh exploitation. Property, in its present form, is based on the antagonism of capital and wage labour. Let us examine both sides of this antagonism.

2.18)    To be a capitalist is to have not only a purely personal, but a social position in production. Capital is a collective product, and only by the united action of many members, nay, in the last resort, only by the united action of all members of society, can it be set in motion.

2.19)    Capital is therefore not only personal; it is a social power.

2.20)    When, therefore, capital is converted into common property, into the property of all members of society, personal property is not thereby transformed into social property. It is only the social character of the property that is changed. It loses its class character.

2.21)  Let us now take wage labour.

2.22)  The average price of wage labour is the minimum wage, *i.e.*, that quantum of the means of subsistence which is absolutely requisite to keep the labourer in bare existence as a labourer. What, therefore, the wage labourer appropriates by means of his labour, merely suffices to prolong and reproduce a bare existence. We by no means intend to abolish this personal appropriation of the products of labour, an appropriation that is made for the maintenance and reproduction of human life, and that leaves no surplus wherewith to command the labour of others. All that we want to do away with is the miserable character of this appropriation, under which the labourer lives merely to increase capital, and is allowed to live only in so far as the interest of the ruling class requires it.

2.23)  In bourgeois society, living labour is but a means to increase accumulated labour. In Communist society, accumulated labour is but a means to widen, to enrich, to promote the existence of the labourer.

2.24)  In bourgeois society, therefore, the past dominates the present; in Communist society, the present dominates the past. In bourgeois society capital is independent and has individuality, while the living person is dependent and has no individuality.

2.25)  And the abolition of this state of things is called by the bourgeois, abolition of individuality and freedom! And rightly so. The abolition of bourgeois individuality, bourgeois independence, and bourgeois freedom is undoubtedly aimed at.

2.26)   By freedom is meant, under the present bourgeois conditions of production, free trade, free selling and buying.

2.27)   But if selling and buying disappears, free selling and buying disappears also. This talk about free selling and buying, and all the other 'brave words' of our bourgeois about freedom in general, have a meaning, if any, only in contrast with restricted selling and buying, with the fettered traders of the Middle Ages, but have no meaning when opposed to the Communistic abolition of buying and selling, of the bourgeois conditions of production, and of the bourgeoisie itself.

2.28)   You are horrified at our intending to do away with private property. But in your existing society, private property is already done away with for nine-tenths of the population; its existence for the few is solely due to its non-existence in the hands of those nine-tenths. You reproach us, therefore, with intending to do away with a form of property, the necessary condition for whose existence is the non-existence of any property for the immense majority of society.

2.29)   In one word, you reproach us with intending to do away with your property. Precisely so; that is just what we intend.

2.30)   From the moment when labour can no longer be converted into capital, money, or rent, into a social power capable of being monopolised, *i.e.*, from the moment when individual property can no longer be transformed into bourgeois property, into capital, from that moment, you say, individuality vanishes.

2.31)   You must, therefore, confess that by 'individual' you mean no other person than the bourgeois, than the middle-class owner of property. This person must, indeed, be swept out of the way, and made impossible.

2.32)   Communism deprives no man of the power to appropriate the products of society; all that it does is to deprive him of the power to subjugate the labour of others by means of such appropriations.

2.33)   It has been objected that upon the abolition of private property, all work will cease, and universal laziness will overtake us.

2.34)   According to this, bourgeois society ought long ago to have gone to the dogs through sheer idleness; for those of its members who work, acquire nothing, and those who acquire anything do not work. The whole of this objection is but another expression of the tautology: that there can no longer be any wage labour when there is no longer any capital.

2.35)   All objections urged against the Communistic mode of producing and appropriating material products, have, in the same way, been urged against the Communistic mode of producing and appropriating intellectual products. Just as, to the bourgeois, the disappearance of class property is the disappearance of production itself, so the disappearance of class culture is to him identical with the disappearance of all culture.

2.36)   That culture, the loss of which he laments, is, for the enormous majority, a mere training to act as a machine.

2.37)   But don't wrangle with us so long as you apply, to our intended abolition of bourgeois property, the standard of your bourgeois notions of freedom, culture, law, &c. Your very ideas are but the outgrowth of the conditions of your bourgeois production and bourgeois property, just as your jurisprudence is but the will of your class made into a law for all, a will whose essential character and direction are determined by the economical conditions of existence of your class.

2.38) The selfish misconception that induces you to transform into eternal laws of nature and of reason, the social forms springing from your present mode of production and form of property— historical relations that rise and disappear in the progress of production—this misconception you share with every ruling class that has preceded you. What you see clearly in the case of ancient property, what you admit in the case of feudal property, you are of course forbidden to admit in the case of your own bourgeois form of property.

2.39) Abolition [*Aufhebung*] of the family! Even the most radical flare up at this infamous proposal of the Communists.

2.40) On what foundation is the present family, the bourgeois family, based? On capital, on private gain. In its completely developed form, this family exists only among the bourgeoisie. But this state of things finds its complement in the practical absence of the family among the proletarians, and in public prostitution.

2.41) The bourgeois family will vanish as a matter of course when its complement vanishes, and both will vanish with the vanishing of capital.

2.42) Do you charge us with wanting to stop the exploitation of children by their parents? To this crime we plead guilty.

2.43) But, you say, we destroy the most hallowed of relations, when we replace home education by social.

2.44) And your education! Is not that also social, and determined by the social conditions under which you educate, by the intervention, direct or indirect, of society, by means of schools, &c.? The Communists have not invented the intervention of society in education; they do but seek to alter the character of that intervention, and to rescue education from the influence of the ruling class.

2.45)    The bourgeois clap-trap about the family and education, about the hallowed co-relation of parents and child, becomes all the more disgusting, the more, by the action of Modern Industry, all the family ties among the proletarians are torn asunder, and their children transformed into simple articles of commerce and instruments of labour.

2.46)    But you Communists would introduce community of women, screams the bourgeoisie in chorus.

2.47)    The bourgeois sees his wife a mere instrument of production. He hears that the instruments of production are to be exploited in common, and, naturally, can come to no other conclusion that the lot of being common to all will likewise fall to the women.

2.48)    He has not even a suspicion that the real point aimed at is to do away with the status of women as mere instruments of production.

2.49)    For the rest, nothing is more ridiculous than the virtuous indignation of our bourgeois at the community of women which, they pretend, is to be openly and officially established by the Communists. The Communists have no need to introduce community of women; it has existed almost from time immemorial.

2.50)    Our bourgeois, not content with having wives and daughters of their proletarians at their disposal, not to speak of common prostitutes, take the greatest pleasure in seducing each other's wives.

2.51) Bourgeois marriage is, in reality, a system of wives in common and thus, at the most, what the Communists might possibly be reproached with is that they desire to introduce, in substitution for a hypocritically concealed, an openly legalised community of women. For the rest, it is self-evident that the abolition of the present system of production must bring with it the abolition of the community of women springing from that system, *i.e.*, of prostitution both public and private.

2.52) The Communists are further reproached with desiring to abolish countries and nationality.

2.53) The workers have no country. We cannot take from them what they have not got. Since the proletariat must first of all acquire political supremacy, must rise to be the leading class of the nation, must constitute itself *the* nation, it is, so far, itself national, though not in the bourgeois sense of the word.

2.54) National differences and antagonism between peoples are daily more and more vanishing, owing to the development of the bourgeoisie, to freedom of commerce, to the world market, to uniformity in the mode of production and in the conditions of life corresponding thereto.

2.55) The supremacy of the proletariat will cause them to vanish still faster. United action, of the leading civilised countries at least, is one of the first conditions for the emancipation of the proletariat.

2.56) In proportion as the exploitation of one individual by another will also be put an end to, the exploitation of one nation by another will also be put an end to. In proportion as the antagonism between classes within the nation vanishes, the hostility of one nation to another will come to an end.

2.57)  The charges against Communism made from a religious, a philosophical and, generally, from an ideological standpoint, are not deserving of serious examination.

2.58)  Does it require deep intuition to comprehend that man's ideas, views, and conception, in one word, man's consciousness, changes with every change in the conditions of his material existence, in his social relations and in his social life?

2.59)  What else does the history of ideas prove, than that intellectual production changes its character in proportion as material production is changed? The ruling ideas of each age have ever been the ideas of its ruling class.

2.60)  When people speak of the ideas that revolutionise society, they do but express that fact that within the old society the elements of a new one have been created, and that the dissolution of the old ideas keeps even pace with the dissolution of the old conditions of existence.

2.61)  When the ancient world was in its last throes, the ancient religions were overcome by Christianity. When Christian ideas succumbed in the eighteenth century to rationalist ideas, feudal society fought its death battle with the then revolutionary bourgeoisie. The ideas of religious liberty and freedom of conscience merely gave expression to the sway of free competition within the domain of knowledge.

2.62)  'Undoubtedly,' it will be said, 'religious, moral, philosophical, and juridical ideas have been modified in the course of historical development. But religion, morality, philosophy, political science, and law, constantly survived this change.'

2.63)  'There are, besides, eternal truths, such as Freedom, Justice, etc., that are common to all states of society. But Communism abolishes eternal truths, it abolishes all religion, and all morality, instead of constituting them on a new basis; it therefore acts in contradiction to all past historical experience.'

2.64) What does this accusation reduce itself to? The history of all past society has consisted in the development of class antagonisms, antagonisms that assumed different forms at different epochs.

2.65) But whatever form they may have taken, one fact is common to all past ages, *viz.*, the exploitation of one part of society by the other. No wonder, then, that the social consciousness of past ages, despite all the multiplicity and variety it displays, moves within certain common forms, or general ideas, which cannot completely vanish except with the total disappearance of class antagonisms.

2.66) The Communist revolution is the most radical rupture with traditional property relations; no wonder that its development involved the most radical rupture with traditional ideas.

2.67) But let us have done with the bourgeois objections to Communism.

2.68) We have seen above, that the first step in the revolution by the working class is to raise the proletariat to the position of ruling class to win the battle of democracy.

2.69) The proletariat will use its political supremacy to wrest, by degree, all capital from the bourgeoisie, to centralise all instruments of production in the hands of the State, *i.e.*, of the proletariat organised as the ruling class; and to increase the total productive forces as rapidly as possible.

2.70) Of course, in the beginning, this cannot be effected except by means of despotic inroads on the rights of property, and on the conditions of bourgeois production; by means of measures, therefore, which appear economically insufficient and untenable, but which, in the course of the movement, outstrip themselves, necessitate further inroads upon the old social order, and are unavoidable as a means of entirely revolutionising the mode of production.

2.71)   These measures will, of course, be different in different countries.

2.72)   Nevertheless, in most advanced countries, the following will be pretty generally applicable.

1.  Abolition of property in land and application of all rents of land to public purposes.
2.  A heavy progressive or graduated income tax.
3.  Abolition of all rights of inheritance.
4.  Confiscation of the property of all emigrants and rebels.
5.  Centralisation of credit in the hands of the state, by means of a national bank with State capital and an exclusive monopoly.
6.  Centralisation of the means of communication and transport in the hands of the State.
7.  Extension of factories and instruments of production owned by the State; the bringing into cultivation of waste-lands, and the improvement of the soil generally in accordance with a common plan.
8.  Equal liability of all to work. Establishment of industrial armies, especially for agriculture.
9.  Combination of agriculture with manufacturing industries; gradual abolition of all the distinction between town and country by a more equable distribution of the populace over the country.

10. Free education for all children in public schools. Abolition of children's factory labour in its present form. Combination of education with industrial production, &c, &c.

2.73) When, in the course of development, class distinctions have disappeared, and all production has been concentrated in the hands of a vast association of the whole nation, the public power will lose its political character. Political power, properly so called, is merely the organised power of one class for oppressing another. If the proletariat during its contest with the bourgeoisie is compelled, by the force of circumstances, to organise itself as a class, if, by means of a revolution, it makes itself the ruling class, and, as such, sweeps away by force the old conditions of production, then it will, along with these conditions, have swept away the conditions for the existence of class antagonisms and of classes generally, and will thereby have abolished its own supremacy as a class.

2.74) In place of the old bourgeois society, with its classes and class antagonisms, we shall have an association, in which the free development of each is the condition for the free development of all.

# 3. Socialist and Communist Literature

## 1. Reactionary Socialism

### A. Feudal Socialism

3.1) Owing to their historical position, it became the vocation of the aristocracies of France and England to write pamphlets against modern bourgeois society. In the French Revolution of July 1830, and in the English reform agitation, these aristocracies again succumbed to the hateful upstart. Thenceforth, a serious political struggle was altogether out of the question. A literary battle alone remained possible. But even in the domain of literature the old cries of the restoration period had become impossible.[*]

3.2)   In order to arouse sympathy, the aristocracy was obliged to lose sight, apparently, of its own interests, and to formulate their indictment against the bourgeoisie in the interest of the exploited working class alone. Thus, the aristocracy took their revenge by singing lampoons on their new masters and whispering in his ears sinister prophesies of coming catastrophe.

3.3)   In this way arose feudal Socialism: half lamentation, half lampoon; half an echo of the past, half menace of the future; at times, by its bitter, witty and incisive criticism, striking the bourgeoisie to the very heart's core; but always ludicrous in its effect, through total incapacity to comprehend the march of modern history.

3.4)   The aristocracy, in order to rally the people to them, waved the proletarian alms-bag in front for a banner. But the people, so often as it joined them, saw on their hindquarters the old feudal coats of arms, and deserted with loud and irreverent laughter.

3.5)   One section of the French Legitimists and 'Young England' exhibited this spectacle.

3.6)   In pointing out that their mode of exploitation was different to that of the bourgeoisie, the feudalists forget that they exploited under circumstances and conditions that were quite different and that are now antiquated. In showing that, under their rule,

---

[*] Not the English Restoration (1660–1689), but the French Restoration (1814–1830). [Engels, 1888 English edition.]

the modern proletariat never existed, they forget that the modern bourgeoisie is the necessary offspring of their own form of society.

3.7)　　For the rest, so little do they conceal the reactionary character of their criticism that their chief accusation against the bourgeois amounts to this, that under the bourgeois régime a class is being developed which is destined to cut up root and branch the old order of society.

3.8)　　What they upbraid the bourgeoisie with is not so much that it creates a proletariat as that it creates a *revolutionary* proletariat.

3.9)　　In political practice, therefore, they join in all coercive measures against the working class; and in ordinary life, despite their high-falutin phrases, they stoop to pick up the golden apples dropped from the tree of industry, and to barter truth, love, and honour, for traffic in wool, beetroot-sugar, and potato spirits.*

3.10)　　As the parson has ever gone hand in hand with the landlord, so has Clerical Socialism with Feudal Socialism.

3.11)　　Nothing is easier than to give Christian asceticism a Socialist tinge. Has not Christianity declaimed against private property, against marriage, against the State? Has it not preached in the place of these, charity and poverty, celibacy and mortification of the flesh, monastic life and Mother Church? Christian Socialism is but the holy water with which the priest consecrates the heart-burnings of the aristocrat.

---

* This applies chiefly to Germany, where the landed aristocracy and squirearchy have large portions of their estates cultivated for their own account by stewards, and are, moreover, extensive beetroot-sugar manufacturers and distillers of potato spirits. The wealthier British aristocracy are, as yet, rather above that; but they, too, know how to make up for declining rents by lending their names to floaters or more or less shady joint-stock companies. [Engels, 1888 English edition.]

## B. Petty-Bourgeois Socialism

3.12) The feudal aristocracy was not the only class that was ruined by the bourgeoisie, not the only class whose conditions of existence pined and perished in the atmosphere of modern bourgeois society. The medieval burgesses and the small peasant proprietors were the precursors of the modern bourgeoisie. In those countries which are but little developed, industrially and commercially, these two classes still vegetate side by side with the rising bourgeoisie.

3.13) In countries where modern civilisation has become fully developed, a new class of petty bourgeois has been formed, fluctuating between proletariat and bourgeoisie, and ever renewing itself as a supplementary part of bourgeois society. The individual members of this class, however, are being constantly hurled down into the proletariat by the action of competition, and, as modern industry develops, they even see the moment approaching when they will completely disappear as an independent section of modern society, to be replaced in manufactures, agriculture and commerce, by overlookers, bailiffs and shopmen.

3.14) In countries like France, where the peasants constitute far more than half of the population, it was natural that writers who sided with the proletariat against the bourgeoisie should use, in their criticism of the bourgeois régime, the standard of the peasant and petty bourgeois, and from the standpoint of these intermediate classes, should take up the cudgels for the working class. Thus arose petty-bourgeois Socialism. Sismondi was the head of this school, not only in France but also in England.

3.15) This school of Socialism dissected with great acuteness the contradictions in the conditions of modern production. It laid bare the hypocritical apologies of economists. It proved, incontrovertibly, the disastrous effects of machinery and division of labour; the concentration of capital and land in a few hands; overproduction and crises; it pointed out the inevitable ruin of the petty bourgeois and peasant, the misery of the proletariat, the anarchy in production, the crying inequalities in the distribution of wealth, the industrial war of extermination between nations, the dissolution of old moral bonds, of the old family relations, of the old nationalities.

3.16)    In its positive aims, however, this form of Socialism aspires either to restoring the old means of production and of exchange, and with them the old property relations, and the old society, or to cramping the modern means of production and of exchange within the framework of the old property relations that have been, and were bound to be, exploded by those means. In either case, it is both reactionary and Utopian.

3.17)    Its last words are: corporate guilds for manufacture; patriarchal relations in agriculture.

3.18)    Ultimately, when stubborn historical facts had dispersed all intoxicating effects of self-deception, this form of Socialism ended in a miserable fit of the blues.

## C. German or 'True' Socialism

3.19)    The Socialist and Communist literature of France, a literature that originated under the pressure of a bourgeoisie in power, and that was the expressions of the struggle against this power, was introduced into Germany at a time when the bourgeoisie, in that country, had just begun its contest with feudal absolutism.

3.20) German philosophers, would-be philosophers, and *beaux esprits* [men of letters], eagerly seized on this literature, only forgetting, that when these writings immigrated from France into Germany, French social conditions had not immigrated along with them. In contact with German social conditions, this French literature lost all its immediate practical significance and assumed a purely literary aspect. It was bound to appear to be idle speculation about the true society, about the realisation of the human nature. Thus, to the German philosophers of the eighteenth century, the demands of the first French Revolution were nothing more than the demands of 'Practical Reason' in general, and the utterance of the will of the revolutionary French bourgeoisie signified, in their eyes, the laws of pure Will, of Will as it was bound to be, of true human Will generally.

3.21) The work of the German *literati* consisted solely in bringing the new French ideas into harmony with their ancient philosophical conscience, or rather, in annexing the French ideas without deserting their own philosophic point of view.

3.22) This annexation took place in the same way in which a foreign language is appropriated, namely, by translation.

3.23) It is well known how the monks wrote silly lives of Catholic Saints *over* the manuscripts on which the classical works of ancient heathendom had been written. The German *literati* reversed this process with the profane French literature. They wrote their philosophical nonsense beneath the French original. For instance, beneath the French criticism of the economic functions of money, they wrote 'Alienation of Humanity', and beneath the French criticism of the bourgeois state they wrote 'Dethronement of the Category of the General', and so forth.

3.24)   The introduction of these philosophical phrases at the back of the French historical criticisms, they dubbed 'Philosophy of Action', 'True Socialism', 'German Science of Socialism', 'Philosophical Foundation of Socialism', and so on.

3.25)   The French Socialist and Communist literature was thus completely emasculated. And, since it ceased in the hands of the German to express the struggle of one class with the other, he felt conscious of having overcome 'French one-sidedness' and of representing, not true requirements, but the requirements of Truth; not the interests of the proletariat, but the interests of Human Nature, of Man in general, who belongs to no class, has no reality, who exists only in the misty realm of philosophical fantasy.

3.26)   This German socialism, which took its schoolboy task so seriously and solemnly, and extolled its poor stock-in-trade in such a mountebank fashion, meanwhile gradually lost its pedantic innocence.

3.27)   The fight of the Germans, and especially of the Prussian bourgeoisie, against feudal aristocracy and absolute monarchy, in other words, the liberal movement, became more earnest.

3.28)   By this, the long-wished-for opportunity was offered to 'True' Socialism of confronting the political movement with the Socialist demands, of hurling the traditional anathemas against liberalism, against representative government, against bourgeois competition, bourgeois freedom of the press, bourgeois legislation, bourgeois liberty and equality, and of preaching to the masses that they had nothing to gain, and everything to lose, by this bourgeois movement. German Socialism forgot, in the nick of time, that the French criticism, whose silly echo it was, presupposed the existence of modern bourgeois society, with its corresponding economic conditions of existence, and the political constitution adapted thereto, the very things those attainment was the object of the pending struggle in Germany.

3.29)  To the absolute governments, with their following of parsons, professors, country squires, and officials, it served as a welcome scarecrow against the threatening bourgeoisie.

3.30)  It was a sweet finish, after the bitter pills of flogging and bullets, with which these same governments, just at that time, dosed the German working-class risings.

3.31)  While this 'True' Socialism thus served the government as a weapon for fighting the German bourgeoisie, it, at the same time, directly represented a reactionary interest, the interest of German Philistines. In Germany, the *petty-bourgeois* class, a relic of the sixteenth century, and since then constantly cropping up again under the various forms, is the real social basis of the existing state of things.

3.32)  To preserve this class is to preserve the existing state of things in Germany. The industrial and political supremacy of the bourgeoisie threatens it with certain destruction—on the one hand, from the concentration of capital; on the other, from the rise of a revolutionary proletariat. 'True' Socialism appeared to kill these two birds with one stone. It spread like an epidemic.

3.33)  The robe of speculative cobwebs, embroidered with flowers of rhetoric, steeped in the dew of sickly sentiment, this transcendental robe in which the German Socialists wrapped their sorry 'eternal truths', all skin and bone, served to wonderfully increase the sale of their goods amongst such a public.

3.34)   And on its part German Socialism recognised, more and more, its own calling as the bombastic representative of the petty-bourgeois Philistine.

3.35)   It proclaimed the German nation to be the model nation, and the German petty Philistine to be the typical man. To every villainous meanness of this model man, it gave a hidden, higher, Socialistic interpretation, the exact contrary of its real character. It went to the extreme length of directly opposing the 'brutally destructive' tendency of Communism, and of proclaiming its supreme and impartial contempt of all class struggles. With very few exceptions, all the so-called Socialist and Communist publications that now [1847] circulate in Germany belong to the domain of this foul and enervating literature.*

## 2. Conservative or Bourgeois Socialism

3.36)   A part of the bourgeoisie is desirous of redressing social grievances in order to secure the continued existence of bourgeois society.

3.37)   To this section belong economists, philanthropists, humanitarians, improvers of the condition of the working class, organisers of charity, members of societies for the prevention of cruelty to animals, temperance fanatics, hole-and-corner reformers of every imaginable kind. This form of socialism has, moreover, been worked out into complete systems.

3.38)   We may cite Proudhon's *Philosophie de la Misère* as an example of this form.

---

* The revolutionary storm of 1848 swept away this whole shabby tendency and cured its protagonists of the desire to dabble in socialism. The chief representative and classical type of this tendency is Mr Karl Gruen. [Engels, 1890 German edition.]

3.39) The Socialistic bourgeois want all the advantages of modern social conditions without the struggles and dangers necessarily resulting therefrom. They desire the existing state of society, minus its revolutionary and disintegrating elements. They wish for a bourgeoisie without a proletariat. The bourgeoisie naturally conceives the world in which it is supreme to be the best; and bourgeois Socialism develops this comfortable conception into various more or less complete systems. In requiring the proletariat to carry out such a system, and thereby to march straightway into the social New Jerusalem, it but requires in reality, that the proletariat should remain within the bounds of existing society, but should cast away all its hateful ideas concerning the bourgeoisie.

3.40) A second, and more practical, but less systematic, form of this Socialism sought to depreciate every revolutionary movement in the eyes of the working class by showing that no mere political reform, but only a change in the material conditions of existence, in economical relations, could be of any advantage to them. By changes in the material conditions of existence, this form of Socialism, however, by no means understands abolition of the bourgeois relations of production, an abolition that can be affected only by a revolution, but administrative reforms, based on the continued existence of these relations; reforms, therefore, that in no respect affect the relations between capital and labour, but, at the best, lessen the cost, and simplify the administrative work, of bourgeois government.

3.41) Bourgeois Socialism attains adequate expression when, and only when, it becomes a mere figure of speech.

3.42) Free trade: for the benefit of the working class. Protective duties: for the benefit of the working class. Prison Reform: for the benefit of the working class. This is the last word and the only seriously meant word of bourgeois socialism.

3.43)　It is summed up in the phrase: the bourgeois is a bourgeois—for the benefit of the working class.

## 3.　Critical-Utopian Socialism and Communism

3.44)　We do not here refer to that literature which, in every great modern revolution, has always given voice to the demands of the proletariat, such as the writings of Babeuf and others.

3.45)　The first direct attempts of the proletariat to attain its own ends, made in times of universal excitement, when feudal society was being overthrown, necessarily failed, owing to the then undeveloped state of the proletariat, as well as to the absence of the economic conditions for its emancipation, conditions that had yet to be produced, and could be produced by the impending bourgeois epoch alone. The revolutionary literature that accompanied these first movements of the proletariat had necessarily a reactionary character. It inculcated universal asceticism and social levelling in its crudest form.

3.46)　The Socialist and Communist systems, properly so called, those of Saint-Simon, Fourier, Owen, and others, spring into existence in the early undeveloped period, described above, of the struggle between proletariat and bourgeoisie (see Section I. Bourgeois and Proletarians).

3.47)　The founders of these systems see, indeed, the class antagonisms, as well as the action of the decomposing elements in the prevailing form of society. But the proletariat, as yet in its infancy, offers to them the spectacle of a class without any historical initiative or any independent political movement.

3.48) Since the development of class antagonism keeps even pace with the development of industry, the economic situation, as they find it, does not as yet offer to them the material conditions for the emancipation of the proletariat. They therefore search after a new social science, after new social laws, that are to create these conditions.

3.49) Historical action is to yield to their personal inventive action; historically created conditions of emancipation to fantastic ones; and the gradual, spontaneous class organisation of the proletariat to an organisation of society especially contrived by these inventors. Future history resolves itself, in their eyes, into the propaganda and the practical carrying out of their social plans.

3.50) In the formation of their plans, they are conscious of caring chiefly for the interests of the working class, as being the most suffering class. Only from the point of view of being the most suffering class does the proletariat exist for them.

3.51) The undeveloped state of the class struggle, as well as their own circumstances,* causes Socialists of this kind to consider themselves far superior to all class antagonisms. They want to improve the condition of every member of society, even that of the most favoured. Hence, they habitually appeal to society at large, without the distinction of class; nay, by preference, to the ruling class. For how can people, when once they understand their system, fail to see in it the best possible plan of the best possible state of society?

3.52) Hence, they reject all political, and especially all revolutionary, action; they wish to attain their ends by peaceful means,

---

* Moore renders 'Lebenslage' 'surroundings' but I follow other translators who have, more accurately, opted for 'position in life', 'social status' or 'circumstances in life'. CM.

necessarily doomed to failure, and by the force of example, to pave the way for the new social Gospel.

3.53) Such fantastic pictures of future society, painted at a time when the proletariat is still in a very undeveloped state and has but a fantastic conception of its own position, correspond with the first instinctive yearnings of that class for a general reconstruction of society.

3.54) But these Socialist and Communist publications contain also a critical element. They attack every principle of existing society. Hence, they are full of the most valuable materials for the enlightenment of the working class. The practical measures proposed in them—such as the abolition of the distinction between town and country, of the family, of the carrying on of industries for the account of private individuals, and of the wage system, the proclamation of social harmony, the conversion of the function of the state into a more superintendence of production—all these proposals point solely to the disappearance of class antagonisms which were, at that time, only just cropping up, and which, in these publications, are recognised in their earliest indistinct and undefined forms only. These proposals, therefore, are of a purely Utopian character.

3.55) The significance of Critical-Utopian Socialism and Communism bears an inverse relation to historical development. In proportion as the modern class struggle develops and takes definite shape, this fantastic standing apart from the contest, these fantastic attacks on it, lose all practical value and all theoretical justification. Therefore, although the originators of these systems were, in many respects, revolutionary, their disciples have, in every case, formed mere reactionary sects. They hold fast by the original views of their masters, in opposition to the progressive historical development of the proletariat. They, therefore, endeavour, and that consistently, to deaden the class struggle and to reconcile the class antagonisms. They still dream of experimental realisation of their social Utopias, of founding isolated 'phalansteres', of establishing 'Home Colonies', or setting up a 'Little Icaria'*— duodecimo editions of the New Jerusalem—and to realise all these castles in the air, they are compelled to appeal to the feelings and purses of the bourgeois. By degrees, they sink into the category of the reactionary [or] conservative Socialists depicted above, differing from these only by more systematic pedantry, and by their fanatical and superstitious belief in the miraculous effects of their social science.

3.56) They, therefore, violently oppose all political action on the part of the working class; such action, according to them, can only result from blind unbelief in the new Gospel.

3.57) The Owenites in England, and the Fourierists in France, respectively, oppose the Chartists and the *Réformistes*.

## 4. Position of the Communists in Relation to the Various Existing Opposition Parties

4.1) Section II has made clear the relations of the Communists to the existing working-class parties, such as the Chartists in England and the Agrarian Reformers in America.

---

* *Phalanstéres* were Socialist colonies on the plan of Charles Fourier; *Icaria* was the name given by Cabet to his Utopia and, later on, to his American Communist colony. [Engels, 1880 English edition.]

'Home Colonies' were what Owen called his Communist model societies. *Phalanstéres* was the name of the public palaces planned by Fourier. *Icaria* was the name given to the Utopian land of fancy, whose Communist institutions Cabet portrayed. [Engels, 1890 German edition.]

4.2)   The Communists fight for the attainment of the immediate aims, for the enforcement of the momentary interests of the working class; but in the movement of the present, they also represent and take care of the future of that movement. In France, the Communists ally with the Social-Democrats* against the conservative and radical bourgeoisie, reserving, however, the right to take up a critical position in regard to phases and illusions traditionally handed down from the great Revolution.

4.3)   In Switzerland, they support the Radicals, without losing sight of the fact that this party consists of antagonistic elements, partly of Democratic Socialists, in the French sense, partly of radical bourgeois.

4.4)   In Poland, they support the party that insists on an agrarian revolution as the prime condition for national emancipation, that party which fomented the insurrection of Cracow in 1846.

4.5)   In Germany, they fight with the bourgeoisie whenever it acts in a revolutionary way, against the absolute monarchy, the feudal squirearchy, and the petty bourgeoisie.

4.6)   But they never cease, for a single instant, to instil into the working class the clearest possible recognition of the hostile antagonism between bourgeoisie and proletariat, in order that the German workers may straightway use, as so many weapons against the bourgeoisie, the social and political conditions that the bourgeoisie must necessarily introduce along with its supremacy, and in order that, after the fall of the reactionary classes in Germany, the fight against the bourgeoisie itself may immediately begin.

---

* The party then represented in Parliament by Ledru-Rollin, in literature by Louis Blanc, in the daily press by the *Réforme*. The name of Social-Democracy signifies, with these its inventors, a section of the Democratic or Republican Party more or less tinged with socialism. [Engels, English Edition 1888]

4.7) The Communists turn their attention chiefly to Germany, because that country is on the eve of a bourgeois revolution that is bound to be carried out under more advanced conditions of European civilisation and with a much more developed proletariat than that of England was in the seventeenth, and France in the eighteenth century, and because the bourgeois revolution in Germany will be but the prelude to an immediately following proletarian revolution.

4.8) In short, the Communists everywhere support every revolutionary movement against the existing social and political order of things.

4.9) In all these movements, they bring to the front, as the leading question in each, the property question, no matter what its degree of development at the time.

4.10) Finally, they labour everywhere for the union and agreement of the democratic parties of all countries.

4.11) The Communists disdain to conceal their views and aims. They openly declare that their ends can be attained only by the forcible overthrow of all existing social conditions. Let the ruling classes tremble at a Communistic revolution. The proletarians have nothing to lose but their chains. They have a world to win.

4.12) WORKERS OF ALL COUNTRIES, UNITE!

# Appendix B

## Preface to the 1872 German Edition

The Communist League, an international association of workers, which could of course be only a secret one, under conditions obtaining at the time, commissioned us, the undersigned, at the Congress held in London in November 1847, to write for publication a detailed theoretical and practical programme for the Party. Such was the origin of the following Manifesto, the manuscript of which travelled to London to be printed a few weeks before the February [French] Revolution [in 1848]. First published in German, it has been republished in that language in at least twelve different editions in Germany, England, and America. It was published in English for the first time in 1850 in the *Red Republican*, London, translated by Miss Helen Macfarlane, and in 1871 in at least three different translations in America. The French version first appeared in Paris shortly before the June insurrection of 1848, and recently in *Le Socialiste* of New York. A new translation is in the course of preparation. A Polish version appeared in London shortly after it was first published in Germany. A Russian translation was published in Geneva in the sixties. Into Danish, too, it was translated shortly after its appearance.

However much that state of things may have altered during the last twenty-five years, the general principles laid down in the Manifesto are, on the whole, as correct today as ever. Here and there, some detail might be improved. The practical application of the principles will depend, as the Manifesto itself states, everywhere and at all times, on the historical conditions for the time being existing, and, for that reason, no special stress is laid on the revolutionary measures proposed at the end of

Section II. That passage would, in many respects, be very differently worded today. In view of the gigantic strides of Modern Industry since 1848, and of the accompanying improved and extended organization of the working class, in view of the practical experience gained, first in the February Revolution, and then, still more, in the Paris Commune, where the proletariat for the first time held political power for two whole months, this programme has in some details become antiquated. One thing especially was proved by the Commune, viz., that 'the working class cannot simply lay hold of the ready-made state machinery, and wield it for its own purposes.' (See *The Civil War in France: Address of the General Council of the International Working Men's Association*, 1871, where this point is further developed.) Further, it is self-evident that the criticism of socialist literature is deficient in relation to the present time, because it comes down only to 1847; also that the remarks on the relation of the Communists to the various opposition parties (Section IV), although, in principle still correct, yet in practice are antiquated, because the political situation has been entirely changed, and the progress of history has swept from off the earth the greater portion of the political parties there enumerated.

But then, the Manifesto has become a historical document which we have no longer any right to alter. A subsequent edition may perhaps appear with an introduction bridging the gap from 1847 to the present day; but this reprint was too unexpected to leave us time for that.

Karl Marx & Frederick Engels
June 24, 1872, London

# Appendix C

## Preface to the 1882 Russian Edition

The first Russian edition of the Manifesto of the Communist Party, translated by Bakunin, was published early in the 'sixties by the printing office of the Kolokol [a reference to the Free Russian Printing House]. Then the West could see in it (the Russian edition of the Manifesto) only a literary curiosity. Such a view would be impossible today.

What a limited field the proletarian movement occupied at that time (December 1847) is most clearly shown by the last section: the position of the Communists in relation to the various opposition parties in various countries. Precisely Russia and the United States are missing here. It was the time when Russia constituted the last great reserve of all European reaction, when the United States absorbed the surplus proletarian forces of Europe through immigration. Both countries provided Europe with raw materials and were at the same time markets for the sale of its industrial products. Both were, therefore, in one way of another, pillars of the existing European system.

How very different today. Precisely European immigration fitted North American for a gigantic agricultural production, whose competition is shaking the very foundations of European landed property—large and small. At the same time, it enabled the United States to exploit its tremendous industrial resources with an energy and on a scale that must shortly break the industrial monopoly of Western Europe, and especially of England, existing up to now. Both circumstances react in a revolutionary manner upon America itself. Step by step, the small and middle land ownership of the farmers, the basis of the whole political constitution, is succumbing to the competition of giant farms; at the same time, a mass industrial proletariat and a fabulous concentration of capital funds are developing for the first time in the industrial regions.

And now Russia! During the Revolution of 1848–9, not only the European princes, but the European bourgeois as well, found their only salvation from the proletariat just beginning to awaken in Russian intervention. The Tsar was proclaimed the chief of European reaction. Today, he is a prisoner of war of the revolution in Gatchina*, and Russia forms the vanguard of revolutionary action in Europe.

The Communist Manifesto had, as its object, the proclamation of the inevitable impending dissolution of modern bourgeois property. But in Russia we find, face-to-face with the rapidly flowering capitalist swindle and bourgeois property, just beginning to develop, more than half the land owned in common by the peasants. Now the question is: can the Russian obshchina, though greatly undermined, yet a form of primeval common ownership of land, pass directly to the higher form of Communist common ownership? Or, on the contrary, must it first pass through the same process of dissolution such as constitutes the historical evolution of the West?

The only answer to that possible today is this: If the Russian Revolution becomes the signal for a proletarian revolution in the West, so that both complement each other, the present Russian common ownership of land may serve as the starting point for a communist development.

Karl Marx & Frederick Engels<br>January 21, 1882, London

---

* A reference to the events that occurred in Russia after the assassination, on March 1, 1881, of Emperor Alexander II by Narodnaya Volya members. Alexander III, his successor, was staying in Gatchina for fear of further terrorism.

# Appendix D

## Preface to the 1883 German Edition

The preface to the present edition I must, alas, sign alone. Marx, the man to whom the whole working class of Europe and America owes more than to any one else—rests at Highgate Cemetery and over his grave the first grass is already growing. Since his death [March 14, 1883], there can be even less thought of revising or supplementing the Manifesto. But I consider it all the more necessary again to state the following expressly:

The basic thought running through the Manifesto—that economic production, and the structure of society of every historical epoch necessarily arising therefrom, constitute the foundation for the political and intellectual history of that epoch; that consequently (ever since the dissolution of the primaeval communal ownership of land) all history has been a history of class struggles, of struggles between exploited and exploiting, between dominated and dominating classes at various stages of social evolution; that this struggle, however, has now reached a stage where the exploited and oppressed class (the proletariat) can no longer emancipate itself from the class which exploits and oppresses it (the bourgeoisie), without at the same time forever freeing the whole of society from exploitation, oppression, class struggles—this basic thought belongs solely and exclusively to Marx.

I have already stated this many times; but precisely now is it necessary that it also stand in front of the Manifesto itself.

Frederick Engels
June 28, 1883, London

# Appendix E

## Preface to the 1888 English Edition

The Manifesto was published as the platform of the Communist League, a working men's association, first exclusively German, later on international, and under the political conditions of the Continent before 1848, unavoidably a secret society. At a Congress of the League, held in November 1847, Marx and Engels were commissioned to prepare a complete theoretical and practical party programme. Drawn up in German, in January 1848, the manuscript was sent to the printer in London a few weeks before the French Revolution of February 24. A French translation was brought out in Paris shortly before the insurrection of June 1848. The first English translation, by Miss Helen Macfarlane, appeared in George Julian Harney's *Red Republican*, London, 1850. A Danish and a Polish edition had also been published.

The defeat of the Parisian insurrection of June 1848—the first great battle between proletariat and bourgeoisie—drove again into the background, for a time, the social and political aspirations of the European working class. Thenceforth, the struggle for supremacy was, again, as it had been before the Revolution of February, solely between different sections of the propertied class; the working class was reduced to a fight for political elbow-room, and to the position of extreme wing of the middle-class Radicals. Wherever independent proletarian movements continued to show signs of life, they were ruthlessly hunted down. Thus the Prussian police hunted out the Central Board of the Communist League, then located in Cologne. The members were arrested and, after eighteen months' imprisonment, they were tried in

October 1852. This celebrated 'Cologne Communist Trial' lasted from October 4 till November 12; seven of the prisoners were sentenced to terms of imprisonment in a fortress, varying from three to six years. Immediately after the sentence, the League was formally dissolved by the remaining members. As to the Manifesto, it seemed henceforth doomed to oblivion.

When the European workers had recovered sufficient strength for another attack on the ruling classes, the International Working Men's Association sprang up. But this association, formed with the express aim of welding into one body the whole militant proletariat of Europe and America, could not at once proclaim the principles laid down in the Manifesto. The International was bound to have a programme broad enough to be acceptable to the English trade unions, to the followers of Proudhon in France, Belgium, Italy, and Spain, and to the Lassalleans in Germany.[*]

Marx, who drew up this programme to the satisfaction of all parties, entirely trusted to the intellectual development of the working class, which was sure to result from combined action and mutual discussion. The very events and vicissitudes in the struggle against capital, the defeats even more than the victories, could not help bringing home to men's minds the insufficiency of their various favorite nostrums, and preparing the way for a more complete insight into the true conditions for working-class emancipation. And Marx was right. The International, on its breaking in 1874, left the workers quite different men from what it found them in 1864. Proudhonism in France, Lassalleanism in Germany, were dying out, and even the conservative English trade unions, though most of them had long since severed their connection with the International, were gradually

---

[*] Lassalle personally, to us, always acknowledged himself to be a disciple of Marx, and, as such, stood on the ground of the Manifesto. But in his first public agitation, 1862–1864, he did not go beyond demanding co-operative workshops supported by state credit.

advancing towards that point at which, last year at Swansea, their president [W. Bevan] could say in their name: 'Continental socialism has lost its terror for us.' In fact, the principles of the Manifesto had made considerable headway among the working men of all countries.

The Manifesto itself came thus to the front again. Since 1850, the German text had been reprinted several times in Switzerland, England, and America. In 1872, it was translated into English in New York, where the translation was published in *Woorhull and Claflin's Weekly*. From this English version, a French one was made in *Le Socialiste* of New York. Since then, at least two more English translations, more or less mutilated, have been brought out in America, and one of them has been reprinted in England. The first Russian translation, made by Bakunin, was published at Herzen's Kolokol office in Geneva, about 1863; a second one, by the heroic Vera Zasulich, also in Geneva, in 1882. A new Danish edition is to be found in *Socialdemokratisk Bibliothek*, Copenhagen, 1885; a fresh French translation in *Le Socialiste*, Paris, 1886. From this latter, a Spanish version was prepared and published in Madrid, 1886. The German reprints are not to be counted; there have been twelve altogether at the least. An Armenian translation, which was to be published in Constantinople some months ago, did not see the light, I am told, because the publisher was afraid of bringing out a book with the name of Marx on it, while the translator declined to call it his own production. Of further translations into other languages I have heard but had not seen. Thus the history of the Manifesto reflects the history of the modern working-class movement; at present, it is doubtless the most wide spread, the most international production of all socialist literature, the common platform acknowledged by millions of working men from Siberia to California.

Yet, when it was written, we could not have called it a *socialist* manifesto. By Socialists, in 1847, were understood, on the one hand the adherents of the various Utopian systems: Owenites in England, Fourierists in France, both of them already reduced to the position of mere sects, and gradually dying out; on the other hand, the most multifarious social quacks who, by all manner of tinkering, professed to redress, without any danger to capital and profit, all sorts of social grievances, in both cases men outside the working-class movement, and looking rather to the 'educated' classes for support. Whatever portion of the working class had become convinced of the insufficiency of mere political revolutions, and had proclaimed the necessity of total social change, called itself Communist. It was a crude, rough-hewn, purely instinctive sort of communism; still, it touched the cardinal point and was powerful enough amongst the working class to produce the Utopian communism of Cabet in France, and of Weitling in Germany. Thus, in 1847, socialism was a middle-class movement, communism a working-class movement. Socialism was, on the Continent at least, 'respectable'; communism was the very opposite. And as our notion, from the very beginning, was that 'the emancipation of the workers must be the act of the working class itself,' there could be no doubt as to which of the two names we must take. Moreover, we have, ever since, been far from repudiating it.

The Manifesto being our joint production, I consider myself bound to state that the fundamental proposition which forms the nucleus belongs to Marx. That proposition is: That in every historical epoch, the prevailing mode of economic production and exchange, and the social organisation necessarily following from it, form the basis upon which it is built up, and from which alone can be explained the political and intellectual history of that epoch; that consequently the whole history of mankind (since the dissolution of primitive tribal society, holding land in common ownership) has been a history of class struggles, contests between exploiting and exploited, ruling and oppressed classes; That the history of these class struggles forms a series of evolutions in which, nowadays, a stage has been reached where the exploited and oppressed class—the proletariat—cannot attain its emancipation from the sway of the exploiting and ruling class—the bourgeoisie—without, at the same time, and once and for all, emancipating society at large from all exploitation, oppression, class distinction, and class struggles.

This proposition, which, in my opinion, is destined to do for history what Darwin's theory has done for biology, we both of us, had been gradually approaching for some years before 1845. How far I had independently progressed towards it is best shown by my 'Conditions of the Working Class in England.' But when I again met Marx at Brussels, in spring 1845, he had it already worked out and put it before me in terms almost as clear as those in which I have stated it here.

From our joint preface to the German edition of 1872, I quote the following:

'However much that state of things may have altered during the last twenty-five years, the general principles laid down in the Manifesto are, on the whole, as correct today as ever. Here and there, some detail might be improved. The practical application of the principles will depend, as the Manifesto itself states, everywhere and at all times, on the historical conditions for the time being existing, and, for that reason, no special stress is laid on the revolutionary measures proposed at the end of Section II. That passage would, in many respects, be very differently worded today. In view of the gigantic strides of Modern Industry since 1848, and of the accompanying improved and extended organization of the working class, in view of the practical experience gained, first in the February Revolution, and then, still more, in the Paris Commune, where the proletariat for the first time held political power for two whole months, this programme has in some details become antiquated. One thing especially was proved by the Commune, viz., that 'the working class cannot simply lay hold of ready-made state machinery, and wield it for its own purposes.' (See *The Civil War in France: Address of the General Council of the International Working Men's Association* 1871, where this point is further developed.) Further, it is self-evident that the criticism of socialist literature is deficient in relation to the present time, because it comes down only to 1847; also that the remarks on the relation of the Communists to the various opposition parties (Section IV), although, in principle still correct, yet in practice are antiquated, because the political situation has been entirely changed, and the progress of history has swept from off the Earth the greater portion of the political parties there enumerated.

'But then, the Manifesto has become a historical document which we have no longer any right to alter.'

The present translation is by Mr Samuel Moore, the translator of the greater portion of Marx's 'Capital.' We have revised it in common, and I have added a few notes explanatory of historical allusions.

Frederick Engels
January 30, 1888, London

# Notes

## Introduction

1. Eco, 2006, p. 23. For Martin Puchner, "[t]he *Communist Manifesto* influenced the course of history more directly and lastingly than almost any other text" (Puchner, 2006, p. 11). A. J. P. Taylor is no admirer of the *Manifesto*'s program, but he allows that, thanks to it, "everyone thinks differently about the politics and society, when he [sic] thinks at all" (Taylor, 1967, p. 7). For Aijaz Ahmad, "[o]ne can say without fear of refutation that the *Manifesto* has been more consequential in the actual making of the modern world than any other piece of political writing" (Ahmad, 1998, p. 12). For Terry Eagleton, "[v]ery few [texts] have changed the course of actual history" as has the *Manifesto* (Eagleton, 2018).

2. Seymour, 2020. See also Seymour, 2019. Most typically, from the right, the collapse of the Eastern Bloc is taken as proof of the *Manifesto*'s world-historical wrongness: "[I]n 1989, it abruptly became clear that the Specter was just that" (Malia, 1998, p. xxvi). By contrast, the same events can be and have been read by some as direct vindication of the *Manifesto* itself (see for example, Hodges, 1999, and, more obliquely, Callinicos, 1991). For an unedifying example of the stiff and deadening supposed fidelity of Stalinism to the *Manifesto*, see Adoratsky, 1938, where the document is deployed in dirge-like hagiography of Stalin ("The triumph of the ideas of the *Manifesto of the Communist Party* was secured by the brilliant perpetuators of the cause of Marx and Engels—Lenin and Stalin, and the Bolshevik Party led by them . . . In all spheres of the national economy of the U.S.S.R., in industry, agriculture and trade, the socialist system has won complete victory . . . The leadership of the Party of

Lenin-Stalin guarantees our forward advance to the building of complete communism", etcetera). The brilliant socialist scholar Hal Draper dismissed this grim artefact as "a consumer fraud" (Draper, 1994, p. 2).

3    See Ash Sarkar's prime-time televised exasperation with Piers Morgan on 12 July 2018, on ITV's *Good Morning Britain*.

4    Cf. Findlay, 2009, p. 23. "In arguing here for the need to read the *Manifesto*, I make two principal claims: for the need to read it for the first time as part of the education of any serious student of nineteenth-century British and European history, culture, and politics; and for the need for novices and experts alike to read it both *in* and *for* our times."

5    <www.oxfam.org/en/5-shocking-facts-about-extreme-global-inequality-and-how-even-it> (accessed November 4, 2020).

6    See, for example, <www.jacobinmag.com/2020/10/bolivia-coup-mas-evo-morales-elections-arce-anez> (accessed June 3, 2021).

7    The history of these various editions is covered with, as he teases himself, "unreasonable completeness" by Hal Draper (Draper, 1994). Draper draws on the pioneering work of Bert Andréas, a short translation of whose seminal book is available at Andréas, 2013.

8    Carver, 1998, p. 55. The whole essay is a fascinating investigation of the issues surrounding translation in general, and of a text already associated with a widely celebrated translation in particular.

9    Hobsbawm, 2012, p. 5.

10   Draper, 1994, p. 31. Draper also clarifies, however, that the authors were less favorably inclined when they encountered Macfarlane's text without knowing its provenance. Beyond the conscious imprimatur of the authors, substantively, various of Macfarlane's formulations that sound oddest to modern ears have eloquent defenders. See, for example, Black, 2014, pp. xxii–xxvi. For an intriguing example of the problems of translation, see the discussion of Jonathan Sperber's rendering of "Alles Ständische und Stehende verdampft" as "everything that firmly exists and all the elements of the society of orders evaporate," over the iconic "all that is solid melts into air," the better to indicate "the dissolution of hierarchical Prussian society by the steam-power of industry" (Evans, 2013). As one correspondent puts it, though "a lot more accurate than the elegant version it seeks to replace," Sperber's version is "well, frankly

hideous" (Jem Thomas, appended to Evans, 2013). Carver offers the definitely less hideous "everything feudal and fixed goes up in smoke."

11 Carver, 1998, p. 51.

12 This doesn't exhaust the possible approaches, of course. There are, for example, important discussions to be had over the *Manifesto*'s fascinating, if highly partial and flawed, approach to culture. These range beyond the remit here, but for perspicacious analyses of the *Manifesto*'s views on "world literature" and its trends, for example, see Ahmad, 2000, and Santucci, 2001.

### Chapter 1. On the *Manifesto* and the Manifesto Form

1 Perloff, 1984, p. 66.

2 Hanna, 2014.

3 Perloff, 1984, p. 65.

4 Indeed, there is a long history of accusing Marx of plagiarizing one or other of these documents. For a withering assessment of some such claims, see Draper, 1994, pp. 16–19. Harold Laski, in his 1948 introduction to the *Manifesto*, moots that Engels may have meant "half-conscious tribute to the memory of the Babouvian *Manifeste des Egaux*", the 1796 *Manifesto of Equals*.

5 Puchner, 2006, p. 11, p. 19, and, *passim*, pp. 11–61. This is a brilliant outline of the influences on *The Communist Manifesto*, and its influence on what came after. "The first revolutionary document to actually bear the title 'manifesto' was written . . . by the radicalized wing of the Puritan Revolution, the Levellers' 'A New Engagement, or, Manifesto' (1648). . . . [T]he word 'manifesto' or 'manifestation' begins to function as a center of gravity." Puchner, 2006, pp. 15–16.

6 Danchev, 2011, p. xxi.

7 Perloff, 1984, p. 76: "Marx and Engels had used boldface headings, capitals, numbered series, and aphorisms, set off from the text, so as to capture the reader's attention."

8 Danchev, 2011, p. xxi. See also Berman, 1983, p. 89.

9 Avineri, 1998.

10 See Perloff, 1984, p. 66. Marinetti's demand for "violence and precision" was, in part, a doomed attempt to break with the *Manifesto*'s radical past.

11 Silva, 1975, Núñez's translation. For other examinations of the style of the *Manifesto*, see Siegel, 1982.

12 Runciman, 2010, pp. 90–95.

13 Fleetwood, 2002, p. 211.

14 All texts are, to a degree, polyvocal, particularly all manifestos. *The Communist Manifesto* is vividly and particularly so. Whatever one thinks of his later trajectory, a useful formulation of generosity is in Kautsky, 1904, with its call for "a criticism . . . which does not limit itself to state how some sentences and turns no longer fit the case; . . . a criticism, furthermore, that endeavours to comprehend it and to comprehend also those sentences which today are obsolete, thus deriving new knowledge from them."

15 Hanna, 2014.

16 Danchev, 2011, p. xx.

17 "To read *The Communist Manifesto* as melodrama isn't to denigrate the work but to set it more accurately in its time." Lansbury, 1986, p. 5. See also Anker, 2015, for a reading of the *Manifesto* as a melodrama of a left-melancholic cast. Barker, 2016, is persuasive on the *Manifesto* as a kind of "dialectical Promethean" tragedy. On comedy, see Holt, 2011, p.19: "[I]n the *Communist Manifesto* Marx and Engels in effect argue that capitalism—the epoch of the bourgeoisie—*fictionalises* the world, turns all relations, material and social, spiritual and temporal, into fictional relations. More specifically, that fictionalisation is understood under— or rather *as*—the comic genre (as opposed to the tragic, the epic, or the lyric). With one vital difference: for Marx and Engels capital isn't humorous. The profound, metaphysical laughter that Bakhtin describes as a defining characteristic of medieval carnival is completely missing in capitalist carnival, which, as Marx and Engels say, drowns things in the icy waters of 'egotistical calculation'". In his otherwise useful discussion of Bertolt Brecht's attempt to translate the *Manifesto* into verse, Spaethling makes the frankly extraordinary claim that "[f]or the most part, the prose [of the *Manifesto*] is dry and academic, a brittle string of words" (Spaethling, 1962, p. 286). This is a bizarre and decidedly minority opinion. For a detailed discussion of Brecht's poem *qua* poem,

and a hugely admirable English translation thereof, see Suvin, 2020, pp. 62–78 and pp. 51–61.

18  Bosmajian, 2013, p. 180: "To a very great extent Marx uses rhetorical stylistic devices which rely for their effectiveness not so much on silent reading as on oral presentation." For an overview of some of the specific linguistic strategies deployed in the text, see Yelland, 1997.

19  Močnik, 2018, p. 498.

20  Puchner valuably develops J. L. Austin's famous theory of speech acts, which excluded theatre, by reference to Kenneth Burke's theory of "dramatism," to clarify how the *Manifesto* attempts to do what it does (Puchner, 2006, pp. 23–7). Also referring to Austin, Jason Barker points out that the final line of the text, "Workers of all countries, unite!" is in part a speech act, given that "there was no international *organization* of workingmen—i.e. no given, ready-made "public"—to whom this statement could have been addressed. Marx and Engels are aiming to bring into existence—precisely, to unify—the addressee—namely, the proletariat—through the act of uttering the statement" (Barker, 2016, p. 321).

21  From Plato's *Gorgias* at <www.gutenberg.org/files/1672/1672-h/1672-h.htm (accessed 28 January 2022).

22  Clews, 1964, p. 31.

23  Schwartz, 2016.

24  Bosmajian, 2013, p. 177. In and of itself, of course, this is no argument for or against the analytical rigour with which the rhetorical flair is accompanied.

25  Anderson, 1984, p. 97. See also Berman's winning response to Anderson, Berman, 1984.

26  Berman, 1983, p. 102.

27  Ibid. p. 91.

28  Anderson, 1984.

29  Gavin, 1989, p. 278, and pp. 275–8.

30  In Wilhelm Liebknecht's words, "Marx attached extraordinary value to pure correct expression and in Goethe, Lessing, Shakespeare, Dante, and Cervantes, whom he read every day, he had chosen the greatest masters. He showed the most painstaking conscientiousness in regard to purity

and correctness in speech" (quoted in Bosmajian, 2013, p. 175). We can quibble with the formulation of "purity" in language choice, but Marx's extreme attention on formulation is clear. Prawer draws attention to the echo-chamber nature of the text, its proliferating layers, its "images, from oral and written literature, from publishing, and from theatrical performance" (Prawer, 1978, p. 138).

31 As Gavin puts it, "Anderson invokes closure by simply asserting that at least some words *do* have a univocal meaning" (Gavin, 1989, p. 283).

32 "[T]here do not exist specific and uniquely semiotic texts . . . all texts contain semiotically relevant components." Broekman and Backer, 2015, p. 21.

33 For a brief discussion of this model, see <raptorvelocity.substack.com/p/the-vibrating-aboutness-cluster> (accessed 21 October 2020).

34 Silva, 1975. I am indebted to Paco Brito Núñez for his unpublished translation.

35 Martin, 2015, pp. 65–6. Elsewhere, Martin is more judicious, seeing logic and rhetoric as in collaboration in the *Manifesto*: "To be persuaded by such a document meant not simply to be reasoned with as an intellectual but also to be recruited to an authoritative and insistent stance from which a distinct political project could be envisaged" (pp. 65–6).

## Chapter 2. *The Communist Manifesto* in its Time

1 For the dual, or double revolution as a backdrop to *The Communist Manifesto*, see among others Struick, 1971, pp. 11–24, and Lamb, 2015, p. 3.

2 The intimate relation of these "new" ideas, and of the French Revolution itself, to early capitalism was important in the model of the *Manifesto*, and of most of the classical Marxist tradition. For an important and contrasting Marxist view, drawing on the seminal work of Robert Brenner and Ellen Wood, for which a failure of the *Manifesto* is intimately related to its failure to see that "[c]apitalism . . . played no part in the origin or the politics of the French Revolution," see Comninel, 2000. The broad sweep of this debate extends far beyond us, but it is worth making the following points. 1) In what follows, I follow more closely the classical Marxist position than Comninel's for reasons laid

out in Miéville, 2005, pp. 214–24, in a discussion of so-called "political Marxism." 2) Comninel himself is clear that irrespective of its relation to capitalism, liberalism and its contested political principles was key to the French Revolution. 3) Even disagreeing with the hard specifics of Comninel's claim, one can agree with his softer corollary that much of what is wrong with the *Manifesto* is due to Marx being "ahead of his time"—too enthused by the bourgeoisie, as we shall see, if not for the reasons Comninel outlines.

3 James, 1963, p. 48.

4 Bracketing its perfidy, the law of 1802 was not particularly successful.

5 For a brilliant deconstruction of the savagery inherent in liberalism, see Losurdo, 2011. For a discussion of the distinction, perhaps at times overly schematic but nonetheless extremely productive, of the "moderate" and "radical" wings of the enlightenment, see Israel, 2001.

6 There is debate about how directly Louverture was inspired by the radical wing of the Enlightenment, and whether his encounter with the Abbé Raynal's call for a "black Spartacus," so powerfully described by James, occurred (see Dubois, 2009, for a brief overview, and Høgsbjerg, 2010, for an argument in favor of the relationship between the black Jacobins and the Radical Enlightenment). What is more certain, per Louverture's letter, is that the slave revolt was framed in terms of such contested revolutionary notions as liberty (James, 1963, p. 149). Roos's poem is quoted scornfully by Anton de Kom in his extraordinary *We Slaves of Suriname* (de Kom, 2022, pp. 225–226, and in a different translation at p.118).

7 See Levin, 1998.

8 See, for example, Schmidt, 2020, p. 1,025.

9 Herres, 2015, p. 16.

10 For a careful examination of Hegel, arguing that the debates between "progressive" and "reactionary" readings of Hegel have obscured as much as they have illuminated, see Losurdo, 2004. See also <hegel.net/en/faq.htm#wasnt-hegel-a-lackey-of-the-prussian-monarchy>, among various invaluable discussions at that site (accessed June 7, 2021).

11 Callinicos, 1995, p. 21.

12  There were too those among them, crucially Feuerbach, for whom matters and the relationship to materialism were more complicated. See, for example, Wright, 1956.

13  See, for example, Wheen, 1999, p. 42. For the full text of Marx's exasperated article, see <marxists.architexturez.net/archive/marx/works/1842/free-press/ch06.htm> (accessed January 28, 2022).

14  Alcantara, 1996, p. 42.

15  As an old man who had clearly been faced with the misrepresentation countless times, Engels, with palpable irritation, countered that "if somebody twists this into saying that the economic factor is the *only* determining one he transforms that proposition into a meaningless, abstract, absurd phrase," stressed that "systems of dogma also exercise their influence upon the course of historical struggles and in many cases determine their *form* in particular," and underlines that, rather, for materialism, "the *ultimately* determining factor in history is the production and reproductions of real life" (Engels in a letter to Joseph Bloch, 1890. Online at <www.marxists.org/archive/marx/works/1890/letters/90_09_21.htm> (accessed February 16, 2022).)

16  From a letter to Feuerbach in August 1844, quoted in Callinicos, 1995 (p. 25), which includes a valuable brief overview of Marx's life, and his political development up to the publication of the *Manifesto* and beyond (see, for example, pp. 19–32), on which I draw here.

17  Marx, 1932.

18  For an invaluable introduction, see Eagleton, 2007.

19  Marx, 1968.

20  In Gasper, 2005, p. 143. These drafts are available at <www.marxists.org/archive/marx/works/1847/06/09.htm> and <www.marxists.org/archive/marx/works/1847/11/prin-com.htm> (accessed 7 June 2021).

21  For an invaluable and detailed look at the specifics of communism in the 1840s, see Stedman Jones, 2002, pp. 38–55.

22  Appendix E.

23  Ibid.

24  "In this militant text there is a strong emphasis on the cataclysmic character of the workers' revolution." Marković, 2013, p. 154.

25  See Toscano, 2021, for an invaluable overview of the development of communism.

26  See again Stedman Jones, 2014, pp. 38–54.

27  Leopold, 2015, p. 35.

28  For an interesting, if dated, overview of these utopian socialists, see Plekhanov, 1913. For Marx and Engels's familiarity with Considerant, for example, see Davidson, 1977.

29  Struick, 1971, p. 58, p. 60.

30  This is reproduced in Gasper, 2005, pp. 128–48.

31  Letter of 23–24 November 1847, quoted in Puchner, 2006, p. 20.

32  Available online at <marxists.architexturez.net/archive/marx/works/1842/cantos/index.htm> (accessed September 7, 2021). I'm grateful to Barnaby Raine for bringing this text to my attention.

33  F. Lessner, quoted in Struick, 1971, p. 61.

34  Struick, 1971, p. 61.

35  For invaluable overviews of the historical context of the writing of the *Manifesto*, see among others Beamish, 1998, Struick, 1971, Stedman Jones, 2019, Lamb, 2015, Herres, 2015, Bender, 2013.

36  This sets this book against the more reductive of a tenacious "Marx versus Engels" cottage industry in scholarship. This approach, if not without any perspicacities, is often devoted not only to pointing out the (uncontroversial) point that the two men did not always agree, nor on distinguishing their thought more systematically, nor even of counterposing them, but of validating the former as the real thinker against the supposedly crude latter. For an overview and critique of such approaches, if one that errs too far in the direction of dismissiveness and dichotomy, see Blackledge, 2020.

37  Rowson, 2018, p. 4. Rowson's book is a splendid and unlikely adaptation of the *Manifesto* into comic-book form.

38  Quoted at <www.speeches–usa.com/Transcripts/alexis_deTocqueville–gale.html>, and in Robenson, 2015, p. 14.

39  Draper, 1994, p. 14.

40  Clark, 2019.

41  Clark, 2019.

42 Fernbach, 2019, p. 32, and throughout, for an invaluable overview of
   Marx's relationship to, and activities during, the 1848 revolutions.

43 "The revolutions of 1848 represented the moment at which the struggle
   between capital and labour took on greater importance than that between
   the bourgeoisie and the old feudal landowning classes." Callinicos, 1995,
   p. 31.

44 Fernbach, 2019, pp. 37–46, and throughout.

45 Fennback, 1973, pp. 193–4.

46 Puchner, 2006, p. 33.

47 Draper, 1994, pp. 22–3.

48 Ibid. p. 27.

49 Ibid. p. 33: "As the last flickers of the revolutionary period guttered out, the
   *Communist Manifesto* too faded from view." See also Stedman Jones, 2014,
   pp. 19–37, for an invaluable overview of the reception of the *Manifesto*.
   "Between 1850 and 1870, the *Manifesto* was remembered by no more
   than a few hundred German-speaking veterans of the 1848 revolutions."
   (Stedman Jones, 2014, p. 23).

50 Carver, 2015, p. 68.

51 This group, often known as the First International, formally disbanded
   in 1876, but was effectively defunct from 1872. It was followed by the
   founding in 1889 of the Second International, a confederation of trade
   unions and left-wing—though by no means all communist—political
   parties. Its heir organization, the Socialist International, founded in
   1951, still exists, as a grouping of worldwide labor parties. The Third
   International, extant from 1919 to 1943, was an international grouping of
   parties affiliated to Russia's Communist Party, and was always dominated
   by the line from Moscow. Subsequently there have arisen—and remain—
   various Fourth Internationals, tiny groups of anti-Stalinist communists.

52 Draper, 1994, pp. 46–78.

53 Puchner, 2006, p. 38.

54 Ibid. p. 36, and see pp. 36–9. See also Trkulja, 2018, p. 642: "The
   attitude towards the *Manifesto* largely depended on the rise and fall
   of working-class and other emancipation movements in Europe and
   worldwide." For a specific local case of Italy, see Musto, 2008.

55 Hobsbawm, 2012, p. 6.

56 See Townshend, 2015, for the spread of the *Manifesto* since its publication, including its influence on "official" and "unofficial" Marxist currents. See also Farr and Ball, 2015, for the *Manifesto*'s intellectual influence, including on its enemies.

57 See Robinson, 2018, for a wry reminiscence on the commodification and marketing of the text.

58 *The Times* of September 11, 2008 reported a 700 percent increase in sales of the *Manifesto* on Amazon.com since the banking collapse.

59 Berman, 2001, p. 254.

60 Traverso, 2021, pp. 7–8.

## Chapter 3. An Outline of the *Manifesto*

1 This is how Terrell Carver translates the phrase "Märchen vom Gespenst" (in Carver and Farr, 2015, p. 237).

2 The comparison of communism to a ghost, and indeed its ambivalence, was not new to the *Manifesto*. "In Central Europe the image was almost commonplace in the late 1840s. For example, in the entry on 'Communism' . . . [for a liberal encyclopedia in 1846] the political economist Wilhelm Schulz noted that 'for a few years in Germany the talk has been about Communism. It has already become a threatening spectre that some fear and others use to strike fear.'" (Stedman Jones, 2014, p. 38.) Since the publication of Jacques Derrida's *Specters of Marx* in 1995, there has been an enormous resurgence of interest in, a veritable academic industry on, Derrida-and-Marx and the spectral dimensions of the *Manifesto* and of Marx's project more generally, under the rubric of Derrida's wincingly punning concept of haunted essence, "hauntology." For examples of a sympathetic and a considerably less sympathetic approach thereto, see Fisken, 2011, and Fowler, 2002, respectively. Fowler's attacks are swingeing, sometimes to the point of philistinism, and not nearly discriminate enough: see, for example, her grouping of Margaret Cohen's brilliant 1993 book *Profane Illumination* together with others she dismisses as "sub-scholarly speculations about the occult" (Fowler, 2002, p. 197). But there is no question that she is right that, for a substantial part of this theoretical current, "*explanation* of the irrational is replaced by *tabooed luxuriance* within it" (Fowler, 2002,

p. 197). For a spirited critique of Derrida's "hauntology" as predicated on a misunderstanding of the nature of the capitalist-spectral, see Thomas, 1998. For Carver, Derrida's figuration of "spectre" as "ghost" is a somewhat tendentious misreading, Marx and Engels's spectre not being something dead and returned, but an illusion, that "horror story," a "red scare" invoked by communism's enemies, which must be laid to rest so that communism itself can rise (Carver, 1998, p. 13).

3   Engels clarifies this in an important footnote to the 1888 English edition, reproduced here below 1.1 in Appendix A.

4   Lamb, 2015, p. 29: "By so presenting class struggle as the key feature of the process of history he [Marx] was, in effect, announcing to his proletarian readers and their representatives that activism would be required on their part."

5   Berman, 1983, p. 92.

6   Schumpeter, 1949, p. 209.

7   "It was only during the next fifteen years that some of the distinctive categories of Marxist economic analyses, such as the distinction between 'labour' and 'labour power,' or the shifting balance between absolute and relative surplus value in the history of capitalism, fully emerged" (Ahmad, 2000, p. 5).

8   Though at the time of writing, Engels was already of the opinion that sections of the peasantry and the lower middle classes might have interests in common with the workers. Marx joined him in this after the experience of the revolutions of 1848 (Gaspar, 2005, p. 55).

9   For general discussions of contemporary negative solidarity, though not ones that foreground the lumpenproletariat, see the discussions between Alex Williams, Jeremy Gilbert and Jason Read, at <splinteringboneashes. blogspot.com/2010/01/negative-solidarity-and-post-fordist.html>, <jeremygilbertwriting.wordpress.com/notes-towards-a-theory-of-solidarity/>, and <thenewinquiry.com/the-principle-of-our-negative-solidarity/> (accessed June 9, 2021).

10  I'm grateful to Matthew Beaumont for this point, and this discussion.

11  A more provocative, alternative riposte to this claim about the dangers of laziness, the dangers of which we have, in any case, no reason to believe, would be, Who cares? See, for the classic exposition of this anti-work

radicalism, Paul Lafargue's 1883 *The Right to be Lazy* at <www.marxists.org/archive/lafargue/1883/lazy/> (accessed October 26, 2020).

12  For an outstanding recent exploration of family-abolitionist communism, see Lewis, 2019. The *Manifesto* doesn't expand on this point, but the fact of such hypocrisy is systemically important. According to any rigorous system of historical materialism, ideas thrown up by and shoring up societies must encompass unspoken assumptions, conflicting and unconscious drives and desires, and disavowal of stated norms. Systemic hypocrisy, the wholesale breaching of stated norms, isn't a pathology, but constitutive of the morality so-breached. This conception of co-constitutive norms and their transgressions can be extended to a whole gamut of "ideals" which liberalism professes, and ritually transgresses.

13  Lamb, 2015, p. 75.

14  Hägglund, 2019, p. 34. See also p. 25: "The aim . . . is to decrease the realm of necessity and increase the realm of freedom by making the relation between the two a democratic question."

15  For a valuable gloss on this, the most opaque section to the modern reader, see Leopold, 2015.

16  Lamb, 2015, p. 87. "Christian socialism had merely provided solace to aristocrats who were ashamed of the exploitation they had once exerted."

17  Macfarlane, in her first English translation, rendered "petty bourgeoisie," memorably and poetically, if tendentiously, as "shopocrat."

18  See, for example, Draper, 1994, p. 293.

19  In 1890 Engels added a footnote describing "the chief representative and classical type of this tendency" as "Mr. Karl Gruen." (See the footnote to paragraph 3.35, Appendix A.)

20  Marx, 1937, p. 101.

21  See Lamb, 2015, p. 94 for a fascinating discussion of the True Socialist approach.

22  Draper, 1994, p. 293. "Instead of fighting bourgeois liberalism because it did not go far enough, they lent themselves and their radical reputations to a reactionary alternative to liberalism."

23  I have engaged with this discussion in Miéville, 2019a. Marx's diary remark about "cookbooks of the future" comes from an 1873 afterword to

*Capital* Volume 1, available (though in a less celebrated translation) here: <www.marxists.org/archive/marx/works/1867-c1/p3.htm> (accessed 28 January 2022).

24 Lamb, 2015, p. 112, for a fuller description of these groups.

25 See also Lamb, 2015, pp. 112–13.

26 See Cunliffe, 1982. Discussing debates about the compatibility of the German strategy outlined in the *Manifesto*, Cunliffe concludes that there is no necessary tension here, on the basis of understanding the *Manifesto*'s vision of "the universal interdependence of nations" as meaning "that the sufficient condition for a successful proletarian revolution in a country in which industrial capitalism is immature is a simultaneous and successful one in all countries in which industrial capitalism is mature" (p. 572). One can further nuance that by understanding "simultaneous" and "all," in his formulation, to have a fair degree of—though not infinite—elasticity. This discussion bears directly on the debate over the internationalisation of capitalism, what is called, in the Marxist tradition, "combined and uneven development," and the political strategies deriving from it, "permanent revolution," particularly with regard to "underdeveloped" countries. See, for example, Moss, 1998, Hoffman, 1998, Paxton, 1998, Saccarelli, 2015.

27 Draper, 1994, p. 270. "The general problem is that of revolutionary strategy immediately after a conquest of power: What . . . [these paragraphs] discuss is solely economic policy—the codicil added a basic political consideration."

28 Lamb, 2015, p. 120.

## Chapter 4. Evaluating the *Manifesto*

1 A classic starting point for the vast and sprawling debate among Marxists over the transition from feudalism to capitalism, bearing directly on the model outlined in the *Manifesto*, is Aston and Philpin, 1985.

2 In a letter to J. Weydemeyer of March 5, 1852.

3 For an introductory overview of the discussion of the dictatorship of the proletariat, see Bottomore (ed.), 1991, pp. 151–2. The article in which Weydemeyer introduces the term was published in New York, in *Turn-Zeitung*, on the first day of the year, 1852, and is available at <libcom.org/

library/dictatorship-proletariat-joseph-weydemeyer> (accessed October 28, 2020).

4  Draper, 2013, pp. 158–9. Šljutic, 2018, for example, wrongly claims that the *Manifesto* proclaimed a "death sentence" on the peasantry (p. 618).

5  George Will, <nypost.com/2015/03/25/why-inequality-can-be-beautiful/> (accessed 28 January 2022).

6  Fisher, 2010.

7  <www.ursulakleguin.com/nbf-medal> (accessed January 28, 2022).

8  See <www.theguardian.com/education/2020/sep/27/uk-schools-told-not-to-use-anti-capitalist-material-in-teaching> (accessed January 28, 2022). As Yanis Varoufakis has it, "Imagine an educational system that banned schools from enlisting into their curricula teaching resources dedicated to the writings of British writers like William Morris, Iris Murdoch, Thomas Paine even. Well, you don't have to. Boris Johnson's government has just instructed schools to do exactly that."

9  Saccarelli, 2015, p. 113.

10  Wright, 2015, p. 110.

11  Gasper, 2005, p. 89.

12  Löwy, 1998. The lesson for Marx and Engels, in Sebastian Haffner's words, was that "who wants the proletarian revolution first wants the bourgeois revolution that is spiritually already transcended and that he cannot really want" (quoted in Bronner, 2012, p. 149).

13  Compare the previous year, when in *The Poverty of Philosophy* Marx expressed a similar trajectory for the proletariat, the transformation of "the mass of the people" by "[e]conomic conditions" "into workers . . . The domination of capital has created for this mass a common situation, common interests. This mass is already a class as against capital, but not yet for itself. In the struggle . . . this mass becomes united, and constitutes a class for itself." Available online at <www.marx2mao.com/m&e/pp47.html> (accessed January 28, 2022).

14  Taylor, 1967, p. 32. This evidence-free jibe is particularly beneath Taylor.

15  This arithmetic model of oppression—class + race + gender + disability + sexual identity, etc.—is the very crudest version of what is sometimes called "intersectionality" theory, discussed below. Such theory is of

course not a single body of thought, and there are far more sophisticated, indispensably insightful versions.

16  Ahmad, 1998, p. 16.

17  This "negative universality of capitalist exploitation is converted into the positive universality of what Marx would elsewhere call the 'poetry of the revolution.'" Ahmad, 1998, p. 16.

18  Gasper, 2005, p. 101.

19  Boyer, 1998, pp. 155–6. This central importance to Engels's work is another reason to credit him as co-author.

20  Harvey, 1998, p. 60.

21  See Thatcher, 1998, pp. 65–6; Wilks-Heeg, 1998, pp. 127–8. Boyer, 1998 (p. 155) is persuasive that though workers' living standards were improving in the long term, they declined in the 1830s and 1840s, giving an immediate context of relative immiseration. For a paradigmatic exposition of the revisionist position, see Bernstein: "[T]he movement means everything for me and . . . what is *usually* called "the final aim of socialism" is nothing." Bernstein, 2013, p. 127. See Mandel, 2013, for the development of Marx's theory of wages in and after the *Manifesto*.

22  Gordon Brown, the ex-Labour leader in the UK, made a career in part of repeating the claim at regular intervals (see <www.theguardian.com/politics/2008/sep/11/gordonbrown.economy> (accessed October 28, 2020)).

23  Gasper, 2005, p. 101, develops this point. See Boyer, 1998, p. 155, for Engels's development of a boom-bust theory.

24  For a high-profile recent example see the claim of the Bridgewater CEO Bob Prince that we've "probably seen the end of the boom-bust cycle" at <www.bloomberg.com/news/articles/2020-01-22/bridgewater-co-cio-bob-prince-says-boom-bust-cycle-is-over> (accessed 28 October 2020).

25  Klein, 2007.

26  Toscano, 2012.

27  For one of the most unbearable and politically illiterate of an unbearable and politically illiterate genre, see Younger and Portnoy, 2018. "As a partner in a corporate advisory firm and a professor of law and finance, we are true believers in free-market capitalism . . . [b]ut we do believe the time is ripe for a rewrite of [the] *Manifesto*."

28 For this point, see, for example, Sassen, 2012, p. 198. For an overview of
Marxist approaches to "globalisation," in the wake of the *Manifesto*, see
Steger, 2015.

29 Ahmad, 2000. See also Löwy, 1998. It is clear that the authors see—and
are critical of—the *domination* involved in this proto-globalization, as
evidenced by their repeated use of the verb "compel" to describe how the
bourgeoisie accomplishes what it supposedly does, but "the brilliant—
and prophetic—analysis of capitalist globalization sketched out . . .
suffers from certain limitations, tensions, or contradictions. These do not
stem from an excess of revolutionary zeal, as most critiques of Marxism
contend, but, on the contrary, from an insufficiently critical stance in
regard to modern bourgeois/industrial civilization." Löwy, 1998, at
<monthlyreview.org/1998/11/01/globalization-and-internationalism>
(accessed January 28, 2022).

30 Dean, 2017, p. 6. Dean's focus on the *Manifesto*'s relevance in
contemporary capitalism is particularly valuable. For David Harvey,
similarly, today's system is one of "turbocharged capitalism" (Harvey,
2017, p. 134).

31 Lamb, 2015, p. 81.

32 Kiernan in Bottomore, 1991, p. 476.

33 Julian Wright calls it "a glimmer" (Wright, 2015, p. 115). Ernst Bloch
famously describes something akin to this sense as "anticipatory
consciousness," or "Not-Yet-Conscious" in *The Principle of Hope*, at
<www.marxists.org/archive/bloch/hope/introduction.htm> (accessed
January 28, 2022). For a rich discussion of the particular Blochian
future-oriented "Marxian uncanny" invoked, particularly, in the *Manifesto*
itself, see Beaumont, 2012, pp. 225–7. Chattopadhyay's suggestion
that the "essential ideas" concerning a post-revolutionary society "are
already found in the *Manifesto* in a condensed form" is only true at
such a very high level of abstraction (Chattopadhyay, 1998). Engels at
times begged Marx to lay out more systematically "the famous Positive,
what you 'really' want." I have outlined an argument for the rigor of
Marx's resistance to this, the importance of *not* thinking that the desired
outcome can be described, in Miéville, 2019a. In Blanqui's words, from
"The Sects and the Revolution," "Even the most clear-sighted among us

have only hazy premonition at best, passing and vague glimpses. Only the revolution, in clearing the terrain, will reveal the horizon, slowly lift the veil, and open up the routes, or rather the multiple paths, that lead to the new order." at <blanqui.kingston.ac.uk/texts/the-sects-and-the-revolution-19-october-1866> (accessed January 28, 2022).

34  Leys and Panitch, 1998, p. 24.

35  Fennbach, 2019, p. 1008.

36  From his 1886 preface to *Capital* Volume 1, available at <www.marxists.org/archive/marx/works/1867-c1/p6.htm> (accessed January 28, 2022).

37  From his introduction to Marx's *The Civil War in France*, available online at <www.marxists.org/archive/marx/works/subject/hist-mat/class-st/intro.htm> (accessed January 28, 2022).

38  See Schaff, 1973, pp. 265–8.

39  On the background of Marx's views in particular on parliamentary and peaceful moves towards socialism, see Hunt, 1984, and Moore, 1963. For one recent vision of a "class-struggle social democratic" to socialism, stressing the peaceful over the forcefully revolutionary, see, for example, Sunkara, 2019.

40  For a debate showing the modern salience of exactly these issues, see the exchange Tabor, 2019, Blanc, 2019, and Parkinson, 2019.

41  This, for example, was the broad trajectory in the early twentieth century of the Czech-Austrian Marxist Karl Kautsky, so towering a figure within the Marxist movement that his "renegacy" was shattering to his comrades and admirers. See, for example, Lenin's incandescent and clearly traumatised 1918 response, *The Proletarian Revolution and the Renegade Kautsky*.

42  D'Amato, 2010.

43  Poulantzas, 2008, p. 338.

44  See the debate between the more orthodox Marxist Henri Weber and Poulantzas in Poulantzas, 2018, p. 339, p. 353, for example. Weber stresses that he and his comrades "don't think that the state is a monolith which must be confronted and broken down exclusively from the outside," that they, too, believe in the slow, patient building up by any means of "hegemony" (normalizing ideas of workers' power, fundamentally

changing the terms of the debate, "shifting the Overton window," etc.), that "we undoubtedly have to fight for the extension of democracy rather than shouting 'elections are for fools' . . . [and] draw support from the internal divisions of the bourgeois state". But for all that he insists that "you have to take a stand" on the issue of whether or not such an approach is in and of itself "the transformation of capitalist society and the capitalist state into a socialist society and a workers state"—which he insists it does not. But, of course, Poulantzas doesn't claim it does either.

45 Poulantzas, 2008, p. 356.

46 "To talk of coordinating the internal struggle with the external struggle does not mean at all that we necessarily avoid talking about rupture. But it means recognizing that the revolutionary break does not inevitably occur in the form of a centralization of a counter-state confronting the state itself en bloc. It can pass through the state, and I think this is the only way it will happen at present." Poultanzas, 2018, pp. 340–41.

47 Klarman, 2016, pp. 611–12. The "frankly anti-democratic" description is from Caplan, 2017. It is Noam Chomsky who considers Klarman the gold standard text (Chomsky, 2020).

48 Ackerman, 2011.

49 See, for example, Perez, 2021.

50 See Miéville, 2017. It is worth mentioning that even Lenin, who insisted in *The State and Revolution* that the narrow range of circumstances Marx had identified in England, the US and the Netherlands as leaving the door open to peaceful transition were closed, was open for the briefest of moments, to that possibility in Russia, late in the revolutionary year itself (in "On The Tasks of the Revolution"). This door closed, yes. But even so intransigent a revolutionary as Lenin held that it had, exceptionally, opened in the first place. For a sour, uncomradely, tendentious example of leftist revolutionism-policing, see Brass, 2019, p. 191.

51 For an outstanding examination of certain dynamics of counter-revolution, see Allinson, 2022. See Neocleous, 1998, for clues about the social forces behind such reaction in the *Manifesto* itself.

52 Lukes, 2012, p. 119.

53 Selsam, 2013, p. 166.

54 Geras, 1989.

55  Ibid.

56  I draw here substantially on Lukes, 2012.

57  Lukes, 2012, p. 125.

58  Quoted in Lukes, 2012, p. 122.

59  Selsam, 2013, p. 170.

60  Ibid.

61  Selsam, 2013, p. 171.

62  The slogan is usually attributed to the great Rosa Luxemburg, who popularized it. Ian Angus is persuasive that it in fact originated not with her, nor with Engels, to whom she attributes it, but with Karl Kautsky. See Angus, 2014.

63  Selsam, 2013, p. 171.

64  Selsam, 2013, p. 169.

65  Engels is quoted in Selsam, 2013, p. 169.

66  One drive behind the honourable tradition of radical liberalism is precisely the disgust at the failure of actually existing liberalism to deliver on its promises: a fidelity, as Richard Seymour has put it in personal communication, to liberal *ideas*, as against the mainstream reactionary liberalism, with its fidelity to the liberal *state*.

67  Engels, 1947.

68  I draw here extensively from Lukes, 2012, p. 131, for whom "[w]hat underlies this explicit rejection of Recht—of the discourse and practice of social justice and rights—is their [Marx and Engels's] denial that the *condition* of Recht, or circumstances of justice, are inherent in human life."

69  <www.marxists.org/archive/marx/works/1875/gotha/cho1.htm> (accessed November 13, 2021).

70  Lukes, 2012, p. 126, p. 125.

## Chapter 5. Criticisms of the *Manifesto*

1  Gasper, 2005, p. 27. I draw extensively on Gasper, 2005, pp. 27–8 in this introductory section.

2  Quoted in Gasper, 2005, p.28.

3  For an excellent and generous recent diagnosis of this tendency, see Raine 2021.

4   See Miéville, 2017, pp. 306–15, for an overview of the Russian degeneration in particular.

5   For a useful brief and introductory overview of Stalinism from a critical socialist perspective, see Post, 2018.

6   See <www.cato.org/policy-report/january/february-2013/how-china-became-capitalist> (accessed June 19, 2021).

7   "If the *Communist Manifesto* was meant to liberate the proletariat, the *Manifesto* itself in recent years needed liberating from Marxism's narrow post-Cold War orthodoxies and exclusive cadres. It has been freed." Buttigieg, 1998.

8   Taylor, 1967, p. 42.

9   See, for example, Chryssis, 1998.

10  Runciman, 2010, p. 95.

11  Kemple, 2009, p. 51.

12  Ibid.

13  Townshend, 1998 (p. 187) is persuasive that one necessary element in nuancing the text's teleology into a more open sense of "historical directionality" of "need and possibility" is the reintegration into the model of the utopian thought, to which we could add its corollary political ethics, somewhat disavowed therein.

14  Townshend, 1997. This is overstatement even for all the qualifications Townshend offers about what this teleology is.

15  Gindin, 1998, pp. 98–9. "Marx brought us the gift of historical optimism, but one hundred and fifty years after the *Manifesto*, doubt threatens to overwhelm us." What if at a certain point, in certain contexts, it is optimism which overwhelms, and doubt which is a gift?

16  Goldmann, 2016, p. 187. Interestingly, Boyer (1998, p. 169) exactly reverses this description, seeing Marx and Engels as "overly pessimistic." As he is discussing their views on the immiseration of the working class and the countervailing pressures they had not, in the *Manifesto*, taken into sufficient account, and the intimate relationship the *Manifesto* imputes between that immiseration and militancy, this pessimism and the optimism Goldmann diagnoses are not in contradiction: if anything, they are the same phenomenon.

17  Harrington, 2013, p. 106.

18  Runciman, 2010, p. 92.

19  For a judicious examination of the gig economy, see Woodcock, 2019.

20  Engels, 1847.

21  Leys and Panitch, 1998, p. 42.

22  Cohen and Moody, 1998, p. 122.

23  Taylor, 1967, p. 28.

24  Runciman, 2010, p. 101.

25  For a classic overview of the debates around shifts in class structure, and "contradictory class positions," see Wright, 1989.

26  Runciman, 2010, p. 103.

27  Davis, 2020.

28  Callinicos describes it as a "bitter and unremitting hatred of sexual oppression, the subjection of women to men." Callinicos, 1995, p. 165.

29  Rowbotham, 1998, p. 14.

30  See Marx and Engels, 1956, specifically at <www.marxists.org/archive/marx/works/1845/holy-family/ch04.htm> (accessed January 28, 2022). Interestingly, it was precisely against a sexist attack that they intervened, ironically turning Bruno Bauer's attack on her supposed "feminine dogmatism" against him.

31  Tronto, 2015, p. 148.

32  For something of that ambivalence, see Gane, 1998, pp. 138–39.

33  Draper, 1994, p. 226.

34  See, for example, Lee, 2013, p. 200.

35  For an invaluable overview, see Bhattacharya, 2017.

36  I draw here extensively on Draper, 1994, p. 264.

37  Gasper, 2005, p. 163.

38  Cowling, 1998, p. 144.

39  Gasper, 2005, p. 67.

40  Quoted in Davis, 2017, p. 45. I draw extensively on Davis here. For an excellent overview of theories of nationalism, see Vanaik, 2018.

41  Anderson, 1983.

42  Borkenau, 1939, p. 94.

43  Nairn, 1975, p. 3. See Davis, 2017, pp. 50–51 for several other examples of what he considers an "old canard."

44 Benner, 1995, p. 50. See also Chapter 1 of Carver, 2018, for the importance of reading Marx's works as theoretically informed political interventions, problematising the generic hierarchies of his work often implied or adduced by commentators.

45 As does work carried out in its wake. See, for example, Davis, 2015.

46 Benner, 1995, p. 55. This passage might also suggest a way between the simple disappearances of nationhood under communism and its instrumentalization under capitalism. This demand on the proletariat takes the frankly ideological "nation" of the ruling bureaucracy as representing an imagined national polity (thus effacing the very different interests of the classes therein), and suggests that the proletariat *might* in fact take that role—because in taking power it will begin overcoming the class struggle and the social problems for which the previous ruling class evaded responsibilities by the invoking of a national first-person plural: "we are all in this together." This radicalized transitional revolutionary—ruptural—sense of the nation is very different from the nation of nationalism, and dovetails intriguingly with recent left discussions about the political trenchancy, or necessity, of thinking in terms of nationhood. Any such move, as Roman Rosdolsky clarifies, isn't a concession to nationalism, but "will only be a transitional stage to a classless and stateless society of the future on an international scale." (Rosdolsky, 1965, p. 337. Emphasis removed.)

47 Benner, 1995, p. 49.

48 Davis, 2015, pp. 53–62.

49 Benner, 1995, p. 48.

50 Ahmad, 2000, p. 18.

51 Davis, 2017. See Okoth, 2019, pp. 107–14, for an outstanding discussion of Afrosocialism.

52 Distressingly to their admirers, Marx and Engels on occasion used unconscionable racist terminology in private. I will not here reproduce Marx's repulsive nickname for his associate Lasalle, for example.

53 Robinson, 2000, p. xxix.

54 As translated in Padover, 1973, p. 275.

55 Kelley, 1998.

56  Satgar, 2019, pp. 4–5. Anderson (2010) has outlined the development of Marx's thought on the question of development according to a Eurocentric unilinearity from the 1840s on, and Lucia Pradella contests, on the basis of Marx's notebooks, the extent to which, as early as 1845, that model inhered (Pradella, 2015). See also Olende, 2019.

57  Five years after the *Manifesto*, in the *New York Daily Tribune*, Marx even more explicitly denounces "[t]he profound hypocrisy and inherent barbarism of bourgeois civilisation" that is "naked" in its brutalities in the colonies. See <www.marxists.org/history/eol/newspaper/vol08/n006/marx/htm> (accessed January 28, 2022). Expanding on the *Manifesto*'s cynicism, he here understands the baroque murderousness of colonial relations as central to the "civilisation" he denounces.

58  Patnaik, 1999, p. 119.

59  This essay is reproduced in Bender, 2013, and the passage in question is at p. 140, but I use here the earlier translation available at <www.marxists.org/archive/trotsky/1937/10/90manifesto.htm> (accessed January 28, 2022).

60  Sinha, 2016, p. 370. See also Toscano, 2021, from whom I draw extensively here. This First International abolitionist-communist nexus also saw a demonstration against the suppression of the Paris Commune by a crowd that included an all-black theatrical quasi-military group known as a Skidmore Guard.

61  Walzer, 2020.

62  See, for example Robinson, 1983. There are also those like Robbie Shilliam for whom the use of the slavery metaphor itself, with regard to wage labor, is evidence of a race-blindness or worse at the heart of Marxism's models (Shilliam, 2015).

63  See, for example, Johnson, 2019, for which "[e]ven Cedric J. Robinson's celebrated *Black Marxism* treats racial ideology as originating in antiquity, an argument we can trace back to the rhetoric of New Negro nationalist soapbox orators and bibliophiles."

64  See Post, 2019, drawing on Botwinick, 2018.

65  Post, 2019.

66  Ignatiev, 2008.

67 Johnson, 2019. Johnson's intervention is powerful and raises important and provocative points, but is ultimately too swingeing, not least because, given the very potential "promiscuity" of "whiteness" that he diagnoses, he too often proceeds to critique the least persuasive and most reductive version of the concept, and to deny a more nuanced iteration the traction it might have.

68 <www.theguardian.com/society/2016/sep/28/hate-crime-horrible-spike-brexit-vote-metropolitan-police> (accessed June 15, 2021). See also Rzepnikowska, 2018, Myślińska, 2016.

69 See Rzepnikowska, 2018, for a good summary of these debates, and Myślińska, 2016, for the invocation of "edges."

70 Fox, Moroşanu, and Szilassy, 2012.

71 Myślińska, 2016.

72 Rzepnikowska, 2018.

73 Post, 2020. This is an invaluable overview of the debate.

74 Available at <www.marxists.org/archive/marx/works/1869/letters/69_12_10-abs.htm> (accessed January 28, 2022).

75 This is from a letter to Sigfrid Mayer and August Vogt, available at <www.marxists.org/archive/marx/works/1870/letters/70_04_09.htm> (accessed January 28, 2022).

76 Du Bois, 1935, p. 700.

77 Roediger, 2017, p. 20.

78 Du Bois, 1935, p. 701.

79 Ibid.

80 Du Bois, of course, isn't beyond criticism, even in such powerful passages. Cedric Johnson (Johnson, 2019) takes reasonable issue, for example, with some of Du Bois's formulations about the extent of this "inferiority complex," diagnosing in it "Du Bois's own bourgeois sensibility," and analogous to "underclass myth making."

81 <www.independent.co.uk/arts-entertainment/books/news/akala-knife-crime-good-morning-britain-piers-morgan-alex-beresford-stabbing-a8827831.html> (accessed June 16, 2021).

82 Patnaik, 1999, p. 113.

83 Heideman, 2018.

84 The text of the speech by Jacques Duclos justifying this decision is at <www.marxists.org/history/algeria/1956/duclos.htm> (accessed January 28, 2022).

85 I draw here, and take the quotations from, CP literature, quoted in Smith, 2008, especially pp. 462–63.

86 For a fascinating example of this, see Smith, 2008, p. 465, for the victory of the CP's West Indian Committee and its allies over the general secretary Harry Pollitt which led to the 1958 edition of the party's canonical *The British Road to Socialism* predicting "voluntary fraternal relations" between a socialist Britain and its erstwhile colonies over the original "fraternal association." On those few words hinged a substantial dispute about political agency, with the West Indian Committee objecting to the "attempt to impose a new form of British-led alliance."

87 Reported in the *Guardian*, available at <www.theguardian.com/world/2018/jul/22/german-leftwingers-woo-voters-with-national-social-stance> (accessed January 28, 2022). For a trenchant criticism of the Brechtian formulation, see Seymour, 2018b.

88 Seymour, 2018a.

89 See, for example, Breunig, Deutscher and To, 2017. For overviews of the evidence see <wol.iza.org/articles/do-immigrant-workers-depress-the-wages-of-native-workers/long>, <www.bbc.co.uk/news/business-46918729> (both accessed June 15, 2021).

90 See Heideman, 2018, D'Amato, 2012, Williams, 2019. For longer treatments, see Kelley, 1990, Naison, 1983, and Maxwell, 1999.

91 Hudis, 2021.

92 Brodber, 2003, p. 123.

93 Toscano, 2021.

94 Césaire, 2010, p. 147, pp. 149–150.

95 Taylor, 2017, p. 20.

96 Knox, 2016, for an outstanding discussion.

## Chapter 6. *The Communist Manifesto* Today

1 Lowith, 2013, p. 171.

2 Rothbard, 1990. See also Tuveson, 1984.

3   See in particular Engels's various works on revolutionary and early Christianity.

4   Berman, 2011.

5   In fact, though tendentious and intended as an attack, Rothbard's essay is a fascinating romp through a history of millenarian sects and their relationship to Marxism.

6   The piece was published in the *Deutsch-Französische Jahrbücher* (see <www.marxists.org/archive/marx/works/1843/critique-hpr/intro.htm> (accessed June 7, 2021)). It was taken from an introduction by Marx to his own work *A Contribution to the Critique of Hegel's Philosophy of Right*, that would be published after his death. The meme itself, winningly rude and almost impossible to describe, is online at <news.knowyourmeme.com/photos/1907590-marxism> (accessed November 13, 2021).

7   This is a distinction invaluably developed by the scholar of religion Rudolf Otto in Otto, 1959. For a comradely debate about the usefulness or otherwise of this tri- versus bi-partite model of rationality in the context of Marxism, see Miéville, 2019a, Fluss and Frim, 2019, and Miéville, 2019b.

8   Wallace, 1974.

9   Some such dissenting doctrines "change the very position of the problem by inserting the present moment into the concrete totality of eschatological or historical time, and by replacing the question What ought I to do? by the essentially different one of How ought I to live?" (Goldmann, 2016, pp. 263–4).

10  See <www.bbc.co.uk/radio4/history/voices/voices_reading_revolt.html> (accessed January 28, 2022).

11  Tismaneanu, 2012, p. 166.

12  Toscano, 2010, p. 17.

13  Davidson, 2015. On the impacts of Covid-19, see Blakeley, 2020.

14  See, for example, Meadway, 2021.

15  Miéville, 2015.

16  See <www.marxists.org/archive/trotsky/1937/10/90manifesto.htm> (accessed January 28, 2022).

17  Wallis, 1998, p. 8.

18  See Nicholas, 1989, pp. 61–3.

19  I am indebted to Alberto Toscano's presentation to HM Online 2020 for
    this insight. As to the *Manifesto*, it implies that "it considers capitalism to
    be 'homoficient,' i.e. producing the same effects in all historical contexts"
    (Močnik, 2018, p. 499).

20  Meillassoux, 1981, p. 97.

21  Toscano, 2012, Osborne, 1998, Ahmad, 2000. See also Toscano, 2012:
    "[T]he story of the sheer dissolution of prior modes of domination,
    and the homogenisation of the conditions of labour and struggle,
    which could be drawn from the manifesto, is one that jars with the
    maintenance and intensification of seemingly pre-capitalist modes of
    domination, which have in many ways been refunctioned by capital, but
    which remain its often indispensable accompaniments."

22  Toscano, 2012.

23  Moos, 2017, p. 17; Booth, 1978, pp. 148–49. For the factory inspectors'
    quote, and a discussion of Marx's considerations on the Acts, see also
    Barker, 2013.

24  Moos, 2017, pp. 19–20.

25  Booth, 1978, pp. 141–43.

26  Marx, 1976, p. 381.

27  Ibid. p. 377.

28  Booth, 1978, p. 137.

29  <www.marxists.org/archive/marx/works/1864/10/27.htm> (accessed
    June 17, 2021).

30  Foot, 2005, p. 98. Harney was talking of universal male suffrage.

31  Foot, 2005, p. 110.

32  Ibid. p. 119, p. 121.

33  Ibid. p. 121.

34  Boyer, 1998, p. 171.

35  The term "woke," the past participle of "wake" in some African-
    American English, has for many decades, originally in particular
    among black Americans, meant "alert to the dangers of injustice in
    society, especially of racism." See, for example, the blues singer Lead
    Belly's 1938 injunction to his listeners, in "Scottsboro Boys," about the
    life-threatening nature of white racism, to "stay woke."

36  See <www.rollingstone.com/politics/politics-news/the-line-that-may-have-won-hillary-clinton-the-nomination-40504/> (accessed June 14, 2021). For more examples of the attacks by Hillary Clinton on Bernie Sanders see Haider, 2020. At the most preposterous and risible end of this sort of technique is the demand by some hipster self-styled progressive partisans for the Israeli state that activists against its settler-colonial policies desist from calling the area Palestine, as this is "deadnaming"—the aggressive and traumatic use of a trans person's name from before they transitioned. That this is sanctimonious trolling, and greeted with braying derision, doesn't make it any less instructive as an extreme example of the tendency under discussion.

37  <thebeet.com/these-vegan-brands-support-black-lives-matter-and-are-doing-something-about-it/> (accessed September 6, 2021); <finance.yahoo.com/news/earth-day-no-evil-foods-162600661.html> (accessed September 6, 2021); and <vegconomist.com/interviews/no-evil-our-goal-is-to-dominate-one-country-at-a-time/> (accessed September 6, 2021).

38  <jacobinmag.com/2020/06/no-evil-foods-unionizing-workers-organizing> (accessed September 6, 2021); <noevilfoods.com> (accessed September 6, 2021).

39  The extraordinary recording is available at <prospect.org/labor/anatomy-of-an-anti-union-meeting> (accessed September 6, 2021).

40  Haider, 2020. "From time to time," he adds sadly, "I ask students if this is the model of social justice they would embrace. The question is always answered with a long silence."

41  <www.smh.com.au/world/europe/glasgow-cop26-summit-nears-deadlock-core-1-5-degree-goal-on-life-support-20211111-p5989a.html> (accessed November 13, 2021).

42  For an excellent, spirited and persuasive defence of Marx, even relatively early in his writing, on issues of ecological sensitivity, see Bellamy Foster, 1998. Even he, however, acknowledges that the *Manifesto*'s approach is inadequate in underestimating the tenacity of capitalism, and thus of ecological crisis as a problem coextensive therewith.

43  See Buck, 2019.

44  For an extended discussion of the debates around this, see Salvage Collective, 2021.

45 See, most famously, Draper, 1973. See also McNally, 2009, for an excellent recent consideration.

46 Bottomore, 1991, p. 408.

47 See, for example, Panitch, 2015, p. 130, on parties "as the very arena in which hegemonically oriented class identity and consciousness were going to be formed."

48 Tad DeLay interviewed on the podcast *The Magnificast*, episode 123, on 26 July 2020. Delay's brilliant, productively tense superposition of psychoanalytical and Marxist categories has been of incomparable importance to my understanding of agency and ideology.

49 DeLay, 2020.

50 Buck-Morss, 2019.

51 Suchting, 1998, p. 163. See also Miéville, 2015.

52 Blouin, 1983, p. 197.

53 Garland, 1990.

54 <floridapolitics.com/archives/10155-john-grant-death-penalty-is-just-a-pain-free-execution-is-not-guaranteed/> (accessed September 6, 2021).

55 See <abcnews.go.com/politics/trump-police-nice-suspects/story?id=48914504> (accessed January 28, 2022).

56 See Miéville, 2019.

57 Mirowski, 2013.

58 For an extensive discussion of such recent sadisms, see Miéville, 2015. See also Seymour, 2019a.

59 See Seymour, 2019a, for a vital analysis of such phenomena.

60 "I'm sorry, *enjoy* your life? Enjoy your *life?* I'm not making some kind of neo-puritan objection to enjoyment. Enjoyment is lovely. Enjoyment is great. The more enjoyment the better. But enjoyment is *one emotion*. The only things in the world that are designed to elicit enjoyment and only enjoyment are products, and your life is not a product" (Spufford, 2012, p. 8).

61 Ehrenreich, 2010.

62 Berlant, 2011.

63 Eagleton, 2018, p. 86.

64 Kollontai, 1923. For illuminating Kollontai's politics of love, I'm indebted to Season Butler for her July 17, 2021 performance at the Berlinische

Gallerie, Berlin, "'Uses of the Erotic: The Erotic as Power' cruises 'Make Way for Winged Eros,'" her provocative pas de deux of texts by Audre Lorde and Kollontai respectively.

65 Gilman-Opalsky, 2020, for the "communism of love," and p. 317 for the quote. Miéville, 2015, for joy versus sadism. Badiou, 2012, for the "love event."

66 See <www.washingtonpost.com/politics/trump-still-wont-apologize-to-the-central-park-five-heres-what-he-said-at-the-time/2019/06/18/32ea4d7e-9208-11e9-b570-6416efdc0803_story.html> (accessed January 28, 2022).

67 Shakespeare, 2014.

68 Armantrout, 2018, p. 112. This rich poem opens, "The market hates itself / almost as much / as you hate it," lines that beg for a reading in terms of the death drive of capitalism itself.

69 Lewis, 2020. I am indebted to Lewis for much, including the introduction to Tronti as a theorist of hate, outlined below.

70 Surin, 2017.

71 Pilbeam, 1993, p. 257.

72 Sparrow, 2017.

73 Baldwin, 2017, p. 12.

74 Benjamin, 1968, p. 260.

75 Tronti, 2019, p. 240, p. 181, p. 150.

76 Shakespeare, 2014.

77 Surin, 2017.

78 Neary, 2017, p. 560.

79 Bosmajian, 2013, pp. 176–77.

80 Kuper, 1981. I draw here on Seymour, 2017.

81 Kuper, 1981, p. 100.

82 Dean, 2017.

83 Amin, 2018, p. 440.

84 Schumpeter, 1949, p. 210. See also Labriola, 1999, p. 5: "Never was funeral oration [for the bourgeoisie] so magnificent." It is worth restating that, per Patnaik's analysis, it may be the inadequate "racing" of capitalism, a failure to integrate a theory of imperialism into the

dynamic, which underpins the exaggerated faith in the Prometheanism of the bourgeoisie (Patnaik, 1999).

85  Stedman Jones, 2018, p. 16.

86  Neary, 2017, p. 560. Neary is critiquing the work of Peter McLaren, but the formulation has far wider applicability.

87  Sparrow, 2017.

88  See, for example, the various libertarian dreams of "seasteading" in working-class-free communities (Miéville, 2008).

89  For an example of crass, ugly, tactically stupid bottom-up class sadism mistaking itself for bracing class hatred, see, for example, *Socialist Worker*, 2411, 8/7/14, "Eton by bear," a celebration of the mauling to death of a child because the victim of the wild animal was from a wealthy background.

90  For a fascinating example of this see the testimony of one activist, Shapovalov, in Russia in 1905, who, to fight his own fear and the disempowerment it engendered, nurses a furious honor in hate. "I came to hate capitalism and my boss"—as avatar thereof— ". . . even more intensely" (Miéville, 2017, p. 26).

91  For an outline of his trolling, both in the direct service of capital accumulation, and simply to be astonishingly unpleasant, see <www.wired.com/story/martin-shkreli-guilty-securities-fraud/> (accessed January 28, 2022).

92  See, for example, Antonov defending the Provisional Government's members from the murderous anger of Red Guards during the storming of the Winter Palace (Miéville, 2017, p. 302).

93  See, for example, the discussion in Kilpatrick, 2013. Kilpatrick splendidly describes Cockburn's as a "joyful hate," an "inspiring hate."

94  This is what lies behind Neary's demand of another writer that he "substantiate his pedagogy of love with a pedagogy of hate."

95  See <www.marxists.org/archive/guevara/1965/03/man-socialism.htm> (accessed January 28, 2022).

# Bibliography

## Books

Adoratsky, V., *The History of the Communist Manifesto of Marx and Engels* (International Publishers, 1938).

Allinson, Jamie, *The Age of Counter-revolution: States and Revolutions in the Middle East* (Cambridge University Press, 2022).

Anderson, Benedict, *Imagined Communities* (Verso, 1983).

Anderson, Kevin, *Marx at the Margins* (University of Chicago Press, 2010).

Armantrout, Rae, *Wobble* (Wesleyan University Press, 2018).

Aston, Trevor and Philpin, C. H. E., *The Brenner Debate: Agrarian Class Structure and Economic Development in Pre-Industrial Europe* (Cambridge University Press, 1985).

Badiou, Alain, *In Praise of Love* (Serpent's Tail, 2012).

Baldwin, James, *I Am Not Your Negro* (Penguin, 2017).

Beaumont, Matthew, *The Spectre of Utopia: Utopian and Science Fictions at the Fin de Siècle* (Peter Lang, 2012).

Bender, Frederic (ed.), Marx, Karl, *The Communist Manifesto*, Second Norton Critical Edition (W. W. Norton, 2013).

Benjamin, Walter, *Illuminations* (Schocken Books, 1968).

Benner, Erica, *Really Existing Nationalisms* (Oxford University Press, 1995).

Berlant, Lauren, *Cruel Optimism* (Duke University Press, 2011).

Berman, Marshall, *All That Is Solid Melts Into Air* (Verso, 1983).

Bhattacharya, Tithi (ed.), *Social Reproduction Theory: Remapping Class, Recentering Oppression* (Pluto, 2017).

Blakeley, Grace, *The Corona Crash* (Verso, 2020).

Blouin, Andrée, *My Country, Africa* (Praeger, 1983).

Borkenau, Franz, *World Communism: A History of the Communist International* (W. W. Norton, 1939).

Bottomore, Tom (ed.), *A Dictionary of Marxist Thought*, 2nd edn (Blackwell, 1991).

Botwinick, Howard, *Persistent Inequalities: Wage Disparities Under Capitalist Competition* (Haymarket Books, 2018).

Brass, Tom, *Revolution and Its Alternatives* (E. J. Brill, 2019).

Brodber, Erna, *The Continent of Black Consciousness* (New Beacon Books, 2003).

Buck, Holly Jean, *After Geoengineering* (Verso, 2019).

Buck-Morss, Susan, *Revolution Today* (Haymarket Books, 2019).

Callinicos, Alex, *The Revenge of History* (Polity Press, 1991).

Callinicos, Alex, *The Revolutionary Ideas of Karl Marx*, 2nd edn (Bookmarks, 1995).

Carver, Terrell, *The Postmodern Marx* (Manchester University Press, 1998).

Carver, Terrell and Farr, James (eds), *The Cambridge Companion to* The Communist Manifesto (Cambridge University Press, 2015).

Carver, Terrell, *Marx* (Polity Press, 2018).

Clews, John C., *Communist Propaganda Techniques* (Praeger, 1964).

Cowling, Mark, *The Communist Manifesto: New Interpretations* (Edinburgh University Press, 1998).

Danchev, Alex (ed.), *100 Artists' Manifestos: From the Futurists to the Stuckists* (Penguin Books, 2011).

Dralyuk, Boris (trans.), *Slap in the Face: Four Russian Futurist Manifestos* (Insert Blanc Press, 2017).

Du Bois, W. E. B., *Black Reconstruction in America 1860–1880* (Harcourt, Brace and Company, 1935).

Eagleton, Terry, *Eagleton: An Introduction*, 2nd edn (Verso, 2007).

Eagleton, Terry, *Why Marx Was Right*, 2nd edn (Yale University Press, 2018).

Ehrenreich, Barbara, *Smile or Die: How Positive Thinking Fooled America and the World* (Granta, 2010).

Engels, Friedrich, *The Condition of the Working Class in England in 1844* (Allen & Unwin, 1892). <http://www.gutenberg.org/cache/epub/17306/pg17306.txt> (accessed November 10, 2020).

Engels, Friedrich, Anti-Dühring (Progress Publishers, 1947) <www.marxists.org/archive/marx/works/download/pdf/anti_duhring.pdf> (accessed January 28, 2022).

Fahs, Breanne, *Burn It Down! Feminist Manifestos for the Revolution* (Verso, 2020).

Fernbach, David (ed.), *The Revolutions of 1848* (Penguin, 1973).

Fernbach, David (ed.), *Karl Marx: The Political Writings* (Verso, 2019).

Fisher, Mark, *Capitalist Realism: Is There No Alternative?* (Zero Books, 2010).

Foot, Paul, *The Vote: How It Was Won and How It Was Undermined* (Penguin Books, 2005).

Garland, David, *Punishment and Modern Society* (University of Chicago Press, 1990).

Gilman-Opalsky, Richard, *The Communism of Love: An Inquiry into the Poverty of Exchange Value* (AK Press, 2020).

Goldmann, Lucien, *The Hidden God: A Study of Tragic Vision in the Pensées of Pascal and the Tragedies of Racine* (Verso, 2016).

Hägglund, Martin, *This Life: Secular Faith and Spiritual Freedom* (Pantheon Books, 2019).

Hodges, Donald Clark, *The Literate Communist: 150 Years of the* Communist Manifesto (Peter Lang, 1999).

Hunt, Richard, *The Political Ideas of Marx and Engels*, vol. 2, *Classical Marxism, 1850–95* (Palgrave Macmillan, 1984).

Ignatiev, Noel, *How the Irish Became White* (Routledge, 2008).

Isaac, Jeffrey C. (ed.), *The Communist Manifesto: Karl Marx and Friedrich Engels* (Yale University Press, 2012).

Israel, Jonathan, *The Radical Enlightenment: Philosophy and the Making of Modernity 1650–1750* (Oxford University Press, 2001).

James, C. L. R., *The Black Jacobins: Toussaint L'Ouverture and the San Domingo Revolution* (Random House, 1963).

Kelley, Robin, *Hammer and Hoe: Alabama Communists During the Great Depression* (University of North Carolina Press, 1990).

Klarman, Michael, *The Framers' Coup: The Making of the United States Constitution* (Oxford University Press, 2016).

Klein, Naomi, *The Shock Doctrine* (Knopf, 2007).

de Kom, Anton, *We Slaves of Suriname* (Polity, 2022).

Kuper, Leo, *Genocide: Its Political Use in the 20th Century* (Yale University Press, 1981).

Lamb, Peter, *Marx and Engels' Communist Manifesto* (Bloomsbury, 2015.)

Lewis, Sophie, *Full Surrogacy Now: Feminism Against Family* (Verso, 2019).

L'Ouverture, Toussaint, *The Haitian Revolution* (Verso, 2008).

Losurdo, Domenico, *Liberalism: A Counter-History* (Verso, 2011).

Losurdo, Domenico, *Hegel and the Freedom of Moderns* (Duke University Press, 2004).

Macfarlane, Helen, *Red Republican: Essays, Articles and her Translation of the* Communist Manifesto (Unkant Publishers, 2014).

Marx, Karl, *Economic & Philosophical Manuscripts of 1844*, 1932. <www.marxists.org/archive/marx/works/download/pdf/economic-philosophic-manuscripts-1844.pdf> (accessed January 28, 2022).

Marx, Karl and Engels, Friedrich, *The Holy Family* (Foreign Languages Publishing House, 1956).

Marx, Karl, *A Critique of The German Ideology*, 1968. <www.marxists.org/archive/marx/works/download/marx-the-german-ideology.pdf> (accessed January 28, 2022).

Marx, Karl, *Grundrisse* (Penguin, 1973).

Marx, Karl, *Capital*, vol. 1 (Penguin Books, 1976).

Maxwell, William, *New Negro, Old Left: African-American Writing and Communism Between the Wars* (Columbia University Press, 1999).

Meillassoux, Claude, *Maidens, Meals and Money: Capitalism and the Domestic Community* (Cambridge University Press, 1981).

Miéville, China, *Between Equal Rights: A Marxist Theory of International Law* (E. J. Brill, 2005).

Miéville, China, *October: The Story of the Russian Revolution* (Verso, 2017).

Mirowski, Philip, *Never Let a Serious Crisis Go to Waste: How Neoliberalism Survived the Financial Meltdown* (Verso, 2013).

Moore, Stanley, *Three Tactics: The Background in Marx* (Monthly Review Press, 1963).

Naison, Mark, *Communists in Harlem During the Depression* (University of Illinois Press, 1983).

Otto, Rudolf, *The Idea of the Holy* (Penguin Books, 1959).

Padover, Saul (ed.), *Karl Marx on America and the Civil War* (McGraw-Hill, 1973).

Panitch, Leo and Leys, Colin, *Socialist Register 1999: The* Communist Manifesto *Now* (Merlin, 1998).

Plekhanov, Georgi, *Utopian Socialism in the Nineteenth Century* (1913), <www.marxists.org/archive/plekhanov/1913/utopian-socialism/index.htm> (accessed October 26, 2020).

Poulantzas, Nicos, 'The State and the Transition to Socialism', in *The Poulantzas Reader*, ed. James Martin (Verso, 2008).

Pradella, Lucia, *Globalisation and the Critique of Political Economy* (Routledge, 2015).

Prawer, S. S., *Karl Marx and World Literature* (Oxford University Press, 1978).

Puchner, Martin, *Poetry of the Revolution: Marx, Manifestos, and the Avant-Garde* (Princeton University Press, 2006).

Roberton, Priscilla, *Revolutions of 1848: A Social History* (Sagwan Press, 2015).

Robinson, Cedric, *Black Marxism* (Second Edition) (University of North Carolina Press, 2000).

Roediger, David, *Class, Race and Marxism* (Verso, 2017).

Rowson, Martin (adapter and illustrator), Marx, Karl and Engels, Friedrich, *The Communist Manifesto* (Self Made Hero, 2018).

Runciman, W. G., *Great Books, Bad Arguments:* Republic, Leviathan, *and* The Communist Manifesto (Princeton University Press, 2010).

Salvage Collective, *The Tragedy of the Worker* (Verso, 2021).

Seymour, Richard, *The Twittering Machine* (Indigo Press, 2019).

Silva, Ludovico, *El estilo literario de Marx* (Siglo XXI Editores, 1975).

Sinha, Manish, *The Slave's Cause: A History of Abolition* (Yale University Press, 2016).

Spufford, Francis, *Unapologetic* (Faber & Faber, 2012).

Struick, Dirk J., *Birth of the Communist Manifesto* (International Publishers, 1971).

Sunkara, Bhaskar, *The Socialist Manifesto* (Verso, 2019).

Suvin, Darko, *Communism, Poetry: Communicating Vessels* (Political Animal Press, 2020).

Taylor, Keeanga-Yamahtta (ed.), *How We Get Free: Black Feminism and the Combahee River Collective* (Haymarket Books, 2017).

Traverso, Enzo, *Revolution: An Intellectual History* (Verso, 2021).

Wheen, Francis, *Karl Marx* (4th Estate, 1999).

Wright, Erik Olin, *The Debate on Classes* (Verso, 1989).

## Introductions to Editions of the *Manifesto*

Dean, Jodi, "Introduction," *The Communist Manifesto* (Pluto Press, 2017).

Draper, Hal, *The Adventures of the Communist Manifesto* (Center for Socialist History, 1994).

Gasper, Phil (ed.), *The Communist Manifesto, Karl Marx and Frederick Engels* (Haymarket Books, 2005).

Harvey, David, "Introduction to the 2008 edition," in *The Communist Manifesto* (Pluto Press. 2017).

Hobsbawm, Eric, "Introduction," in Marx, Karl and Frederick Engels, *The Communist Manifesto: A Modern Edition* (Verso, 2012).

Laski, Harold, "Introduction" 1948. <tribunemag.co.uk/2020/02/labour-and-the-communist-manifesto> (accessed September 7, 2021).

Malia, Martin, "Introduction" in Marx, Karl and Engels, Friedrich, *Communist Manifesto* (Signet Classics, 1998).

Taylor, A. J. P., "Introduction" in Marx, Karl and Engels, Friedrich, *The Communist Manifesto* (Pelican, 1967).

Varoufakis, Yanis, "Introduction" in Marx, Karl and Engels, Friedrich, *The Communist Manifesto* (Vintage, 2018).

## Essays and Articles

Ackerman, Seth, "Burn the Constitution," *Jacobin* (2011). <www.jacobinmag.com/2011/03/burn-the-constitution> (accessed June 18, 2021).

Ahmad, Aijaz, "The *Communist Manifesto* and the Problem of Universality" *Monthly Review*, 50:2 (1998), pp. 12–23.

Ahmed, Aijaz, "*The Communist Manifesto* and "World Literature"," *Social Scientist*, 28:7/8 (2000), pp. 3–30.

Alcantara, Oscar L., "Ideology, Historiography and International Legal Theory" *International Journal for the Semiotics of Law*, IX: 25 (1996), pp. 39–79.

Amin, Samir, "*The Communist Manifesto*, 170 Years Later" *Sociološki pregled/ Sociological Review*, LII:2 (2018), pp. 430–52.

Anderson, Perry, "Modernity and Revolution," *New Left Review*, 1/144 (1984). <newleftreview.org/issues/I144/articles/perry-anderson-modernity-and-revolution> (accessed October 21, 2020).

Andréas, Bert, "A Note on Sources," in Bender, Frederic (ed.), Marx, Karl, *The Communist Manifesto*, Second Norton Critical Edition (W. W. Norton, 2013).

Angus, Ian, "The Origin of Rosa Luxemburg's Slogan 'Socialism or Barbarism'" (2014). <johnriddell.com/2014/10/21/the-origin-of-rosa-luxemburgs-slogan-socialism-or-barbarism/> (accessed November 13, 2021).

Anker, Elisabeth, "The *Manifesto* in a Late-Capitalist Era: Melancholy and Melodrama," in Carver, Terrell and Farr, James (eds), *The Cambridge Companion to* The Communist Manifesto (Cambridge University Press, 2015).

Avineri, Shlomo, "*The Communist Manifesto* at 150," *Dissent* (1998).

Barker, Colin, "Marx on the Factory Acts" (2013). <www.academia. edu/5138882/2013_Marx_on_the_Factory_Acts> (accessed June 17, 2021).

Barker, Jason, "Epic or Tragedy? Karl Marx and Poetic Form in *The Communist Manifesto*," *Filozofia*, 71:4 (2016), pp. 316–27.

Beamish, Rob, "The Making of the *Manifesto*," in Panitch, Leo and Leys, Colin, *Socialist Register 1999: The* Communist Manifesto *Now* (Merlin, 1998).

Bellamy Foster, John, "The Communist Manifesto and the Environment," in Panitch, Leo and Leys, Colin, *Socialist Register 1999: The* Communist Manifesto *Now* (Merlin, 1998).

Bender, Frederic, "Introduction," in Bender, Frederic (ed.), Marx, Karl, *The Communist Manifesto*, Second Norton Critical Edition (W. W. Norton, 2013).

Benjamin, Walter, "The Concept of History" aka "Theses on the Philosophy of History" (1940). <www.sfu.ca/~andrewf/CONCEPT2.html> (accessed June 10, 2021).

Berman, Marshall, "The Signs in the Street: A Response to Perry Anderson," *New Left Review*, I/144 (1984). <newleftreview.org/issues/i144/articles/marshall-berman-the-signs-in-the-street-a-response-to-perry-anderson> (accessed May 4, 2021).

Berman, Marshall, "Unchained Melody," in *Adventures in Marxism* (Verso, 2001).

Berman, Marshall, "Tearing Away the Veils: The *Communist Manifesto*," *Dissent* (2011). <www.dissentmagazine.org/online_articles/tearing-away-the-veils-the-communist-manifesto> (accessed October 21, 2020).

Bernstein, Edouard, "Revising the *Communist Manifesto*," in Bender, Frederic (ed.), Marx, Karl, *The Communist Manifesto*, Second Norton Critical Edition (W. W. Norton, 2013 (1898)).

Black, David, "Helen Macfarlane: A Biographical-Philosophical Introduction," in Macfarlane, Helen, *Red Republican: Essays, Articles and her Translation of the* Communist Manifesto (Unkant Publishers, 2014).

Blackledge, Paul, "Engels vs Marx?: Two Hundred Years of Frederick Engels," *Monthly Review* (2020). <monthlyreview.org/2020/05/01/engels-vs-marx-two-hundred-years-of-frederick-engels/> (accessed June 8, 2021).

Blanc, Eric, "The Democratic Road to Socialism: Reply to Mike Taber" (2019). <cosmonaut.blog/2019/04/11/the-democratic-road-to-socialism-reply-to-mike-taber/> (accessed June 17, 2021).

Booth, Douglas E., "Karl Marx on State Regulation of the Labor Process: The English Factory Acts," *Review of Social Economy*, 36:2 (1978), pp, 137–57.

Bosmajian, Haig A., "A Rhetorical Approach to the *Communist Manifesto*," in Bender, Frederic (ed.), Marx, Karl, *The Communist Manifesto*, Second Norton Critical Edition (W. W. Norton, 2013 (1963–4)).

Boyer, George R., "The Historical Background of the *Communist Manifesto*," *Journal of Economic Perspectives*, 12:4 (1998), pp. 151–74.

Broekman, Jan M. and Catá Backer, Larry, "Eco and the Text of the Communist Manifesto," in Broekman, Jan M. and Catá Backer, Larry, *Signs in Law – A Source Book* (Springer, 2015).

Bronner, Stephen Eric, "The *Communist Manifesto*: Between Past and Present," in Isaac, Jeffrey C. (ed.), *The Communist Manifesto: Karl Marx and Friedrich Engels* (Yale University Press, 2012).

Bruenig, Robert, Deutscher, Nathan and To, Hang Thi, "The Relationship between Immigration to Australia and the Labour Market Outcomes of Australian-Born Workers," *Economic Record*, 93:301 (2017), pp. 255–76.

Buttigieg, Joseph, "Marking the Anniversary of '*The Communist Manifesto*,'" *Chronicle of Higher Education* (1998). <www.chronicle.com/article/marking-the-anniversary-of-the-communist-manifesto/> (accessed November 12, 2020).

Caplan, Lincoln, "A Conservative Counterrevolution," *Harvard Magazine* (2017). <www.harvardmagazine.com/2017/01/a-conservative-counterrevolution> (accessed June 18, 2021).

Carver, Terrell, "Re-translating the *Manifesto*: New Histories, New Ideas," in Cowling, Mark, *The Communist Manifesto: New Interpretations* (Edinburgh University Press, 1998).

Carver, Terrell, "The *Manifesto* in Marx's and Engels's Lifetimes," in Carver, Terrell and Farr, James (eds), *The Cambridge Companion to* The Communist Manifesto (Cambridge University Press, 2015).

Césaire, Aimé, "Letter to Maurice Thorez," *Social Text*, 103, 28.2 (2010), pp. 145–52.

Chattopadhyay, Paresh, "*Communist Manifesto* and Marxian Idea of Post-Capitalist Society," *Economic and Political Weekly*, 33:32 (1998), pp. 2165–7.

Chomsky, Noam, "Noam Chomsky: Fight the Class Struggle or Get it in the Neck," *Jacobin* (2020). <www.jacobinmag.com/2020/12/noam-chomsky-class-struggle-constitution-justice-us-imperialism> (accessed June 18, 2021).

Chryssis, Alexander, "The Cunning of Production and the Proletarian Revolution in the *Communist Manifesto*," in Cowling, Mark, *The Communist Manifesto: New Interpretations* (Edinburgh University Press, 1998).

Clark, Christopher, "Why should we think about the Revolutions of 1848 now?," *London Review of Books*, 41:5 (2019). <www.lrb.co.uk/the-paper/ v41/n05/christopher-clark/why-should-we-think-about-the-revolutions-of-1848-now> (accessed October 26, 2020).

Cohen, Sheila and Moody, Kim, "Unions, Strikes and Class Consciousness Today," in Panitch, Leo and Leys, Colin, *Socialist Register 1999: The Communist Manifesto Now* (Merlin, 1998).

Comninel, George, "Revolution in History: The *Communist Manifesto* in Context," in Moggach, Douglas and Leduc Browne, Paul (eds), *The Social Question and the Democratic Revolution: Marx and the Legacy of 1848* (University of Ottawa Press, 2000).

Cowling, Mark, "Marx and Engels, Marxism and the Nation," in Cowling, Mark, *The Communist Manifesto: New Interpretations* (Edinburgh University Press, 1998).

Cunliffe, John, "Marx's Politics – The Tensions in the *Communist Manifesto*," *Political Studies*, XXX:4 (1982), pp. 569–74.

D'Amato, Paul, "Marxists and Elections," *International Socialist Review*, 59 (2010). <isreview.org/issue/13/marxists-and-elections> (accessed June 17, 2021).

D'Amato, Paul, "The Communist Party and Black Liberation in the 1930s," *International Socialist Review*, 70 (2012). <isreview.org/issue/1/ communist-party-and-black-liberation-1930s> (accessed June 15, 2021).

Danchev, Alex, "Introduction," in Alex Danchev (ed.), *100 Artists' Manifestos: From the Futurists to the Stuckists* (Penguin Books, 2011).

Davidson, Neil, "Neoliberalism as an Agent of Capitalist Self-Destruction," *Salvage*, 1 (2015). <salvage.zone/in-print/neoliberalism-as-the-agent-of-capitalist-self-destruction/> (accessed October 29, 2020).

Davidson, Rondel V., "Reform versus Revolution: Victor Considerant and the *Communist Manifesto*," *Social Science*, 58:1 (1977), pp. 74–85.

Davis, Ben, "The Anarchist in the Network," *Salvage*, 9 (2020).

Davis, Dominic, "From Communism to Postcapitalism: Karl Marx and Friedrich Engels' *The Communist Manifesto* (1848)", in Davis, D., Lombard, E. and Mountford, B. (eds), *Fighting Words: Fourteen Books that Shaped the Postcolonial World: Race and Resistance Across Borders in the*

*Long 20th Century* (Peter Lang, 2017). <openaccess.city.ac.uk/21578/> (accessed November 12, 2020).

Davis, Mike "Marx's Lost Theory," *New Left Review* (2019), pp. 45–66.

Delany, Samuel R., "Racism and Science Fiction," *New York Review of Science Fiction* (1998). <www.nyrsf.com/racism-and-science-fiction-.html> (accessed November 13, 2021).

DeLay, Tad, "Gallows and Political Death Drive," *The Bias Magazine* (2020). <christiansocialism.com/trump-covid-psychoanalysis/> (accessed November 12, 2020).

Draper, Hal, "The *Communist Manifesto* and the Myth of the Disappearing Middle Classes," in Bender, Frederic (ed.), Marx, Karl, *The Communist Manifesto*, Second Norton Critical Edition (W. W. Norton, 2013).

Draper, Hal, "Anatomy of the Micro-Sect" (1973). <www.marxists.org/archive/draper/1973/xx/microsect.htm> (accessed June 19, 2021).

Dubois, Laurent, "Reading 'The Black Jacobins' Seven Decades Later" (2009). <nacla.org/article/reading-"-black-jacobins'-seven-decades-later> (accessed October 26, 2020).

Eco, Umberto, "On the Style of *The Communist Manifesto*," in *On Literature* (Vintage, 2006).

Engels, Friedrich, "Draft of a Communist Confession of Faith" (1847). <www.marxists.org/archive/marx/works/1847/06/09.htm> (accessed January 28, 2022).

Evans, Richard J., "Marx v. The Rest: Marx in His Time," *London Review of Books*, 35:10 (2013).

Farr, James and Ball, Terrence, "The *Manifesto* in Political Theory: Anglophone Translations and Liberal Receptions," in Carver, Terrell and Farr, James (eds), *The Cambridge Companion to* The Communist Manifesto (Cambridge University Press, 2015).

Fernbach, David, "Introduction 1," in Marx, Karl, *The Political Writings* (Verso, 2019).

Findlay, Len, "*Manifest der Kommunistischen Partei/The Communist Manifesto* (review)," *Victorian Review*, 35:1 (2009), pp. 22–27.

Fisken, Tim, "The Spectral Proletariat: The Politics of Hauntology in *The Communist Manifesto*," *Global Discourse*, 2:2 (2011), pp. 17–31.

Fleetwood, Steve, "The Continuing Relevance of the *Communist Manifesto*," *Critique: Journal of Socialist Theory*, 30:1 (2002), pp. 211–20.

Fluss, Harrison and Frim, Landon, "The More You Know: In Defense of Enlightenment Marxism" (2019). <www.patreon.com/posts/26625714> (accessed June 1, 2021).

Fowler, Bridget, "On Fetishism, Ghosts and State Magic: *The Communist Manifesto*, Derrida's *The Spectres of Marx* and Bourdieu's *The State Nobility*," *Critique*, 30:1 (2002), pp. 197–209.

Fox, J., Moroşanu, L. and Szilassy, E., "The Racialization of the New European Migration to the UK," *Sociology*, 46:4 (2012), pp. 680–95.

Gane, Mike, "The *Communist Manifesto*'s Transgendered Proletarians," in Cowling, Mark, *The Communist Manifesto: New Interpretations* (Edinburgh University Press, 1998).

Garcia Linera, Álvaro, "The *Communist Manifesto* and Our Present: Four Theses on Its Historical Actuality," in *Plebeian Power: Collective Action and Indigenous Working-Class and Popular Identities in Bolivia* (E. J. Brill, 2014).

Gavin, William, "Text Vs. Context: Irony and '*The Communist Manifesto*,'" *Studies in Soviet Thought*, 37 (1989), pp. 275–85.

Geras, Norman, "The Controversy About Marx and Justice," in Alex Callinicos (ed.), *Marxist Theory* (Oxford University Press, 1989). <www.marxists.org/reference/subject/philosophy/works/us/geras.htm> (accessed June 18, 2021).

Gindin, Sam, "Socialism with Sober Senses: Developing Workers' Capacities," in Panitch, Leo and Leys, Colin, *Socialist Register 1999: The Communist Manifesto Now* (Merlin, 1998).

Haider, Asad, "How calling someone a "class reductionist" became a lefty insult," *Salon* (2020). <www.salon.com/2020/07/25/how-calling-someone-a-class-reductionist-became-a-lefty-insult/> (accessed November 13, 2020).

Hanna, Julian, "Manifestos: A Manifesto," *The Atlantic* (2014). <www.theatlantic.com/entertainment/archive/2014/06/manifestos-a-manifesto-the-10-things-all-manifestos-need/372135/> (accessed October 8, 2020).

Harrington, Michael, "The Democratic Essence of Socialism," in Bender, Frederic (ed.), Marx, Karl, *The Communist Manifesto*, Second Norton Critical Edition (W. W. Norton, 2013 (1972)).

Harvey, David, "The Geography of the Manifesto," in Panitch, Leo and Leys, Colin, *Socialist Register 1999: The* Communist Manifesto *Now* (Merlin, 1998).

Heideman, Paul, "Socialism and Black Oppression," *Jacobin* (2018). <www.jacobinmag.com/2018/04/socialism-marx-race-class-struggle-color-line> (accessed June 14, 2021).

Herres, Jürgen, "Rhineland Radicals and the '48ers," in Carver, Terrell and Farr, James (eds), *The Cambridge Companion to* The Communist Manifesto (Cambridge University Press, 2015).

Hoffman, John, "The *Communist Manifesto* and the Idea of Permanent Revolution," in Cowling, Mark, *The Communist Manifesto: New Interpretations* (Edinburgh University Press, 1998).

Høgsbjerg, Christian, "CLR James and the Black Jacobins," *International Socialism*, 126 (2010). <isj.org.uk/clr-james-and-the-black-jacobins/#126hogsbjerg48> (accessed October 26, 2020).

Holt, Matthew, "Capital as Fiction: The *Communist Manifesto*," in Marks, Peter (ed.), *Literature and Politics: Pushing the World in Certain Directions* (Cambridge Scholars Publishing, 2011).

Hudis, Peter, "Raya Dunayevskaya's Marxist Humanism and the Alternative to Capitalism," *Jacobin* (2021). <www.jacobinmag.com/2021/06/raya-dunayevskaya-marxist-humanism-anti-racism-capitalism-alienation> (accessed June 17, 2021).

Isaac, Jeffrey C., "Introduction: Rethinking the *Communist Manifesto*," in Isaac, Jeffrey C. (ed.), *The Communist Manifesto: Karl Marx and Friedrich Engels* (Yale University Press, 2012).

Johnson, Cedric, "The Wages of Roediger: Why Three Decades of Whiteness Studies Has Not Produced the Left We Need," *Nonsite* (2019). <nonsite.org/the-wages-of-roediger-why-three-decades-of-whiteness-studies-has-not-produced-the-left-we-need/#> (accessed June 17, 2021).

Kautsky, Karl, "To What Extent is the *Communist Manifesto* Obsolete?" 1904. <www.marxists.org/archive/kautsky/1904/xx/manifesto.htm> (accessed June 19, 2021).

Kelley, Robin, "Race and the *Communist Manifesto*" (1998). <www.marxists.org/history/etol/ewspaper/atc/1159.html> (accessed October 29, 2020).

Kemple, Thomas M., "Post-Marx: Temporal Rhetoric and Textual Action in *The Communist Manifesto*," *Rethinking Marxism*, 12:2 (2000), pp. 44–60.

Kilpatrick, Connor, "Alexander Cockburn: The Last Polemicist," *Jacobin* (2013). <jacobinmag.com/2013/09/alexander-cockburn-the-last-polemicist> (accessed June 19, 2021).

Knox, Robert, "Valuing race? Stretched Marxism and the logic of imperialism," *London Review of International Law*, 4:1 (2016), pp. 81–126.

Kollontai, Alexandra, "Make Way for Winged Eros: A Letter to Working Youth" (1923). <www.marxists.org/archive/kollonta/1923/winged-eros. htm> (accessed September 6, 2021).

Kuljić, Todor D., "The Long Shadows of the *Manifesto of the Communist Party*," *Sociološki pregled/Sociological Review*, LII:2 (2018), pp. 453–70.

Labriola, Antonio, 1999, "In Memory of the *Communist Manifesto*," *Social Scientist*, 27:1/4 (1999), pp. 3–48.

Lansbury, Coral, "Melodrama, Pantomime and the *Communist Manifesto*," *Browning Institute Studies*, 14 (1986), pp. 1–10.

Lee, Wendy Lynne, "Socialist Feminist Critique and the *Communist Manifesto*, in Bender, Frederic (ed.), Marx, Karl, *The Communist Manifesto*, Second Norton Critical Edition (W. W. Norton, 2013 (2002)).

Leopold, David, "Marx, Engels and Other Socialisms," in Carver, Terrell and Farr, James (eds), *The Cambridge Companion to* The Communist Manifesto (Cambridge University Press, 2015).

Levin, Michael, "'The Hungry Forties': The Socio-economic Context of the *Communist Manifesto*," in Cowling, Mark, *The Communist Manifesto: New Interpretations* (Edinburgh University Press, 1998).

Lewis, Sophie, "Hello to My Haters: Tucker Carlson's Mob and Me," *Dissent*, Winter 2020 (2020). <www.dissentmagazine.org/article/hello-to-my-haters-tucker-carlsons-mob-and-me> (accessed November 13, 2020).

Löwith, Karl, "Marx's Prophetic Messianism," in Bender, Frederic (ed.), Marx, Karl, *The Communist Manifesto*, Second Norton Critical Edition (W. W. Norton, 2013 (1964)).

Löwy, Michael, "Globalization and Internationalism: How Up-to-date is the Communist Manifesto?," *Monthly Review* (1998).

Lukes, Steven, "The Morals of the *Manifesto*," in Isaac, Jeffrey C. (ed.), *The Communist Manifesto: Karl Marx and Friedrich Engels* (Yale University Press, 2012).

McNally, David, "The Period, the Party and the Next Left" (2009). <socialistworker.org/2019/03/22/the-period-the-party-and-the-next-left> (accessed June 19, 2021).

Mandel, Ernest, "Marx's Theory of Wages in the *Communist Manifesto* and Subsequently," in Bender, Frederic (ed.), Marx, Karl, *The Communist Manifesto*, Second Norton Critical Edition (W. W. Norton, 2013 (1971)).

Marković, Mihailo, "The State and Revolution in the *Communist Manifesto*," in Bender, Frederic (ed.), Marx, Karl, *The Communist Manifesto*, Second Norton Critical Edition (W. W. Norton, 2013 (1974)).

Martin, James, "The Rhetoric of the *Manifesto*," in Carver, Terrell and Farr, James (eds), *The Cambridge Companion to* The Communist Manifesto (Cambridge University Press, 2015).

Maycroft, Neil, "Marxism, Communism and Utopia," *Studies in Marxism*, 4 (1997).

Meadway, James, "Neoliberism is Dead—and Something Even Worse is Taking Its Place" (2021). <novaramedia.com/2021/06/29/neoliberalism-is-dead-and-something-even-worse-is-taking-its-place/> (accessed September 7, 2021).

Miéville, China, "Floating Utopias," in Davis, Mike and Monk, Daniel (eds), *Evil Paradises: Dreamworlds of Neoliberalism* (The New Press, 2008).

Miéville, China, "On Social Sadism," *Salvage*, 2 (2015). <salvage.zone/in-print/on-social-sadism/> (accessed November 13, 2021).

Miéville, China, "Silence in Debris: Towards an Apophatic Marxism," *Salvage* 6 (2019a). <salvage.zone/in-print/silence-in-debris-towards-an-apophatic-marxism/> (accessed October 26, 2020).

Miéville, China, "Response" (2019b). <www.patreon.com/posts/26625714> (accessed June 1, 2021).

Mitrović, Ljubiša R., "Crossroads and Alternatives of the Contemporary Left (Marginalia on the Occasion of the 170 Years since the First Edition of the *Communist Manifesto*)," *Sociološki pregled/Sociological Review*, LII:2 (2018), pp. 471–97.

Močnik, Rastko, "On Historical Regression: A Note at the Occasion of the 170th Anniversary of the *Manifesto*," *Sociološki pregled/Sociological Review*, LII:2 (2018), pp. 498–522.

Moos, Katherine A., "The Political Economy of State Regulation: The Case of the English Factory Acts," *Umass Economics Working Papers*, 233 (2017). <scholarworks.umass.edu/econ_workingpaper/233> (accessed June 16, 2021).

Moss, Bernard, "Marx and the Permanent Revolution in France: Background to the Communist Manifesto," in Panitch, Leo and Leys, Colin, *Socialist Register 1999: The* Communist Manifesto *Now* (Merlin, 1998).

Musto, Marcello, "Dissemination and Reception of *The Communist Manifesto* in Italy: From the Origins to 1945," *Critique: Journal of Socialist Theory*, 36:3 (2008), pp. 445–56.

Myślińska, Dagmar Rita, "Post-Brexit hate crimes against Poles are an expression of long-standing prejudices and contestation over white identity in the UK" (2016). <blogs.lse.ac.uk/brexit/2016/09/29/post-brexit-hate-crimes-against-poles-are-an-expression-of-long-standing-prejudices-and-contestation-over-white-identity-in-the-uk/> (accessed June 15, 2021).

Nairn, Tom, "The Modern Janus," *New Left Review*, I:94 (1975).

Neary, Mike, "Pedagogy of Hate," *Policy Futures in Education*, 15:5 (2017), pp. 555–63.

Neocleous, Mark, "Revolution? Reaction? Revolutionary Reaction?," in Cowling, Mark, *The Communist Manifesto: New Interpretations* (Edinburgh University Press, 1998).

Nicholas, Colin, "Theories of Development and the Underdevelopment of the Orang Asli," *Akademika*, 35 (1989), pp. 55–68.

Olaloku-Teriba, Annie, "Afro-Pessimism and the (Un)Logic of Anti-Blackness," *Historical Materialism* 26.2 (2018). <www.historical materialism.org/articles/afro-pessimism-and-unlogic-anti-blackness> (accessed November 13, 2021).

Olende, Ken, "Marx and Race: A Eurocentric Analysis?," *International Socialism Journal*, 162 (2019).

Okoth, Kevin Ochieng, "The Flatness of Blackness: Afro-Pessimism and the Erasure of Anti-Colonial Thought," *Salvage*, 7 (2019), pp. 79–114.

Osborne, Peter, "Remember the Future? The *Communist Manifesto* as Historical and Cultural Form," *Socialist Register*, 34 (1998), pp. 190–204.

Panitch, Leo and Leys, Colin. "The Political Legacy of the Manifesto," in Panitch, Leo and Leys, Colin, *Socialist Register 1999: The* Communist Manifesto *Now* (Merlin, 1998).

Panitch, Leo, "The Two Revolutionary Classes of the *Manifesto*," in Carver, Terrell and Farr, James (eds), *The Cambridge Companion to* The Communist Manifesto (Cambridge University Press, 2015).

Parkinson, Donald, "Revolution or the Democratic Road to Socialism? A Reply to Eric Blanc" (2019). <cosmonaut.blog/2019/04/13/revolution-or-the-democratic-road-to-socialism-a-reply-to-eric-blanc/> (accessed June 17, 2021).

Patnaik, Utsa, "The Promethean Vision: *The Communist Manifesto* and the Development of Capitalism after 150 Years," *Social Scientist*, 27:1/4 (1999), pp. 112–26.

Paxton, Steve, "The *Communist Manifesto*, Marx's Theory of History and the Russian Revolution," in Cowling, Mark, *The Communist Manifesto: New Interpretations* (Edinburgh University Press, 1998).

Perez, Andrew, "The Filibuster Is the Ultimate Excuse for Democrats," *Jacobin* (2021). <www.jacobinmag.com/2021/06/filibuster-democratic-party-joe-manchin-legislation> (accessed June 18, 2021).

Perloff, Marjorie, "'Violence and Precision': The Manifesto as Art Form," *Chicago Review*, 34:2 (1984), pp. 65–101.

Pilbeam, Pamela, "The Insurrectionary Tradition in France 1835–48," *Modern and Contemporary France*, 1:3 (1993), pp. 253–64.

Post, Charles, "Actually Existing "Socialism"—A Critique of Stalinism," *New Socialist* (2018). <newsocialist.org/actually-existing-socialism-a-critique-of-stalinism/> (accessed June 19, 2021),

Post, Charles, "Marxism and the race problem," *Marxist Sociology Blog* (2019). <marxistsociology.org/2019/01/marxism-and-the-race-problem> (accessed June 20, 2021).

Post, Charles, "Beyond 'Racial Capitalism': Toward a Unified Theory of Capitalism and Racial Oppression," *The Brooklyn Rail* (2020). <brooklynrail.org/2020/10/field-notes/Beyond-Racial-Capitalism-Toward-

A-Unified-Theory-of-Capitalism-and-Racial-Oppression> (accessed November 13, 2020).

Raine, Barnaby, "Left Fukuyamaism: Politics in Tragic Times," *Salvage* 11 (2021), pp. 13–31.

Robinson, Colin, "Selling the Communist Manifesto at Barneys," *Jacobin* (2018). <jacobinmag.com/2018/05/communist-manifesto-marketing-class-struggle-barneys> (accessed May 10, 2021).

Rosdolsky, Roman, "Worker and Fatherland: A Note on a Passage in the *Communist Manifesto*," *Science and Society*, 29:3 (1965), pp. 330–37.

Rothbard, Murray N., "Karl Marx: Communist as Religious Eschatologist," *Review of Austrian Economics*, 4 (1990), pp. 123–79.

Rowbotham, Sheila, "Dear Dr Marx: A Letter from a Socialist Feminist," in Panitch, Leo and Leys, Colin, *Socialist Register 1999: The* Communist Manifesto *Now* (Merlin, 1998).

Rzepnikowska, Alina, "Racism and xenophobia experienced by Polish migrants in the UK before and after Brexit vote," *Journal of Ethnic and Migration Studies* (2018). <www.tandfonline.com/doi/full/10.1080/136918 3X.2018.1451308> (accessed June 15, 2021).

Saccarelli, Emanuele, "The Permanent Revolution in and around the *Manifesto*," in Carver, Terrell and Farr, James (eds), *The Cambridge Companion to* The Communist Manifesto (Cambridge University Press, 2015).

Said, Edward, "Thoughts on Late Style," *London Review of Books*, 26:15 (2004). <www.lrb.co.uk/the-paper/v26/n15/edward-said/thoughts-on-late-style> (accessed November 13, 2021).

Salami, Minna, "Why I don't believe the word 'black' should always have a capital 'b,'" *The Guardian* (2021). <www.theguardian.com/commentisfree/2021/jun/03/word-black-capital-letter-blackness> (accessed November 13, 2021).

Salgado, Pedro, "The Transition Debate in Brazilian History: The Bourgeois Paradigm and its Critique," *Journal of Agrarian Change* (2020). <onlinelibrary.wiley.com/doi/full/10.1111/joac.12394> (accessed October 28, 2020).

Santucci, Antonio A., "Economy and *Weltliteratur* in the *Communist Manifesto*," *Rethinking Marxism*, 13:2 (2001), pp. 19–29.

Sassen, Saskia, "Marxism and Globalization: Revisiting the Political in the *Communist Manifesto*" in Isaac, Jeffrey C. (ed.), *The Communist Manifesto: Karl Marx and Friedrich Engels* (Yale University Press, 2012).

Satgar, Vishwas, "The Anti-Racism of Marxism: Past and Present," in Satgar, Vishwas (ed.), *Racism After Apartheid: Challenges for Marxism and Anti-Racism* (Wits University Press, 2019).

Schaff, Adam, "Marxist Theory on Revolution and Violence," *Journal of the History of Ideas*, 34:2 (1973), pp. 263–70.

Schmidt, J, "The German Labour Movement, 1830s–1840s: Early Efforts at Political Transnationalism," *Journal of Ethnic and Migration Studies*, 46: 6 (2020), pp. 1025–39.

Schumpeter, Joseph A., "The *Communist Manifesto* in Sociology and Economics," *Journal of Political Economy*, 57:3 (1949), pp. 199–212.

Schwartz, Pedro, "Karl Marx, the Perennial Prophet" (2016). <www.econlib.org/library/Columns/y2016/SchwartzMarx.html> (accessed August 8, 2021).

Selsam, Howard, "The Ethics of the *Communist Manifesto*," in Bender, Frederic (ed.), Marx, Karl, *The Communist Manifesto*, Second Norton Critical Edition (W. W. Norton, 2013 (1948)).

Seymour, Richard, "The parliamentary state of mind" (2017). <www.leninology.co.uk/2017/07/the-parliamentary-state-of-mind.html> (accessed November 13, 2021).

Seymour, Richard, "Reinventing the Anti-Immigrant Wheel" (2018a). <www.patreon.com/posts/20945069?fbclid=IwAR3BqfnnNQ1DrcaXidQkg277-XmpPUgJXgmyGSr8P3QeU6oOGGTrzPC1GPM> (accessed June 15, 2021).

Seymour, Richard, "Note on Moralism" (2018b) <www.patreon.com/posts/note-on-moralism-20258569> (accessed June 15, 2021).

Seymour, Richard, "Anticommunism without communism" (2019b). <www.patreon.com/posts/23818607> (accessed October 21, 2020).

Seymour, Richard, "Why is the nationalist right hallucinating a 'communist enemy'?" *The Guardian* (2020). <www.theguardian.com/commentisfree/2020/sep/26/communist-enemy-nationalist-right-trump-us-bolsonaro-brazil> (accessed October 7, 2020).

Shakespeare, Steven, "Theology of Hate" (2014). <itself.blog/2014/09/16/theology-of-hate/> (accessed November 13, 2020).

Shilliam, Robbie, "Decolonizing the *Manifesto*: Communism and the Slave Analogy," in Carver, Terrell and Farr, James (eds), *The Cambridge Companion to* The Communist Manifesto (Cambridge University Press, 2015).

Siegel, Paul N., "The Style of the *Communist Manifesto*," *Science and Society*, 46:2 (1982), pp. 222–29.

Šljukić, Srdan Lj., "*Communist Manifesto* and the Peasantry of the 21st Century," *Sociološki pregled/Sociological Review*, LII:2 (2018), pp. 607–27.

Smith, Evan, "'Class Before Race': British Communism and the Place of Empire in Postwar Race Relations," *Science & Society*, 72:4 (2008), pp. 455–81.

Spaethling, Robert H., "Bertolt Brecht and the *Communist Manifesto*," *The Germanic Review: Literature, Culture, Theory*, 37:4 (1962), pp. 282–91.

Sparrow, Jeff, "Trump and Brexit left progressives aghast—they should be emboldened," *The Guardian* (2017). <www.theguardian.com/commentisfree/2017/jan/02/trump-brexit-left-progressives-aghast-they-should-be-emboldened> (accessed November 13, 2020).

Steger, Manfred B., "The Specter of the *Manifesto* Stalks Neoliberal Globalization: Reconfiguring Marxist Discourse(s) in the 1990s," in Carver, Terrell and Farr, James (eds), *The Cambridge Companion to* The Communist Manifesto (Cambridge University Press, 2015).

Suchting, Wal, "What is Living and What is Dead in the *Communist Manifesto?*," in Cowling, Mark, *The Communist Manifesto: New Interpretations* (Edinburgh University Press, 1998).

Suvin, Darko, "Brecht's 'Manifesto' Today (2002)," in Suvin, Darko, *Communism, Poetry: Communicating Vessels* (Political Animal Press, 2020).

Taber, Mike, "Kautsky, Lenin, and the Transition to Socialism: A Reply to Eric Blanc" (2019). <cosmonaut.blog/2019/04/10/kautsky-lenin-and-the-transition-to-socialism-a-reply-to-eric-blanc/> (accessed June 17, 2021).

Thatcher, Ian D., "Past Receptions of the *Communist Manifesto*," in Cowling, Mark, *The Communist Manifesto: New Interpretations* (Edinburgh University Press, 1998).

Tismaneanu, Vladimir, "Reflections on the Fate of Marxism in Eastern Europe: Fulfillment or Bastardization?," in Isaac, Jeffrey C. (ed.), *The Communist Manifesto: Karl Marx and Friedrich Engels* (Yale University Press, 2012).

Toscano, Alberto, "The Manifesto Revisited (Transitions to and from Capitalism)," (2012). <cartographiesoftheabsolute.wordpress.com/2012/05/11/the-manifesto-revisited-transitions-to-and-from-capitalism/> (accessed November 13, 2021).

Toscano, Alberto, "Communism," in Toscano, Alberto, Farris, Sara and Skeggs, Bev, *The Sage Handbook of Marxism* (Sage, 2021).

Townshend, Jules, "*The Communist Manifesto*: The Riddle of History Solved?," *Studies in Marxism*, 4 (1997).

Townshend, Jules, "The *Communist Manifesto* and the Crises of Marxism," in Cowling, Mark, *The Communist Manifesto: New Interpretations* (Edinburgh University Press, 1998).

Townshend, Jules, "Marxism and the *Manifesto* after Engels," in Carver, Terrell and Farr, James (eds), *The Cambridge Companion to* The Communist Manifesto (Cambridge University Press, 2015).

Trkulja, Jovica D., "*Manifesto of the Communist Party*—Reception and Criticism," *Sociološki pregled/Sociological Review*, LII:2 (2018), pp. 628–52.

Tronto, Joan C., "Hunting for Women, Haunted by Gender: The Rhetorical Limits of the *Manifesto*," in Carver, Terrell and Farr, James (eds), *The Cambridge Companion to* The Communist Manifesto (Cambridge University Press, 2015).

Trotsky, Leon, "On the Ninetieth Anniversary of the *Communist Manifesto*," in Bender, Frederic (ed.), Marx, Karl, *The Communist Manifesto*, Second Norton Critical Edition (W. W. Norton, 2013 (1945)).

Tuveson, Ernest L., "The millenarian structure of *The Communist Manifesto*," in Patrides, C. A. and Wittreich, Joseph Anthony (eds), *The Apocalypse in English Renaissance Thought and Literature: Patterns, Antecedents and Repercussions* (Manchester University Press, 1984).

Vanaik, Achin, "Marxism and Nationalism" (2018). <www.versobooks.com/blogs/3578-marxism-and-nationalism> (accessed June 20, 2021).

Wallace, Dewey, "From Eschatology to Arian Heresy: The Case of Francis Kitt," *Harvard Theological Review*, 67, 4 (1974), pp. 459–73.

Wallis, Victor, "The *Communist Manifesto* and Capitalist Hegemony after 150 Years," *Socialism and Democracy*, 12:1 (1998), pp. 7–13.

Walzer, Michael, "A Note on Racial Capitalism," *Dissent* (2020). <www.dissentmagazine.org/online_articles/a-note-on-racial-capitalism> (accessed November 13, 2020).

Whittaker, Nicholas, "Case Sensitive: Why We Shouldn't Capitalize 'Black,'" *The Drift* (2021). <www.thedriftmag.com/case-sensitive/> (accessed January 6, 2022).

Wilks-Heeg, Stuart, "The *Communist Manifesto* and Working-class Parties in Western Europe," in Cowling, Mark, *The Communist Manifesto: New Interpretations* (Edinburgh University Press, 1998).

Williams, Matt, "When Communism Became Black" (2019). <www.rosalux.de/en/publication/id/40161/when-communism-became-black> (accessed June 15, 2021).

Woodcock, Jamie, "The Impact of the Gig Economy," in BBVA, *Work in the Age of Data* (BBVA OpenMind, 2019). <www.bbvaopenmind.com/en/articles/the-impact-of-the-gig-economy/> (accessed September 6, 2021).

Wright, John G., "Feuerbach—Philosopher of Materialism," *International Socialist Review*, 17:4 (1956), pp. 123–6, 136–7. <www.marxists.org/history/etol/writers/wright/1956/xx/feuerbach.htm> (accessed June 7, 2021).

Wright, Julian, "A Lesson in Revolution: Karl Marx and Fridrich Engels, *The Communist Manifesto*," in Hammersley, Rachel (ed.), *Revolutionary Moments: Reading Revolutionary Texts* (Bloomsbury, 2015).

Yelland, Cris, "*The Communist Manifesto*: The Linguistic Approach," *Studies in Marxism*, 4 (1997), pp. 47–58.

Younger, Rupert and Portnoy, Frank, "What Would Karl Marx Write Today?," *Financial Times* (March 9, 2018). <www.ft.com/content/603b3498-2155-11e8-a895-1ba1f72c2c11> (accessed January 28, 2022).

# Acknowledgments

I'm deeply grateful to everyone whose help, insight, patience, and support has made this book possible. My thanks to all at Head of Zeus, including Matilda Singer, Kathryn Colwell, Nicola Bigwood, Ben Prior, and Nicolas Cheetham, for all their work and help, and especially to Neil Belton, my editor, for suggesting this book, and for his immense patience and help during the writing of it. I'm grateful to all who took the time to give detailed thoughts and responses to drafts and sections of the work, including Matthew Beaumont, Neil Belton, Sebastian Budgen, Season Butler, Mic Cheetham, Meehan Crist, Charlotte Heltai, Sophie Lewis, John McDonald, Tessa McWatt, Sue Powell, Barnaby Raine, and Alberto Toscano. I am immeasurably in the debt of my fellow editors of *Salvage*, Jamie Allinson, Richard Seymour, and Rosie Warren, for their solidarity and friendship, and for being constant sources of political and intellectual inspiration. My thanks to the members of the Frightful Hobgoblins group for comradeship, discussion, and inspiration. For indispensable support, my thanks to Gurru Corominas, Cassia Corominas-Miéville, Indigo Corominas-Miéville, and Jemima Miéville. I'm grateful to Canon Jessica Martin for her invaluable insights, and for directing me to the Psalms; to Stathis Kouvelakis; to Kerin Ogg; and to Enzo Traverso for his inspirational work, which introduced me to the Spassky image that looms large in these pages. For such great generosity with their expertise to a non-specialist, and for thoughtful and invaluable responses to the book, I am profoundly grateful to Terrell Carver and Gregor McLennan. For generous permission to use their words, I am deeply grateful to Rae Armantrout, Agnes Denes, Mira Mattar, Ash Sarkar, and Rebecca Solnit. And I'm more thankful than I can express, for more than I can express, to Season Butler.

---

For this edition, I extend my deep gratitude and solidarity to all at Haymarket Books. My thanks in particular go to Anthony Arnove, Rachel Cohen, Julie Fain, Jamie Kerry, Jim Plank, and to my friend and comrade John McDonald, for all his work on this book, and for much more besides.

# Index

# About Haymarket Books

Haymarket Books is a radical, independent, nonprofit book publisher based in Chicago. Our mission is to publish books that contribute to struggles for social and economic justice. We strive to make our books a vibrant and organic part of social movements and the education and development of a critical, engaged, international left.

We take inspiration and courage from our namesakes, the Haymarket martyrs, who gave their lives fighting for a better world. Their 1886 struggle for the eight-hour day—which gave us May Day, the international workers' holiday—reminds workers around the world that ordinary people can organize and struggle for their own liberation. These struggles continue today across the globe—struggles against oppression, exploitation, poverty, and war.

Since our founding in 2001, Haymarket Books has published more than five hundred titles. Radically independent, we seek to drive a wedge into the risk-averse world of corporate book publishing. Our authors include Noam Chomsky, Arundhati Roy, Rebecca Solnit, Angela Y. Davis, Howard Zinn, Amy Goodman, Wallace Shawn, Mike Davis, Winona LaDuke, Ilan Pappé, Richard Wolff, Dave Zirin, Keeanga-Yamahtta Taylor, Nick Turse, Dahr Jamail, David Barsamian, Elizabeth Laird, Amira Hass, Mark Steel, Avi Lewis, Naomi Klein, and Neil Davidson. We are also the trade publishers of the acclaimed Historical Materialism Book Series and of Dispatch Books.

# Also Available from Haymarket Books

*Assata Taught Me: State Violence, Racial Capitalism, and the Movement for Black Lives*
Donna Murch

*Breaking the Impasse: Electoral Politics, Mass Action, and the New Socialist Movement in the United States*
by Kim Moody

*C. L. R. James and Revolutionary Marxism*
*Selected Writings of C.L.R. James 1939-1949*
Edited by Paul Le Blanc and Scott McLemee

*Elite Capture: How the Powerful Took Over Identity Politics (And Everything Else)*
Olúfémi O. Táíwò

*Fighting Fascism: How to Struggle and How to Win*
Clara Zetkin, edited by John Riddell and Mike Taber

*Socialism From Below*
Hal Draper

*Speaking Out of Place: Getting Our Political Voices Back*
David Palumbo-Liu

*Struggle Makes Us Human: Learning from Movements for Socialism*
Frank Barat and Vijay Prashad